EXAMINING THE SECONDARY SCHOOLS OF WALES 1896–2000

Examining the Secondary Schools of Wales 1896–2000

by

†W. GARETH EVANS, ROBERT SMITH AND
GARETH ELWYN JONES

UNIVERSITY OF WALES PRESS
CARDIFF
2008

© †W. Gareth Evans, Robert Smith and Gareth Elwyn Jones 2008

The right of †W. Gareth Evans, Robert Smith and Gareth Elwyn Jones to be identified as authors of this work has been asserted by them in accordance with sections 77 and 78 of the Copyright, Designs and Patents Act 1988.

All rights reserved. No part of this book may be reproduced, stored in a retrieval system, or transmitted, in any form or by any means, electronic, mechanical, photocopying, recording or otherwise, without clearance from the University of Wales Press, 10 Columbus Walk, Brigantine Place, Cardiff, CF10 4UP.

www.uwp.co.uk

British Library Cataloguing-in-Publication Data

A catalogue record for this book is available from the British Library.

ISBN 978-0-7083-2149-2

Typeset by Columns Design Ltd, Reading
Printed in Great Britain by Antony Rowe Ltd, Chippenham, Wiltshire

To the Memory of/Er Cof
W. Gareth Evans
1941–2000

Contents

Preface	xi
Note on references	xv
Chapter 1 Sacrifice or Opportunity? 1896–1918	1
Introduction	1
English	12
Welsh	18
French	22
Latin	29
Geography	31
History	36
Scripture	39
Mathematics	45
Science subjects	50
Physics	51
Chemistry	53
Botany	55
Conclusion	56
Chapter 2 A Means of Escape 1918–1949	63
Introduction	63
English	75
Welsh	79
French	81
Latin	84
Geography	87
History	90
Scripture	93
Mathematics	96
Science subjects	101
Physics	102
Chemistry	103

CONTENTS

Botany, biology and zoology	105
Conclusion	107
Chapter 3 Continuity in Change 1949–1970	115
Introduction	115
English	121
Welsh	124
French	126
Latin	128
Geography	129
History	129
Scripture	131
Mathematics	132
Science subjects	134
Physics	135
Chemistry	139
Botany	140
Biology	142
Conclusion	145
Chapter 4 Comprehensive Examinations? 1970–1988	149
Introduction	149
English	153
Welsh	158
Modern languages	161
French	162
German	163
Latin	164
Geography	165
Geology	168
History	169
Scripture	172
Mathematics	173
Science subjects	177
Physics	178
Chemistry	179
Biology	180
Art and design	182
Woodwork and metalwork	185
Home economics	187
Conclusion	189

CONTENTS

Chapter 5	Examining the New Wales 1988–2000	197
	Introduction	197
	English	208
	Welsh	210
	Modern languages	213
	Geography	214
	History	216
	Religious studies	219
	Mathematics	220
	Science subjects	221
	Physics	222
	Chemistry	222
	Biology	223
	Integrated science	224
	Art and design	226
	Home economics	228
	Conclusion	230
Index		237

Preface

This history book has a history. When Dr W. Gareth Evans, Reader in the Department of Education, University of Wales, Aberystwyth died at the turn of this millennium at the age of fifty-eight he had already made an indelible mark on the study of the history of education in Wales. His publications ranged from a history of Llandovery College to an analysis of the role of education in female emancipation in nineteenth-century Wales, the most important of his works. His most recent book was a history of the Central Welsh Board (CWB). In the course of his researches he had turned his thoughts to a successor volume which would make use of a hitherto untapped source of printed primary documents, the annual examination reports of the CWB and its successor body, the Welsh Joint Education Committee (WJEC).

He had already worked through material covering the period from 1896 to 1970 and had written up accounts of a number of individual subjects. He was about to devote himself full-time to finishing the work with the aid of a Leverhulme Foundation Research Fellowship when it became obvious that he would not live to do so. He sought the help of Prof Geraint Jenkins, director of the Centre for Advanced Welsh and Celtic Studies in Aberystwyth, to ensure its completion. Given its originality, it seemed wholly unacceptable to allow this study to wither on the vine. The Leverhulme Foundation graciously agreed to release part of the funding which had been awarded to Dr Evans to allow Prof Jenkins to commission Dr Robert Smith to bring the project to fruition. Under the direction of Prof Jenkins and the then head of the education department at the University of Wales, Aberystwyth, Prof Richard Daugherty, Dr Smith advanced the work substantially. He researched and wrote the last two chapters, as well as introductory sections to Chapters 2 and 3. With the end in sight, he was appointed head of research at the National Foundation for Educational Research in Wales and found it impossible to devote more time to the project. Following a considerable hiatus the existing drafts were passed on to me. I wrote sections of Chapters 1–3, and brought the book to a publishable state. Gareth Pierce and subject specialists in the WJEC were kind enough to provide some additional material. The publication process was then handled in the usual impeccable manner by the staff of the University of Wales Press, with financial support from the Higher Education Funding Council for Wales and from the University of Wales, Aberystwyth by means of the Sir David Hughes Parry Awards. Throughout, Dr Evans's close family gave this protracted project their unstinting support.

One of the ambitions which drove Dr Evans to undertake this study was a belief that he would be able to make judgements about an issue of contemporary resonance, that of comparative academic standards in external examinations. After all, the nomenclature of the subjects which formed the staple diet of pupils in Wales in the 1890s bore an uncanny resemblance to that of the components of the National Curriculum inaugurated in the 1990s. However, at an early stage he became less convinced that his research would allow him to make such assessments, simply because it was impossible to compare like with like. Indeed, it is this latter element which turns out to be one of the fascinating aspects of his study. Not only have the mechanics of examining changed out of all recognition over the last century, with the virtual demise of the ubiquitous essay format and the adoption of coursework at all levels, but also the matter within similarly named subjects to be examined in the 1890s would be scarcely recognizable to a candidate in the early years of the twenty-first century. Many will want to comment on relative standards on this basis alone, but such judgements will be a matter of prejudice rather than objectivity.

Whatever their merits, general comments in the published annual reports by those who examined on behalf of the CWB and WJEC cannot per se be taken to furnish evidence of a rise or fall in educational standards in Wales. The work of individual candidates was the crucial factor and it is impossible to arrive at firm conclusions on the basis of impressions about an entire cohort. Also, the reports merely reflect the particular priorities and preconceptions of the succession of academics who, as chief examiners, wrote them. What can be said is that a wide range of work was examined each year and anxieties expressed about the work submitted. What we may infer from examiners' reports about academic priorities, teaching methods and, equally interesting, the vested interests of examiners, casts a fascinating light on current ill-founded generalizations about, for example, A level qualifications being the 'gold standard', as if their exchange rate were testimony to immutability both of examinations in themselves and their currency in higher education and the job market.

Wider insights into the history of Welsh education are also evident in this study. Above all it reinforces our understanding of how far the examination system in Wales is one thread in a pattern of what might be termed 'paradoxical devolution' as it has evolved from the end of the nineteenth century to the present day. For example, Dr Evans pointed out in his history of the CWB that it had elements of a national education body for Wales. When the Welsh Intermediate schools were established as a consequence of the Welsh Intermediate and Technical Education Act of 1889 there was no state system of secondary education in England and therefore no obvious inspecting and examining body to report on how efficiently state money was being spent. The CWB had, therefore, to be invented to undertake these tasks in Wales. In little more than a decade it was to incur the bitter enmity of the newly founded Welsh Department of the Board of Education, which regarded itself as the rightful arbiter of all educational matters in Wales.

Far less well-known is the earlier rivalry of the CWB with the University of Wales, whose senior academics wanted to control secondary education in Wales from the start. Ostensibly, they failed to do so, and gave in to the CWB rather more gracefully than did the Welsh Department of the Board of Education. The result was that a national representative body, composed substantially of local authority elected members, controlled external examinations in Wales, while in England this function was performed by examination boards under the auspices of universities. Here was, seemingly, a fundamental difference between the arrangement of education in the two nations. Much was illusion. In practice, not only did the University of Wales control the structure of examinations through its matriculation requirements but also the following pages reveal how some of the most noted scholars of the University of Wales dominated the ranks of examiners across the academic subjects. They could therefore determine priorities, comment on teaching methods and, for better or worse, generally cast their long shadow over the content and approach employed in the intermediate/grammar schools of Wales.

On two counts, therefore, this book makes an important contribution to our understanding of the history of education in Wales. There is much of interest in the detail of the examiners reports in the various subjects; in turn, these shed light on wider aspects of the politics and practice of an aspect of Welsh history increasingly seen as being central to Welsh social history generally.

Those who have contributed to ensuring that this book appears in print cannot be certain that its content and format are precisely as their originator would have wished. It is possible that, if the research had not been brought to such a sadly premature end, he would have extended his study to cover all subject areas across each period, particularly the more practical subjects, even though these attracted relatively few candidates. Nevertheless, if some elements are incomplete it remains the case that the research on which the book is based is original and illuminating. It is with this conviction that it has been contextualized and augmented so as to bring it to a wider audience and serve as a lasting tribute to Dr W. Gareth Evans.

Gareth Elwyn Jones
Swansea, October 2007

Note on references

References follow the normal pattern. However, referencing each of the observations made by examiners in the subject sections would involve tedious repetition. Therefore only direct quotations are acknowledged. Where Dr Evans provided page references in his notes these have been included. Comments, opinions and observations of examiners are taken principally from two sources, the yearly *Report on the Inspection and Examination of County Schools* published by the Central Welsh Board from 1897/8 until its demise and the *Annual Reports of the Examiners* published by the Welsh Joint Education Committee after 1950. Each report contains sections on individual subjects, written by the chief examiners at the different levels. The reports were consulted at two locations: the National Library of Wales in Aberystwyth; and the headquarters of the Welsh Joint Education Committee in Cardiff.

Chapter 1
Sacrifice or Opportunity? 1896–1918

Introduction

Wales was a buoyant country at the time of the creation of its unique state secondary education system. Its population of about two million had more then trebled since the beginning of the nineteenth century. The dramatic expansion of the coal, iron and steel industries had produced disproportionate growth in Glamorgan and Monmouthshire. Glamorgan, in particular, had experienced phenomenal expansion, its population increasing to one-and-a-quarter million by 1901. To some extent this population rise in industrial Wales had been at the expense of the rural counties, as labour was being sucked in to work in the south Wales coalfield. But people were also pouring in at an unprecedented rate from neighbouring English counties – in 1890, 16 per cent of the south Wales population had originated in England.

The imbalance of population growth reflected an imbalance of relative prosperity. Landlord-dominated, conservative rural Wales regularly saw its tenant farmers and labourers facing economic meltdown. In the 1880s and 1890s, while industrial Wales grew at such a phenomenal rate, the rural counties experienced an agricultural depression which fuelled an exodus from the land. But in all parts of Wales disparities of wealth were dramatic. Landowners and industrialists could build houses and indulge in lifestyles which landless labourers and miners could scarcely imagine.

Nevertheless, in overall terms, Wales prospered as never before. Although industrialization brought dire penalties in terms of pollution, accidents, ill-health, lack of sanitation and appalling working conditions, it also resulted in relative individual and communal prosperity, the like of which Wales had not experienced previously. At the end of the nineteenth century, therefore, Wales was at the centre of the British economy, itself the centre of an imperial economy.

Economic buoyancy was accompanied by a burgeoning of Welsh achievement in religion, culture and politics, and increasing numbers of the population were aware of each of these dimensions in national terms. Arguably, education, or the lack of it, had been the catalyst. The 1847 *Report of the Commissioners into the State of Education in Wales* (the Blue Books) had justifiably castigated the education system but had gone beyond this to malign the ethics and morality of a whole nation. The explosive response had helped to radicalize the politics of Wales and to foster a national spirit.

Within half a century the image of Wales had been transformed as a result of a combination of practical achievement and the cultivation of a myth counter to that of the 1847 Blue Books. The Nonconformist dynamic, translating some of Wales's new wealth into impressive, occasionally opulent chapel buildings, linked religious fervour with moral respectability, whatever currents there may have been beneath the surface. The image of respectability was reinforced by Welsh cultural achievement which, through resurgent *eisteddfodau* and the iconic achievements of Welsh choirs, intertwined the religion of Wales with its culture. Preachers and writers did their best to cultivate an image of Wales as *gwlad y menyg gwynion,* the land of the white gloves, symbolic of freedom from crime. Welsh politicians, most notably Tom Ellis and David Lloyd George towards the end of the century, but with a very considerable supporting cast, were both a product of and helped to forge a new nationalist dimension, both cultural and political, which resulted in practical achievement. In 1893 the University of Wales got its charter, and, by the end of the first decade of the twentieth century, Wales had a National Museum, a National Library and a Welsh Department of the Board of Education which brought a significant measure of devolution. Even the disestablishment of the Church of England in Wales was on its way.

One of the earliest major practical outcomes of this new Wales, drawing on political influence and a desperate desire for progress and respectability, was the Aberdare Committee

Report of 1881 which investigated the state of education in Wales in a rather different climate from that of the 1847 commissioners. The Aberdare Committee recommended, in the face of evidence of the parlous state of secondary and higher education, that university colleges be established in north and south Wales and that a system of intermediate secondary schools be set up. The eventual achievement of both these aspirations was little short of a political miracle because it required a regular injection of state money into Welsh secondary and higher education for the first time ever. But it also required that this Treasury grant be provided for Wales only, thus recognizing the existence of Wales as a political unit far more significantly than the only other piece of independent Welsh legislation since Cromwellian times, the Welsh Sunday Closing Act of 1881.

After eight years of hard graft, setbacks and fluctuations in political fortunes, by dint of a combination of individual political skill and some cross-party support, Parliament recognized the relative deficiencies of non-state education in Wales and passed the Welsh Intermediate and Technical Education Act 1889 which injected money into both its university system and its secondary schools. Given its context in the political and social history of Wales, this was one of the most remarkable political achievements of the nineteenth century. The 'treason' of 1847 could hardly have been given a more dramatic counterpoint.

The subjects which would be examined during the early years of public examinations in Wales were conditioned by the system of state secondary schools resulting from this crucial Act of Parliament. The Welsh Intermediate and Technical Education Act of 1889 provided for the establishment of joint education committees in each county of Wales. Their task was to plan the creation and integration of post-elementary schools which would provide a secondary education for a minority of pupils between the ages of approximately ten and sixteen. Committees were quickly established in all the Welsh local authorities and resulted in schools opening across Wales in the 1890s. By 1898 ninety-five schools had been opened and their number included most, though not all, of the former endowed grammar schools.[1] The intermediate schools were not, however, dependent on endowments because, for the first time in England or Wales, central grants from the Treasury were to be combined with local authority rates to provide permanent support for the system. Pupil fees, regarded at the time as an essential status symbol for secondary education, were also to be charged, though at a much lower rate than in traditional grammar schools, and provision was made for between 10 and 20 per cent of places to be financed by scholarships. Essentially, Wales had its unique system of secondary education.[2]

It was not a completely homogeneous system by any means. Contemporary thinking on secondary education was still conditioned by the notion underpinning the recommendations of the 1868 Taunton Report that there should be three grades of secondary education, associated with specific types of curriculum and access to associated occupations. For example, no school could aspire to first grade status if its curriculum did not include Latin and Greek, which in any case were required for entry to the universities of Oxford and Cambridge and subsequently to the highest posts in the Civil Service, the Church, the army and other professions. That such grading should be an integral part of the Welsh secondary school structure was taken as axiomatic by the Aberdare Committee in 1881, the recommendations of which provided the essential spur to subsequent legislation. From the outset, the status of a school was inextricably linked with its curriculum, and ambitious headteachers attempted to provide a classical curriculum.[3]

Nevertheless, the society which Welsh secondary schools were intended to serve was very different from that of England. Thinking about its schools could not therefore be conditioned just by Taunton Report notions but had to take into account the realities of a Welsh occupational structure relatively deficient in professional opportunities and relatively poorer than England, particularly in the agricultural areas. At the same time, there were high aspirations to economic and professional mobility, as well as demand in local economies for skilled workers in both mining and agricultural areas. These virtually irreconcilable demands made of the new secondary system provide a fascinating case study in how an education system reflects the complexities of the society which gives rise to it. Curriculum and examinations were to play an important part as signifiers in the complex interplay of secondary schools and their constituencies which dominated the development of Welsh secondary education in the years before the First World War.

Aspects of this inter-relationship in an economy dominated by extractive industries and agriculture were already evident in the Aberdare Committee's curricular blueprint for the proposed schools:

> The expression 'Intermediate Education' means a course of education which does not consist chiefly of elementary instruction in reading, writing and arithmetic, but includes Latin, Greek, and the Welsh and English language and literature, modern languages, mathematics, natural and applied science, or in some such studies, and generally in the higher branches of knowledge.[4]

The Welsh Intermediate and Technical Education Act itself defined the technical education which should be available, including any subject qualifying for Department of Science and Art grant, working in clay, wood or other material, commercial arithmetic, commercial geography, book keeping and shorthand, and any subject proposed by a joint education committee relating to agriculture, industry, trade or commerce suited to local needs.[5]

Such curricular demands on the intermediate secondary schools were unprecedented and, at the time, impossible to reconcile. The academic and commercial/technical 'sides' came from different traditions, enjoyed dramatically different status and served different social and occupational demands. It was virtually inevitable that headteachers and staff would pull the schools one way or another and, given their own status aspirations, it was inevitable that that way would be the academic. The curriculum was, and would continue to be, the chief instrument for defining the status of the school. The examination system would reinforce curricular choices, if such they can be called, if only because they were the means of determining university matriculation.

A second branch of secondary education was grafted on to the Welsh secondary school system after 1902. Under the Education Act of that year local education authorities were empowered to open municipal secondary schools. By 1920 twelve such schools had been created in industrial south Wales and helped to fill the gap caused by the under-provision of intermediate schools in such areas.[6] However, it did bring the secondary system in Wales more closely into the orbit of the Board of Education, with its own curricular priorities. Furthermore, secondary school headteachers in Wales became even more conscious of the place of their school in the pecking order determined substantially by the kind of curriculum on offer and reinforced by the level of success in external examinations.

The creation of the Welsh intermediate secondary schools predated the state secondary system created in England after 1902, and no precedent existed for the systematic inspection and examination of such schools to ensure that state money was being expended judiciously. The consequent necessity for a regulatory body resulted in the creation of the Central Welsh Board (CWB) in 1896.[7] Its purpose was to inspect Welsh intermediate schools in respect of the award of Treasury grant and to provide and administer examinations. While the CWB was never the inspecting body for the municipal schools created after 1902 (this was exercised from 1907 by the Welsh Department of the Board of Education, which also had the right to inspect the intermediate schools), it did assume the function of administering external examinations in local authority schools. Indeed, in this period none of the secondary schools in Wales remained outside its examining orbit.

The interplay of curriculum and examinations in Welsh secondary schools from 1896 was particularly complex. In the years between 1896 and 1902, within the overall template laid down in the 1889 Act, headteachers and inspectors moulded the curriculum according to an inherited assumption that status in the new secondary schools would be determined by how far they aspired to, and reflected, the curriculum of the traditional grammar schools.[8] After 1902, the curriculum was far more tightly regulated by the Board of Education and, after 1907, by the Welsh Department of that Board. The Education Act 1902 itself had been predicated on Robert Morant's[9] belief that the segregation of middle-class education by means of secondary schools was in danger of being undermined by the activities of school boards in creating higher elementary schools and should be much more rigorously safeguarded. Various instruments were available for the purpose, including school leaving age, but chief among them were the curriculum and the examination system. The result was that from 1902, reform of the curriculum of secondary schools was determined by the Board of Education and substantially endorsed by its Welsh Department after 1907. So it was that in 1907 the curriculum of the Welsh secondary schools laid down by the Welsh Department of the Board of Education, 'should provide instruction in the English language and literature, at least one language other than English, geography, history, mathematics, science and drawing. Where Welsh is spoken the language, or one of the languages, other than English should be Welsh.'[10] The regulations also designated the time to be made available for the teaching of these subjects, although this was modified after 1908.

It is hardly surprising that relations between the two national bodies involved in the administration of secondary education in Wales so early on in its development should be constantly fraught. It is almost inconceivable that the CWB would ever have been established if the Welsh Department of the Board of Education had existed in 1896. As it was, the CWB's legal responsibilities for inspection could not be denied, but once the Welsh Department, with its aspirations to empire building and control of education in Wales, had been created it was inevitable that it would conflict not only with the CWB but with the Board of Education as well.

The pecking order soon became clear. Officials of the Board of Education regarded the Welsh Department as a nuisance and its Permanent Secretary, A. T. Davies, as someone whose ambitions should be headed off. The Welsh Department, similarly, regarded the CWB as an annoyance and its influence in the Welsh intermediate schools an interference with administrative tidiness. More than that, the Chief Inspector of the Welsh Department, O. M. Edwards, whose status as scholar and educator was legendary in Wales, and whose prime position in the Welsh Department gave him considerable power over the direction of Welsh education, regarded the examinations administered by the CWB as distorting his conception of what constituted an appropriate, genuine and stimulating Welsh education.[11]

Until the examination system was rationalized the CWB administered four examinations in Welsh intermediate and secondary schools, as follows:[12]

a) The Junior examination was intended to be taken two years after entry. It was instituted in 1899 and was not formally killed off until 1924, although in practice it was phased out some years before this.
b) The Senior examination was intended to be the culmination of the normal four-year secondary course. If taken in sufficient subjects approved by the universities and passed at credit level in one sitting, it allowed entry to university at the intermediate stage. It was re-christened the School Certificate in 1923 and was not replaced until after the Second World War, when the Ordinary level of the General Certificate of Education was inaugurated.
c) The Higher Certificate examination was taken two years after the Senior examination, and allowed entry to the first year of a three-year degree course.
d) Finally, the Honours examination, which disappeared during the First World War, was an advanced version of the Higher.

While the School and Higher Certificates have always been associated with the Welsh secondary schools it is often forgotten that originally there were also Technical and Commercial Certificates. Their significance lies in the fact that hardly any pupils sat the relevant examinations.

The secondary schools were thus dominated by regular external examinations which were, in turn, substantially determined by the universities – it was they who stipulated which subjects should be allowed for matriculation purposes. Essentially, therefore, the curriculum of the schools, ostensibly determined by the Welsh Department of the Board of Education, was in fact dominated by the demands of university matriculation. It was reported in 1911 that only 15 per cent of the 2,000 or so pupils who left the intermediate schools of Wales proceeded to higher education. Of the 1,700 remaining pupils, three-quarters took the CWB examination in Latin, 80 per cent the French examination.[13]

The irony was that Wales had acquired a system of secondary education which, by providing for relatively low school fees and access for pupils from elementary rather than private schools, gave an opportunity to children from skilled working-class and even unskilled working-class homes to gain an education denied to most of their counterparts in England. In theory, a judicious blend of academic and technical education could have allowed them, at least while the relevant jobs existed, to meet demands across the whole spectrum of Welsh occupational life. In practice, education for all those in secondary schools was dominated by the demands of the minority who went on to university.

Widespread practice within the individual subjects was that the staple method of teaching was by rote learning of factual information which could be regurgitated in examinations. Edwards was only the most high profile of Welsh educationists to object to the aridity which resulted,[14] but he was naive to vent his wrath solely on the CWB as the examining body. That body was in the grip of wider academic and social forces. Not that this detracts from the sentiments expressed in an anonymous pamphlet of 1912 which regarded the examination system as 'an annual orgy of worship of a strange god. Annually in July, the CWB passes the children of the nation through the fire of overwork to this their Moloch-god – and burns all initiative out of their intellect.'[15]

It was the examination system which brought about the most public rift between the Chief Inspector of the Welsh Department of the Board of Education and the chief national examining body in Wales. In his report on education in Welsh schools in 1909, Edwards wrote:

> the minds of the children seem to be very mechanical, their memory is overburdened where the reasoning power should have been developed ... the Central Welsh Board should now consider to what extent their rigid examination system may be the cause of the wooden and unintelligent type of mind of which their examiners

complain. The elasticity and adaptability of the curriculum and the development of differentiation among schools are difficult under such a highly centralised system of examinations ... there is a danger ... that the system of education in Wales may become stereotyped and ineffective.[16]

Evidence to support Edwards's castigations is not difficult to find in examiners' reports, as we shall see.

Perhaps the ultimate irony was that those examiners who complained about the quality of mind exhibited in their scripts were themselves usually university academics. They included some of the most eminent of Welsh scholars. The verdicts of such luminaries as (Sir) John Morris-Jones[17] and W. J. Gruffydd[18] provide the weightiest of academic opinion about standards in Welsh secondary schools, but these must have been forbidding judgements from distinguished intellects and always emerged through the prism of the research scholar. We may conclude that in their turn, however unwittingly, they contributed to the arid approaches they so often deprecated. It remained, despite the efforts of as dynamic and influential figure as Edwards, that the overwhelming criterion of success for a secondary school in Wales was the performance of its pupils in external examinations.

The fascinating element in the CWB's defence of its system of examinations from the time of its first report was that, by providing a systematic examination structure sufficiently rigorous to command credibility, it had actually rationalized and minimized the effect that examinations were having on secondary education, saving the schools from the 'grinding tyranny of external examination'.[19] It is salutary to recall that in 1897 pupils from Cardiff Intermediate School for Girls successfully passed examinations of the University of London, the Cambridge Local Examinations Board, the Oxford and Cambridge Examination Board, the National Froebel Union, the Associated Board of the Royal Academy and Royal College of Music, the Trinity College of Music and the Royal Drawing Society.[20]

During the early years of the existence of the CWB, therefore, the examination system in Wales, for all the shortcomings to which Edwards drew attention, provided a system of school certificates accepted by the various professional bodies, which allowed the schools to ignore the multiplicity of professional examinations for which parents might otherwise have forced them to prepare. By 1907–8 the Board's Senior Certificate was recognized by the University of Wales, the General Medical Council, the Board of Education (for entry to training colleges), the Pharmaceutical Society, the Royal Institute of British Architects, the Institute of Chartered Accountants, the Surveyors Institute, the Institute of Civil Engineers, the National Froebel Union, Royal Holloway College, the Society of Accountants and Auditors, the North and South Wales Bank, the Law Society and the Army.[21]

Thus it is the case that, just as the intermediate secondary schools of Wales pre-dated any state secondary system in England, the examination system in the schools, centred on the CWB, was rationalized before this happened in England. In England, before 1904, multiple external examinations, with different requirements from a variety of professional and other bodies, imposed conflicting curricular demands on secondary schools. In 1904 the Board of Education took action to limit the number of examinations for which pupils under the age of fifteen were allowed to sit. It was not until 1909 that the problem of examinations was referred to a Consultative Committee and 1911 before that Committee reported.[22]

The Committee's conclusions resembled those of Edwards. Examinations imposed restrictions on the curriculum, encouraged uniformity of teaching and restricted the initiative of teachers – arguments which have been common to all strict external testing regimes, including those in force now. The Consultative Committee therefore recommended that external examinations in secondary schools should be restricted to a School Certificate examination at the age of sixteen, to be taken by the whole class rather than selected pupils, although an examination suitable to the attainment of pupils aged eighteen should also be available.[23]

It took years of negotiation, lasting until 1917, for agreement to be reached on how the suggested rationalization should take place. Even allowing for the context of the First World War, this was a long-drawn-out process. Nevertheless, the School Certificate and the Higher School Certificate rationalized the previous plethora of examinations.

The examination which all secondary school pupils who lasted the four-year course were expected to take was the School Certificate, based on groups of subjects. There were to be three main groups: English, foreign languages, and science and mathematics, with candidates required to pass in the three groups. A fourth group, practical subjects, was significantly not included in the scheme because, according to the Board of Education, practical subjects could not be tested by written examination.[24] The body charged with coordinating and moderating the new order was the Secondary Schools Examination Council, established in 1917. With relatively few exceptions the pattern from that time until after the Second World War was that the CWB, along with the other examination boards, was subject to the overriding authority of the Secondary Schools Examination Council in respect of its examining function. By 1918, then, the pattern of external examinations had been consolidated, with the overwhelming majority of pupils being presented for examination in English, French, mathematics, the sciences, geography, history, Latin, Welsh and, to a lesser extent, the subject called, since the 1980s, religious education but which began life as scripture.[25] This was the staple diet of the pupils who attended those secondary schools which had such a crucial educational and social role in the history of Wales. It is to a detailed investigation of the examination of a range of these subjects that we now turn.

English

During the late nineteenth century and the early years of the twentieth the syllabus for examination in English was based on the model for the teaching of Latin and Greek. It emphasized the importance of grammar and syntax, with pupils expected to master complex rules, be able to parse sentences (an analysis involving the separation of sentences into their component members and the consideration of their precise relationship) and analyse textual material. In addition, Old and Middle English and philology were part of the courses studied by pupils at the Higher Certificate level. Pupils were also expected to show competence in comprehension, taught by means of an intensive study of the prose and poetry of recognized authors which pupils were expected to memorize. The 'composition' element emphasized style, correct spelling and punctuation, sentence construction and correct paragraphing. Less attention was paid to English literature, although the work of, for example, Chaucer, Spenser, Shakespeare, Carlyle, Macaulay, Gibbon and Milton gradually gained a place on the syllabus. They were studied primarily from the perspective of their commentary on morality and their historical importance.

In the years immediately before the First World War, voices were raised which questioned the methods and aims of teachers of English. The syllabus was criticized for reflecting too closely the approach adopted in teaching Latin and Greek. Prominent figures within Welsh education, notably Edwards, maintained that these methods were in dire need of reform. The narrow, utilitarian emphasis ingrained by the Revised Code of 1862, which married examination success with payment of grant in the elementary schools, was increasingly criticized, as was the tendency of examination schedules to emphasize factual information rather than literary appreciation.

During the first half of the twentieth century, examiners of English based their comments on well-established, unchanging criteria which emphasized both knowledge and skills and distinguished rigidly between language and literature. The English language examination sought to test candidates' mastery of grammar analysis, précis, comprehension and essay writing, while English literature was judged from the standpoint of textual and contextual knowledge, analysis and criticism.

Early syllabuses and examination papers reflected this approach which was to mould the study of English for many decades.[26] Grammar and composition were given detailed attention, while the study of English literature heavily emphasized the classical approach which included mastering a vast amount of information on the structure and technicalities of the language.

The emphasis on grammar required pupils to demonstrate a thorough grasp of the principles governing the structure of language. Grammar was not intended to be mere note-work but a measure of pupils' intelligence. The need to know the difference between conjugations, relative adverbs and pronouns was emphasized, and parsing was also deemed to be an essential linguistic ability. It was contended that the analysis of a sentence had a practical value as it promoted an understanding of the use of language, and gave pupils a thorough training in the logic of language.[27] In the early years of the twentieth century, examiners continually justified the emphasis on this part of the syllabus. The report on the Senior examination in 1909 maintained that sentence analysis had proved to be 'a good test of sustained thinking power'[28] and that understanding the derivation of words, particularly at the Higher level, meant that candidates had gained a thorough knowledge of historical grammar. At the same time, the translation of passages of Old and Middle English was an important examination component for many years at the Senior stage. This meant pupils had to be aware of the growth of English vocabulary over the centuries and of the relative contributions made in different periods. Candidates had to demonstrate an awareness of the influence of other languages, notably Latin and French, on English, compare 'Middle' and 'Modern' English forms and prepare notes on particular words and phrases.

At the Junior level, correct spelling and accurate punctuation were adjudged the important features of work of quality. Composition work, which included the study and imitation of recognized authors, was of major importance. This part of the syllabus was normally taught through constant practice and attention to good models in composition textbooks. Examiners regularly emphasized that grammar should not be an end in itself but should be learnt in conjunction with composition, so that knowledge of grammar assisted pupils to write clear and correct English.

Examiners regularly highlighted the key attributes of successful essays. Pupils needed to be able to marshal ideas on a subject, express themselves accurately, use correct grammar and punctuation and treat topics intelligently and imaginatively. They needed to choose appropriate vocabulary and avoid the use of slang in order to express thoughts elegantly. Style was particularly important for effective essays.

In English literature, examiners emphasized the need for sound textual knowledge and thoughtful independent judgement. Pupils were expected to study the specified text rather than rely on notes provided by their teachers, to be able to draw their own conclusions from the words of the author and show evidence of appreciation of the literary features of the text. At the same time, pupils were expected to read texts in the context of the broader political and social history of the periods studied and be aware of the relevant classical background. For instance, it was maintained that the study at Honours level of Shakespeare's plays required the capacity to appreciate individual liberty and the concept of the divine right of kings. At this level, work of quality should show awareness of key developments in literature over specific periods and utilize texts to illustrate those periods. As with English language examinations, candidates were expected to conform to a particular style in answering questions on English literature. Essays required illustrative quotations, while relevance and an effective style should be encouraged.

In these early years of the century, wide differences were noted in the quality of teaching English in the schools of Wales. Carmarthen Girls' School in 1900 was commended for the excellent way in which English literature was taught, and the teaching at Grove Park Girls' School in Wrexham was similarly complimented. A report on Aberystwyth and Cardigan schools in 1900 noted that pupils who had been taught Welsh grammar appeared to be in a particularly advantageous position to cope with the complexities of English grammar. In 1903, teachers were urged to follow similar rules of composition in correcting an English essay as they would in correcting a piece of Latin prose and, it was argued, should read and discuss standard passages of English prose from the standpoint of style and structure. The appropriateness of the diction, the balance and length of the sentences and paragraphs, punctuation and the gradual development of the topic needed to be highlighted.

Nevertheless, a staple of examiners' reports was to comment on incorrect spelling and punctuation. In 1906, spelling in some essays was said to be distinctly bad, and at the Junior stage in 1913:

> Punctuation was often weak; many pupils made the full stop almost their only support, and some had the detestable habit of sprinkling dots like full stops meaninglessly over their paper. In a few schools the English was extremely ungrammatical.[29]

In 1914 examiners found that the standard of composition was generally good, with a marked absence of the Welsh idiom observed in previous years. In 1916 examiners concluded that the results were better than could be expected in view of the effect of the First World War on the homes and minds of pupils, although the standard of achievement in English literature had declined, owing mainly to the shortage of textbooks in a number of schools.

Attention had been regularly drawn to a wide range of linguistic and cognitive problems which affected the performance of pupils in examinations in English. In 1898 examiners drew attention to the poor standard of composition.

> It is evident that Composition is not regarded in the majority of the Schools as either an art or a science, but as an accomplishment of little examinational or practical value, which may properly be left to the unaided intelligence of the Pupil. The value of words, the management of sentences, the construction of paragraphs, the arrangement of facts and ideas, the elements, in short, of Composition have not been systematically studied.[30]

Significantly, examiners did not believe those weaknesses derived from the fact that English was, for many pupils, a second language but rather contended that pupils had not been taught the art of expressing themselves correctly, lucidly and precisely. Examiners maintained that pupils needed more practice in preparing essay plans. They should be taught that every answer must have a beginning, a middle and an end, encouraged to treat one idea at a time, and arrange material appropriately.

The art of précis also needed greater attention. Many pupils at the Senior level were said to have but a faint idea of what was required and few were able to discriminate between essential and non-essential information. The adoption of a limited range of teaching approaches was also criticized. In 1898 the examiner, Prof W. Macneil Dixon of Mason College, Birmingham, noted that answers showed that, because of poor teaching methods, pupils had memorized but not understood what had been taught. In 1918 'faults due to obviously bad teaching' emerged in the scripts of pupils 'carefully crammed with cut-and-dried' answers to likely questions.[31]

The tendency to teach grammar as an end in itself and not in conjunction with the study of composition was also a problem. In 1898 it was contended that: 'The study of Grammar may easily become a species of fetish worship, and more be expected from it than the subject is able to supply, while the real value of a study of *Composition* is overlooked.'[32]

Inspectors' reports underlined the conclusions of the examiners. At Brecon in 1901, the need for grammatical theory to be always exemplified by reference to the actual practice of the language was emphasized, while at Bala Girls' School, lessons in grammar were 'somewhat mechanical' and failed to awaken interest. Many pupils appeared to recognize no difference between colloquial and literary language, wrote disconnected sentences and committed errors of syntax. In 1908 it was evident that many pupils at the Junior level had only vague and inaccurate ideas concerning abstract nouns, the definite article and auxiliary verbs. At Tregaron in 1900, 'slang and colloquialisms' were commonplace, whilst spelling and sentence-formation required attention at Llanelli Girls' School. At Bethesda many pupils lacked a firm grasp of English, whilst at Gelligaer many were found to have difficulty in expressing themselves. Similarly at Botwnog in 1902, pupils had 'considerable difficulty' in expressing themselves in English, while at Llandeilo it was recommended that pupils needed training in precise and accurate expression.[33]

Effective teaching of literature, in the judgement of examiners, required the awakening of interest in literary appreciation and the instilling of literary taste. Pupils needed to be given time to assimilate the subject-matter set, analyse it, reason upon it and compare and contrast it with other material. Questions requiring independent judgement needed to be set as school exercises and answers presented in a clear and orderly manner.

Examiners attributed the weaknesses evident from the written examinations to the poor quality of teaching in many schools. Answers often highlighted insufficient knowledge of the set texts, and there was evidence that pupils were learning passages by heart without understanding their meaning. Teachers were accused of relying too much on dictating notes and editorial comment rather than on guiding pupils through the prescribed texts. Pupils generally avoided questions requiring independent thought and many had not received adequate instruction on the use of apt quotation. These methods often led to the regurgitation of irrelevant material instead of individual responses to meet the precise demands of a question. In 1910 at the Senior stage, examiners commented on the tendency of many candidates to rely on memory rather than to exercise their independent judgement, and in 1912 noted that some candidates paid closer attention to notes than to the text itself. Quotations were often introduced in an unintelligent manner and literary terms sometimes misunderstood. The impressions gleaned by the examiners again echoed comments made by inspectors during the same period. The inspectors' report on Newtown Girls' School in 1902 noted that there was little self-reliance in answering questions on English literature, while at Swansea Grammar School the questions on 'Milton' were said to be 'quite beyond a large number of the pupils who seemed to have had no experience in basing their conclusions on personal observation and investigation of the poems'.[34]

Welsh

In the first decade of the twentieth century, examiners emphasized the need for candidates sitting CWB examinations in Welsh language and literature to demonstrate a thorough knowledge of grammar, including accidence, the mutation of initial consonants, the conjugation of verbs and prepositions, and the analysis of sentences. The importance of parsing as a 'whetstone' in grammatical training was emphasized and it was deemed essential that pupils understood the government and relationship of different words in a sentence as this would ensure that they gained an awareness of the distinctive rules of the Welsh language. Considerable emphasis was placed on candidates' ability to translate prepared and unprepared passages into English. Translation was viewed as a means of promoting linguistic competence in both Welsh and English because teachers would have the opportunity to discuss the meaning of words in both languages. Pupils at the most advanced stages were expected to demonstrate an understanding of linguistic features such as the Latin element in Welsh and be able to answer questions on the style, manners, vocabulary and orthography of the prepared texts. Remarkably, most of the examination was conducted through the medium of English, although a limited number of questions could be answered in Welsh. In an era dominated by the emphasis on mastering grammar and translation skills, little attention was devoted to the study of Welsh literature, although during the years immediately before the First World War works such as *Cartrefi Cymru* by Edwards, *Drych y Prif Oesoedd* by Theophilus Evans and *Cywydd Hiraeth am Fôn* and *Cywydd y Farn Fawr* by Goronwy Owen were studied.

Examiners emphasized the understanding of Welsh grammar as a crucial aspect of pupils' work. Morris-Jones maintained that the study of Welsh grammar was an important scientific training which exercised pupils' intelligence:

> Welsh grammar is a science based upon facts already for the most part in their possession; it exercises their intelligence without burdening their memory. Hence, although Welsh is a difficult language, its study can be carried by them to a higher stage in a given time than that of any other language; by this means they may be brought at a much earlier age than would otherwise be possible to realise the nature of grammatical rules, to understand figures of speech, to gave some idea of what is meant by style.[35]

The quality of work in Welsh was regarded as being generally satisfactory during these years. Nevertheless, some aspects caused concern to the examiners. It was noted that some pupils had not mastered the names of the different mutations. In 1909, Gruffydd found that the pupils in some districts 'seemed to have no ear for even the most ordinary mutations'. Similarly, in dealing with the inflection of the verb, pupils were reported to have shown insufficient care in distinguishing between good and bad forms. Parsing was also a problem for many pupils. In 1900 Thomas Powel[36] noted that this aspect was the weakest part of the examination and examples of accurate, complete and well-arranged parsing were rare at any stage.

Morris-Jones emphasized the need for candidates to be able to parse each word separately if the construction of the Welsh sentence were to be understood. In 1903 he tendered advice on the art of parsing to assist teachers and pupils:

> In *gwelais dy dy frawd* the noun *brawd* is related to the rest of the sentence by being dependent upon *ty*, which is the object of the verb. Sufficient attention had not been given to the parsing of verbs containing their own subjects: in the sentence just quoted, *ty* was frequently given as the subject of *gwelais*; in some cases, where it was dimly perceived that *ty* was the object, the verb *gwelais* was said to be the subject of *ty*! One other point perhaps deserves mention: the subject of the verb 'to be,' as of other verbs in Welsh, follows it; in the sentence – *gwaith ofer oedd iddo geisio cloi'r enaid* – set in the Honours grammar paper, *gwaith* is the complement of the verb, the subject is *ceisio*; *cloi* depends upon this in the genitive, and *enaid* is similarly dependent upon *cloi*; the literal meaning of the sentence is 'to him the seeking of the locking of the soul was vain work'.[37]

Examiners reflected contemporary ideas in emphasizing the role of translation from Welsh into English in the development of skills in English composition. They maintained that, unless correct English were insisted upon, pupils would not appreciate the significance of the Welsh or English idiom and emphasized that effective translation required more than a mere word-for-word translation. In order to achieve this aim, teachers were advised to encourage pupils to read widely in both English and Welsh. It was important that pupils should be able to choose the most appropriate English word and the correct English idiom. Words such as *rhagluniaeth* proved difficult for some candidates and it was noted in 1909 that it had been translated as predestination, government, influence, power and prophecy in different scripts. *Plant athrylith* was given as sons of talent, plain children, educated boys, and children of labour, while *mursenyddion* appeared in one translation as members of parliament.

Translation from English into Welsh also generated problems. Many pupils were unable to provide the Welsh names of large towns in Wales and examiners noted that colloquial and anglicized forms of expression were common, even in Higher papers. In 1909, Gruffydd wrote:

> Not more than about twenty pupils in South Wales could translate a negative question 'haven't you seen?' correctly, the common formula being *oes mo chwi wedi gweld?* The following were common mistakes: *triodd, gwneudyr* (N. Wales for *gwydr*); *mynachlog, mynachen, gwraig mynach* (for fem. of *mynach*); 'lady-like mansion' *(annedd foneddigaidd)*; *cyrodd (curodd)*; *ombwyty* and *abwyti; doniol* (for 'strange').[38]

Many pupils experienced difficulty in explaining the Latin equivalent of the Welsh word. For instance, in 1912 it was found that some pupils believed that the Welsh word *po* was derived from the Latin *quo* and that *paham*, was a derivation of *quam*. Nevertheless, Morris-Jones maintained that questions on the influence of Latin were a crucial part of the examination. He maintained that teachers should endeavour to teach Welsh in the following way:

> The Latin verb should be explained by means of the Welsh verb; the use of the Latin imperfect tense may be compared with that of the Welsh imperfect; and similarly the use of the subjunctive mood, the omission of the pronominal subject of a verb, the agreement of noun and adjective, and so on. It will be found most instructive to point out the correspondences of Welsh and French syntax. A passage from a Latin or Greek text-book read by the pupils should be occasionally set for translation into Welsh; it will undoubtedly stimulate the pupils to a better understanding of the original, besides being an excellent exercise in Welsh composition. A Latin or Greek author might even at times be translated into Welsh in class.[39]

Throughout this period examiners emphasized the need for Welsh to be taught by those with a specialist training in the subject. The argument was propagated forcefully by Gruffydd before the First World War and was reiterated in the inter-war period. Some school governors and headteachers considered Welsh to be a subject which could be taught by non-specialists, despite examiners maintaining that each school should have an honours graduate in Welsh on the staff.

The precarious status of Welsh as a subject is evident. It was grouped with French, and candidates in that subject were invariably more numerous than those in Welsh. The attitudes in schools in which Welsh occupied a vulnerable position reflected the views of many parents who regarded a qualification in Welsh as of less worth in the world of employment than one in French. That the schools did not make greater efforts to counteract such attitudes was a serious matter for the fate of the language. It is true that, in 1891, nearly 55 per cent of the population could speak Welsh and there were more Welsh speakers at the end of the nineteenth century than at the beginning. Nevertheless, the pressures on the language were inexorable as anglicization and the English language ate steadily into Welsh-speaking communities, especially in the industrial areas. In no sector of the Welsh education system was the preservation of the Welsh language a priority and the secondary schools' curriculum did nothing at this stage to enhance the status of Welsh as an academic subject.

French

During the nineteenth century, modern foreign languages struggled to gain recognition as acknowledged academic subjects. Their study received little attention at universities and this omission was reflected in the school curriculum. In the early decades of the twentieth century, however, modern languages gained a firmer position in the universities and in a number of schools, not least because of a campaign by the Modern Languages Association. It based its efforts on the argument that a training in a modern language offered a valuable means of disciplining the mind, rather than on ensuring pupils gained an oral proficiency in the language, which was viewed at the time as less significant. The Board of Education's Regulations for Secondary Schools, issued in 1904, advocated the teaching of one modern language for at least 3.5 hours a week, and after the First World War the position of modern languages in the secondary school curriculum was strengthened by the Leathes Report of 1918.[40] Even so, the development of modern languages teaching proved very slow, not least because of the difficulty experienced in attracting qualified teachers. Many schools relied on the services of teachers with no specialist training and there were comparatively few graduate teachers of modern languages. Moreover, there was a tendency in some circles to regard the introduction of modern languages as a further encumbrance, especially in Welsh-speaking areas where it became the custom not to commence studies in modern languages until the second year of secondary schooling. It was also clear that, despite the efforts of the Modern Languages Association, few schools offered any choice other than French. This was attributed to the historical links which existed between Britain and France and also the fact that there were more French teachers available than teachers of any other language.[41] At the Senior Stage in 1914, 1,127 candidates were entered for examination in French, compared with only 18 in German.

Throughout the early part of the twentieth century, the teaching of French concentrated on ensuring that pupils knew the basics of French grammar and they were expected to be proficient in translation skills. The emphasis lay firmly on the written rather than the spoken word and examination candidates were expected to show mastery of philology and sentence analysis.

In the years immediately before the First World War, aims and methods of teaching were challenged by reformers who wanted a greater emphasis on oral skills; some went as far as to advocate the introduction of the direct method of teaching. This method favoured the use of the target language as much as possible and regarded fluent communication as the chief objective. The movement was deeply influenced by the work of linguists such as W. Victor, Francis Gouin, Henry Sweet and Otto Hesperen and gained same support among teachers. The CWB made a concession by producing a Direct Method alternative syllabus, although few schools chose to adopt it. However, an increasing number of schools did make greater use of oral work. In 1901 examiners noted that the increase in attention to oral skills had succeeded in raising the overall performance of pupils and the importance of this aspect was reiterated in 1909. Nevertheless, it remained the case that many teachers were very unhappy about the way in which the subject was taught. For instance in 1912 J. De Gruchy Gaudin, a teacher at Caernarfon County School, noted that the examination schedules were responsible for generating a distaste for the subject, the syllabuses were unsuitable and the questions on grammar too difficult. At the same time, traditionalists warned that the learning of correct grammar should be the key feature of modern language teaching. By 1912 the Board of Education was itself expressing reservations about the lack of attention devoted to grammatical accuracy by those teachers who taught by the Direct Method.

The Direct Method was also questioned by the Leathes Report in 1918. It reiterated the need for grammatical accuracy[42] although it also conceded the need for some reform of the syllabus in order to place greater weight on oral proficiency. CWB Inspectors, notably Sadie Price, similarly emphasized the importance of oral work alongside formal grammar.

At this time, the syllabus for modern languages deliberately sought to emulate the aims and methods adopted in teaching the classical languages of Latin and Greek. The syllabus and examination schedules sought to ensure that pupils had mastered grammar and philology, and emphasized the skills of translation and composition. The emphasis was on knowledge of the written word, with only a few schools introducing an element of oral work. For most pupils, learning modern languages meant translating prepared and unprepared texts into English and some translating from English into French. Pupils were expected to convey the meaning of those passages accurately and in correct and idiomatic English. Some examiners underlined the importance of translation:

Strange as it may seem, it is evidently necessary to point out to those who clamour for its abolition, that no test will be more frequently required than this of the scholar in after life. From an educational standpoint, too, there are few finer intellectual exercises, rightly understood. But we in this country have never rightly understood the value or the true method of translation, which should be prepared and not extempore work, and should consist neither in the niggard expression of the literal sense of a passage in very questionable English nor in a loose and imaginative paraphrase. The one object should be to combine precision and elegance, which will result in each sentence and each part of a sentence receiving its logical and, in the higher forms, its literary equivalent. This continual wrestling with the text would undoubtedly develop the mental facilities of the pupils, and their style in the mother tongue would benefit from the exercise to an extent on which I need not enlarge. Time of course should be given for several rough copies of the passage to be written before the final version is drafted. This method forms the basis of literary instruction in French schools and its effects are clearly perceptible in the ease and grace of style so conscious among well educated French ... I should be glad if the teachers of French in the Welsh Secondary schools, with the natural enthusiasm and the quick perception which distinguishes them among all home-trained teachers of a foreign tongue, would boldly take the initiative in this direction as in others previously mentioned.[43]

Examiners continually emphasized the need for pupils to acknowledge the importance of adopting the English idiom when translating from French. They regularly complained that translations were 'too literal' or 'wooden' and that the translation of prepared passages appeared to be based on memory rather than on understanding of meaning. Moreover, examiners complained that some pupils' answers revealed evidence of guesswork, leading to instances of utter nonsense. Teachers were urged to ensure that pupils gained practice in translating both unseen and prepared passages and that their vocabulary was sufficient to enable them to tackle the task with ease.

It was also deemed essential that pupils demonstrate their understanding of the general meaning of passages instead of concentrating their efforts on individual words or phrases. Examiner Newall criticized those candidates who omitted unfamiliar words, and even at the Higher stage it was noted that there was too much 'wild and unintelligent guessing', one examiner in 1914 stating:

> In translation into English, out of 126 pupils only some half a dozen obtained 75 per cent and over, while about a score were failures. The majority gave bad renderings. Many showed much ignorance of common idioms and constructions.[44]

Translation into French was also required at the end of the nineteenth century, although by 1902 candidates were given the option of writing a French composition rather than attempting the translation. Again the examiners highlighted frequent cases of carelessness on the part of candidates who clearly needed more regular practice in writing passages of prose and in oral training to enlarge their vocabulary. In 1901 examiners noted that the quality of the work was often feeble and that Higher standards were only achieved by those at the Honours level. Many prose compositions were marred because candidates did not have a command of French vocabulary and made mistaken use of tenses. At the Senior stage in 1912 the pupils' French vocabulary was also found to be very uneven, whilst at the Higher stage the following year there was 'too much literalness' evident in the translation exercise. Many teachers had taken the view that prose composition was easier than translation into French, a view which had led to some dubious teaching methods. In 1908, for instance, it was noted that some pupils reproduced memorized sentences when writing a prose essay even though they had nothing whatever to do with the set subject. The examiner noted:

> The free composition of those pupils taking unprepared work was not very good on the whole. The most popular and the best done subject was Welsh scenery, the pupils generally having the necessary vocabulary and confining themselves to single sentences. Oliver Cromwell, the subject next in popularity, made more demands on their syntax, and was not well done in most cases. Amongst the pupils taking set books, some did good free compositions on Germain; but few who attempted the characters in *Britannicus* were successful. The pupils taking the special paper sent in a few good free compositions on the set books.[45]

In 1910 the examiners noted that the average pupil could not produce an acceptable piece of French prose due to weaknesses in grammar and idiom.

The quality of response to questions on grammar also drew regular criticism from the examiners. In 1898 Frederick Spencer[46] noted that many papers were spoiled by inaccuracies and that few pupils, even in the Higher examinations, displayed adequate knowledge of French grammar and syntax. Throughout the early years of the twentieth century pupils were criticized for defective parsing, gender inaccuracies and errors in the application of grammatical rules. Etymologies were not explained properly and only the most rudimentary questions on methodology were attempted. In 1910 examiners noted that questions on grammar at the Senior level indicated the subject was studied as theory without sufficient oral and written practice.

Questions on French literature were also not answered to the satisfaction of the examiners. Candidates were expected to demonstrate their knowledge of the texts themselves, to appreciate their style and be aware of the broader context of the period in which the literature had been written. Nevertheless, many answers were criticized for superficiality and for making sweeping statements, while many candidates made broad comments which rarely addressed the points raised by the questions.

Although oral proficiency was not a compulsory part of the examinations, many pupils were tested in oral skills. In 1898 Spencer commended the decision to introduce oral French into the syllabus and urged more schools to adopt it. Oral ability was tested by means of reading and dictation and many schools based their teaching on conventional methods of instruction. In 1900 it was stated:

> In most instances, the reports on reading and pronunciation were distinctly good. The general results of the dictation tests in all the Stages this year were considerably better than those in the preceding one. In fact, the improvements throughout the schools were as great as could reasonably be expected in a single year. In a few schools, some of the dictation exercises were practically faultless. On the other hand, there were some schools in which it was tolerably evident that the pupils had had little or no practice in

writing passages from dictation. This fault should be remedied, and, in every school, at least one half-hour a week should be devoted to an exercise in dictation.[47]

Examiners predicted that the introduction of oral French would emphasize the fact that it was a modern, living language and they complimented progressive teachers who gave attention to this aspect whilst not neglecting other aspects such as grammar and sentence structure. Other examiners remained cautious. Whilst recognising the value of oral work, one rejected the tendency to teach French through the Direct Method. Moreover, he warned that there was a danger that in some schools French conversation lessons took a stereotyped form in which pupils were only able to respond to a very narrow range of questions. Such comments were reiterated in 1911:

> Although there was ample evidence of steady and painstaking work in the majority of schools as well as of diligence and intelligence among the pupils yet the French teaching does not appear to be on sound lines except in a small number of schools. In most schools there is considerable room for improvement. In some the French teaching is evidently bad. The reports of the Oral Examiners fully confirmed the impression made by the written work. The majority of the schools showed weakness in reading, pronunciation, and conversation. There is little doubt that this state of things was largely due to the neglect of the study of the sounds of the language. It cannot be too strongly emphasised or repeated too often that, no matter what method be employed, the study of a language must be based on a knowledge of its sounds, without which a full appreciation of its poetry or literary prose is impossible.[48]

The quality of French teaching in Welsh schools was affected by the upheaval of the First World War as shortages and frequent changes of staff meant that a growing number of classes were taught by teachers who had no specialist training in French. Nevertheless, few changes were made to the examination schedules. Proficiency in French continued to be measured primarily by reference to written work, the oral test remaining optional and carrying few marks. The influence of the universities on the kind of topics examined was strong, especially at the Higher Certificate level. Examiners continued to focus on the need for accuracy and knowledge of the rules of grammar, although gradually the emphasis on theoretical grammar and on philology diminished.

Latin

By the time of the establishment of the Welsh intermediate schools the position of Latin in the school curriculum was firmly established. Latin and Greek were accorded a central role in the work of the English public schools, upon which so many headteachers in Wales tried to model their institutions. Pupils were expected to undertake a systematic study of the language by considering grammatical forms, the features of accidence, verb forms and gender rules. Translation was also viewed as a key skill, and proficiency in prose composition was regarded as a means of testing pupils' ability to apply the grammatical knowledge they had learned. The Board of Education continually underlined the importance of Latin. The Secondary Schools Regulations of 1904 stipulated that if two languages other than English were to be taught one had to be Latin. Even so, many contemporary commentators expressed doubts about the need to give such prominence to it in the school curriculum. By 1914 commentators were criticizing the emphasis on grammar[49] and individuals such as William Lewis, headmaster of Llanelli County School, regarded the emphasis on Latin as being responsible for the 'pronounced academic bias of the schools'.[50] Other commentators drew attention to the 'classical bias' prevailing at the Board of Education. The insistence on Latin as a compulsory subject for matriculation for the University of Wales was also criticized.[51] By 1916 the place of Latin on the school curriculum had become a burning issue in Welsh education circles. Increasingly, commentators questioned the emphasis on a dead language and it was contended that other languages were as effective as Latin in promoting mental discipline.[52]

In the early years of intermediate education, examination papers sought to test pupils' competence in Latin grammar, their ability to translate prepared and unprepared passages of Latin into English, and to translate English sentences into Latin. The syllabus mirrored the courses adopted in England, although pupils in Wales rarely studied Latin before the age of twelve, three years later than their English counterparts, and despite fewer hours being allocated to the subject in Wales. Thus the CWB regulations required pupils to master a syllabus similar to that pursued by English pupils in a much shorter period of time.

Examiners also made detailed comments about the quality of the teaching. In 1905 it was noted that it varied considerably, much depending on the personality and enthusiasm of the teacher. Examiners' reports referred to failures in pupils' understanding of Latin grammar. It was noted that some pupils paid little attention to elementary principles of grammar and syntax. For instance, case-construction received only superficial attention. These weaknesses were clearly in evidence when pupils attempted to translate English sentences into Latin. Such questions sought to test candidates' knowledge of the rules of syntax, required mastery of constructions and a grasp of the principles of Latin prose, and were regarded as a means of stimulating thought and developing a thorough understanding of the language. The standard of work varied immensely. Many candidates showed that their command of Latin idioms was very limited and failed to cast a sentence or paragraph in a way that set its clauses in the Latin order. In 1908, examiners complained that even at the Honours level there was a tendency for candidates to adopt English sentence structures, and in the Higher examination in 1912 it was noted that some candidates wrote with a disregard of gender, declension and conjugation.

The quality of the translations submitted also drew adverse comments from the examiners. J. Mortimer Angus,[53] for example, maintained that candidates ought to be able to choose appropriate English words and present their translations in the English idiom. He maintained that teachers should drill pupils in the meaning of words and the grammatical construction of sentences. It was maintained that translation into English of unseen passages was a good test of these skills. The main weakness highlighted by the examiners was loose phrasing, by means of which candidates sought to convey the general meaning of a passage instead of a proper translation. This was noted at all levels of examination, with teachers being reminded of the need for pupils to be given adequate practice in the art of translating unseen passages. Such comments contributed to the improvement in the quality of unseen translations noted by examiners in the years immediately before the First World War. In 1913 and 1914 examiners commented that the quality of this aspect of the examination had improved, attributing this to the better methods adopted by teachers.

Translation of prepared passages generated its own problems. Examiners complained of candidates failing to choose appropriate English words, while many candidates' work suggested they had been taught to commit entire passages to memory without fully understanding the meaning. The problem was exemplified by a comment in the examiners' report for 1905:

> In one of the extracts from Caesar the first word had been changed in the printed paper for the sake of clearness; but about a quarter of the pupils translated the text which was not before them; while in the Ovid it was no unusual thing for the translation to begin or end a line too soon or too early – in one case a wholly different passage of the same length was substituted; moreover, it was apparent that in some cases the words used were misunderstood.[54]

Examiners noticed instances of sentences which had been translated correctly appearing in the wrong place. In some cases, the same mistakes were repeated in numerous papers submitted from the same school. Other candidates suffered because of loose style and poor English – a point regularly emphasized by examiners.

Nevertheless, examiners noted that the majority of schools appeared to be committed to retaining Latin as a key element of the school curriculum, made evident by the fact that increased numbers were being entered for the examination throughout the 1920s.

Geography

The late nineteenth century was a period of considerable significance for the academic study of geography. The Taunton Report of 1868 noted that the subject was given little attention in the curriculum of the endowed grammar schools in Wales and a similar conclusion was reached in the Aberdare Report in 1881. In the early years of the new intermediate schools there was also a considerable reluctance on the part of Welsh education leaders to devote attention to the subject and this, combined with the absence of qualified specialist teachers, meant little had been achieved by the end of the century. Geography teaching relied heavily on second-rate textbooks which rigidly separated the physical and political aspects, and which tended to see the subject as an appendix to geology on the one hand and history on the other. Pupils were trained to learn the names of rivers, mountains and towns, with little effort made to teach the skills of applying that factual knowledge.

The malaise affecting the teaching of geography was, however, challenged during the last years of the nineteenth century. Under the leadership of pioneering geographers such as Halford J. Mackinder a new approach was adopted which emphasized the scope and potential of the subject. Mackinder maintained that the subject had to be regarded as 'the science of distribution' which traced the arrangement of things in general on the earth's surface. He also stressed the need for pupils to be able to provide explanations of human life on the earth's surface, to show an understanding of the relationship between man and his environment, and to be able to apply the factual knowledge they had learned. His ideas strongly influenced the principles of 'New Geography' which exerted a growing influence on the teaching of the subject at both university and schools during the early years of the twentieth century.[55]

The position of geography in Welsh schools was strengthened further by the influence of H. J. Fleure, whose pioneering work at the University College of Wales at Aberystwyth[56] ensured that geography gained due recognition as a serious academic discipline. He was a major influence on United Kingdom geography, serving as honorary secretary of the Geographical Association and honorary editor of the *Geographical Teacher* for nearly thirty years from 1917. Due to Fleure's significance the Geographical Association had its headquarters at Aberystwyth from 1917 until 1930 when he moved to Manchester. In his role as chief examiner in geography for the CWB, Fleure also contributed perceptive comments on the need to include the fruits of academic research in the classrooms of the intermediate schools of Wales, an approach endorsed by fellow examiners such as James Fairgrieve, W. R. Whitehouse and C. Daryll Forde. Gradually, anthropology and historical geography were given a place in the school syllabus and geography gained recognition as a valid discipline. By 1921, 80 per cent of all candidates at the School Certificate level sat the examination in geography.

The changing nature of school geography is illustrated in the syllabus studied by pupils in Wales. At the end of the nineteenth century pupils sat two papers, the first on physical geography and the other a general paper covering a broad range of topics. Physical geography was influenced by advances in geology and physiography, pupils being expected to demonstrate their knowledge of volcanoes, terrains, mountain ranges and plains, and to be aware of the processes by which those physical features had evolved. The syllabus demanded a broad span of knowledge, including the physical characteristics of different continents. For instance, in 1898 pupils attempting the physical geography examination were expected to be able to describe the physical structure of North America and to compare it with other continents. The emphasis on factual knowledge was also evident in the general geography paper. The paper required pupils to demonstrate knowledge of the major towns and cities of continental Europe and the United States, as well as the chief ports of Asia, Africa and South America. In addition, the geography syllabus gave pupils a detailed knowledge of the British Empire. At the same time, however, the syllabus emphasized knowledge of the home locality and the physical and political geography of Wales. Candidates were questioned on their knowledge of the main Welsh towns and the physical features of the surrounding countryside. As early as 1898 examiners had expressed alarm at the 'discreditable ignorance' shown of many famous Welsh localities.[57] The following year schools were criticized for neglecting the study of Wales, considered 'wrong, both educationally and nationally'.[58] The physical geography of Wales in particular had been neglected, with many teachers choosing to illustrate examples of physical phenomena from other parts of the world, even though such examples could have been drawn from the immediate locality. Despite the continuing emphasis on the need for pupils to acquire factual knowledge, examiners in Wales were acutely aware of the way in which geography, as an academic discipline, was increasingly emerging as a scientific subject rather than one which adopted a descriptive approach based on the recall of such knowledge. In 1900 teachers were reminded that geography was far more than a catalogue of facts to be learned by rote and that, in addition to testing recall, examiners would expect pupils to show an understanding of underlying causes and the influence of the environment on human life. For instance, it was stated that pupils needed greater familiarity with the relationship between geographical factors and the growth of towns, together with the influence of geology on the economy of the relevant areas.

These aspects of geography were continually emphasized by Fleure, who served as examiner for geography after 1909. The author of pioneering studies at Aberystwyth which stressed the interaction between man and his environment, Fleure was convinced of the need to use the examination system to improve the quality of geography teaching. He exerted considerable influence on the development of a syllabus which sought to ensure that pupils who studied geography gained more than bald factual information.

In 1910 teachers were told that geography was a study of relationships, and the examination schedules at Junior Certificate level specified the need for pupils to be able to compare and contrast relationships between man and his physical environment in different regions of the world. This meant that pupils had to gain a knowledge of life in tropical forests, deserts, the mountains of the Himalayas, the South Sea Islands and the frozen north, as well as the general geography of the continent of Europe. The syllabus for the Junior stage also stipulated that the study of the physical geography of Britain should consider its effects on the economy. For instance, a geographical study of London would include consideration of the factors which led 'a tidal swamp and its islets and promontories' to become the site of the first city of the world. In addition, pupils were expected to gain an understanding of the factors which fostered long-distance trade and its influence on the political geography of the world.

Although the syllabus continued to stress knowledge and understanding of the geography of the world, special attention was to be devoted to local geography through the study of a particular locality, the idea being that the skills and interest generated should be nurtured and applied to the study of world geography. By 1914, therefore, examiners were determined that the study of geography should centre on skills as much as factual knowledge, and that pupils should be encouraged to think broadly and exercise individual judgement. Pupils should understand geographical principles and be able to apply their factual knowledge to questions which tested understanding of those principles.

The need for geography to be taught by specialist teachers was continuously highlighted by examiners in the early years of the twentieth century. As a subject, it did not enjoy the status afforded to the like of mathematics or physical science. As early as 1901, the CWB was urged to put pressure on the University of Wales to recognize geography as a qualifying subject for matriculation which could be studied to degree level. This, examiners felt, would ensure that specialist teachers, qualified in modern geographical methods, would end the humdrum and lifeless teaching of the subject. In 1906, examiners emphasized the importance of good teaching for the future of the subject: 'Earnest and efficient teachers are wanted; for pupils, in whatever environment, will always respond to such teachers and adequate equipment would necessarily follow.'[59]

At the same time, examiners maintained that the resources available to geography teachers were often inadequate. The use of maps and lantern slides, together with the introduction of practical fieldwork, was strongly advocated, and examiners insisted that such work could only be undertaken if classrooms were equipped with the appropriate apparatus. They recommended the creation of geography laboratories where it would be possible to undertake detailed map work.

Despite the encouragement given by examiners, the supply of qualified teachers remained inadequate. In 1918, Fairgrieve complained that in many schools the subject was taught by people with no specialist training in geography and the time allocated was inadequate.

History

Throughout the twentieth century examiners have been conscious of their role in the development of history as an academic discipline. They have sought to guide teachers and pupils by emphasising the need for examination candidates to demonstrate sound historical knowledge and understanding, together with a range of skills and competencies. During the early years examiners highlighted the need for accurate factual detail and for pupils to demonstrate a sense of time, conceptual understanding, breadth of perspective and an awareness of the impact of historical research. In addition, examiners regularly drew attention to issues such as the danger that those studying history specialize in too narrow a range of topics. They were particularly critical of the neglect of medieval history and the fact that Welsh history merited little attention in many schools.

The primary objective of history teachers at this time was to ensure that pupils gained a factual knowledge of the history of England and Wales. The sixteen papers set for the 1898 examination covered aspects of the history of England and Wales between 55 BC and 1815. By 1904, when there were twenty-one syllabuses, only two, covering the periods 416–1273 and 1789–1915, examined the history of Europe. The schedules indicated that for the Senior examination, attention should focus on the history of England and Wales and should concentrate on issues such as the growth of the constitution, the chief characters and movements of the period, the social consequences of great wars, the relations between Church and state, and the influences of Europe in British history.

Examiners insisted that pupils needed to show understanding as well as factual recall. In 1897 candidates were expected to be able to distinguish between significant and insignificant facts. Examination questions demanded more than the mere regurgitation of factual knowledge but examiners regretted that those questions which required pupils to give evidence of independent thought were generally avoided and few pupils were able to demonstrate a critical faculty. There was little indication of insight or evaluation: the power to read behind events was the exception rather than the rule.

Examination reports made detailed suggestions as to the means by which the teaching of history could be improved. Examiners insisted that lessons should be planned to combine effective methodology and teaching styles, as well as appropriate learning activities designed to ensure that pupils acquire understanding and skills. It was recognized that teaching history to those under fourteen years of age was difficult. Examiners were conscious of the need to change a teaching approach entirely dependent on a disconnected set of notes, dictated to the pupils, which were often misunderstood. Teachers and pupils were therefore reminded of the need to embrace modern interpretations and to renounce antiquated historical notions. This, it was emphasized, would overcome the wide-ranging cognitive difficulties which adversely affected the quality of learning in history.

Inspectors' reports on individual schools reflected the evidence gleaned by the examiners. Schools such as Grove Park School, Wrexham, were complimented for the way in which pupils were encouraged to look beneath the surface to determine principles. Elsewhere a different picture emerged. The work of pupils at Llanelli Girls' School in 1900 suggested that there was too much reliance on one superficial textbook, leading to serious deficiencies.

The status of the history of Wales in the intermediate schools was low. This reflected contemporary academic fashions which dictated that the history which was worth studying was that of the state. Sir John Edward Lloyd's magisterial study of Wales[60] was of a period in which Wales had at least limited independence from England. It is true that O. M. Edwards had written a history of more recent events in Wales which served the different purpose of eulogising rural Wales and the moral and cultural achievements of its inhabitants.

Edwards's *Wales*[61] served as a textbook for generations. But suitable resources for the teaching of Welsh history in secondary schools were minimal and attitudes to Welsh history among teachers and parents were not dissimilar to those relating to the teaching of the Welsh language.

Examiners did their best to bolster the status of the history of Wales but with little success. Teachers were reminded of its value in stimulating the imagination, and training judgement. Welsh history, it was maintained, should not be regarded as of less educational value than other sections of the syllabuses. Nevertheless, the problems continued. Ernest Hughes[62] claimed there was no attempt to teach the history of Wales in some schools, and there was evidence that many pupils adopted the expedient of applying to Wales what they had learned about England. 'Thus the Wesley brothers and Whitfield were occasionally described as Welshmen who by preaching to their fellow countrymen in their native tongue brought about the religious revival in Wales.'[63] Moreover, it was evident from pupils' work that Welsh history was taught to the majority in the form of dictated notes on a few important episodes and a few great careers. Intervening periods – decades or centuries as the case might be – were treated as 'blank spaces of time'.[64]

History examiners, like those in geography, stressed the need for suitably qualified and trained specialist teachers. In 1899 it was contended that history was not given equal status with subjects like classics, mathematics and science. Whilst special knowledge and technical skill were deemed essential for those subjects, school authorities were content seemingly to commit the teaching of history to instructors who are devoid of any particular qualification or training therefor.[65]

With 'amateur teachers', pupils were subject to 'the unintelligent reproduction of the statements and even the phraseology of textbooks'.[66] In 1902 it was noted that where trained historians were responsible for the teaching, its quality stood out. In addition, examiners maintained that more attention should be given to securing effective linkage between history and other subjects, notably geography and English literature. In 1904 and 1906 history examiners found a 'deeply rooted ignorance of geography' which prevented many pupils from gaining a clear and intelligent perspective on the periods studied. Teachers were therefore urged to make use of maps in their lessons so that geography became the handmaiden of history. In addition, linguistic difficulties were identified. These included restricted vocabulary, a tendency to verbosity, weakness of style and failures of grammar and spelling, as well as a misunderstanding of key terms and concepts. Although some examiners attributed these weaknesses to the fact that English was not the first language of many candidates, it was noted that similar problems also existed in English-speaking parts of Wales.

Scripture

The study of religion, and religions, in the state schools of England and Wales has caused more controversy than that of any other subject over the last century, whether it has been called scripture, religious instruction, religious education or religious studies.

Such controversy is rooted deep in the history of state education. The Christian religion and denominational affiliations within it played a central role in the establishment of both elementary and secondary schools in the nineteenth century. For example, the impact of the National and British Societies in providing a network of elementary schools in the early decades of that century was central to the voluntary effort preceding the involvement of the state. Nevertheless, the negative impact of denominational rivalry on the progress and acceptance of state education cast a long shadow over successive Education Acts well into the twentieth century and had a particularly significant impact in Wales, with its majority of Nonconformist worshippers. The Board schools set up in the wake of the 1870 Education Act, which soon came to dominate elementary education in Wales, operated under the Cowper Temple clause which stated that 'no religious catechism or religious formulary distinctive of any particular denomination shall be taught in any state-provided school'.[67] But the many voluntary schools continued to provide denominational religious instruction. Since most such schools were

Anglican, religious controversy accompanied all attempts at state reform of the system.

While the Cowper Temple clause contemplated simple biblical teaching in all schools, the teaching of religion in elementary schools was such a delicate matter that either it was taught ineffectually or not at all. Sensitivities in Wales were dramatically heightened at the time of the 1902 Education Act which extended the provision of rate support for voluntary denominational schools. Lloyd George's purple prose had it that 'for hours this House swirled round and round in the vortex of a mad frenzy of theological controversy'[68] and he was to orchestrate the 'Welsh revolt' against financial support for denominational schools which brought most of Wales into direct constitutional conflict with the Westminster government.

Victorian grammar schools had been regarded with suspicion by Welsh Nonconformists because of their Anglican connections and proselytizing potential. The newly established intermediate schools were intended for pupils of any and all denominations, and Anglicans and Nonconformists alike attempted to avoid religious controversy. The result was that other subjects were given a much higher priority in the curriculum of the newly established schools. The Intermediate and Technical Education Act 1889 had echoed the Cowper Temple clause in stipulating that no catechism or formulary should be taught, and that pupils might opt out of any religious instruction.

It is therefore not surprising that, despite its central role in Welsh society, religion was a Cinderella of the secondary school curriculum for much of the twentieth century. The teaching of scripture knowledge was haphazard and the numbers of examination candidates low. For example, in 1906, 33 schools presented 422 candidates at Junior Certificate level, 16 schools entered 96 pupils for the Senior Certificate and there was one candidate at Honours level. In the CWB examinations in 1914, there were candidates from only 29 schools – 435 at the Junior stage, 139 at the Senior stage and none for the Higher certificate. Twenty-five years later, only 36 secondary schools in Wales entered candidates for external examinations

– 564 at School Certificate level, 3 at the Higher level. Even by 1950, when there were 988 candidates at School Certificate level, only 20 were presented at the Higher stage.

Examiners regularly expressed regret that so few pupils took examinations in Scripture but its controversial context was not the only reason. The situation was exacerbated by the congested curriculum. In many schools scripture was only allocated a meagre amount of time and often abandoned before the School Certificate stage. There was also a school of thought which held that religion could not be taught because it demanded a spiritual response which had to be spontaneous if it was to be sincere. The examiner for scripture knowledge in 1913 held that the low priority given to the subject was practical: 'it does not seem to add anything to the pupils' equipment for the immediate utilitarian demands of life'.[69] The other major reason for its low priority was the notion that it was the job of the Sunday schools to inculcate religious knowledge. In 1916 it was argued that more thorough instruction in Bible history was now more urgent because attendance at Sunday schools appeared to be dwindling. The Revd J. E. Hughes, the examiner in 1917, was particularly concerned that the spiritual element in schools was suffering:

> Since the Scriptures are generally taken as a basis of such an element in most schools, it does appear strange that Scripture Knowledge should not be pursued to such a point as to enable pupils to submit themselves to the test of an examination at least at the Junior stage, without much extra effort.[70]

Hughes returned to this theme in succeeding years. In 1918 he found that not a single pupil from sixty-seven county schools was entered for external examinations in scripture knowledge. In 1919 he found the attitude of more than half the county schools in Wales incomprehensible when they presented no pupils for examination: 'when the moral and spiritual factors should certainly be more emphasised than lightly regarded in our national system of education is it not advisable to make more general use of the Scriptures to this end'.[71] This was a refrain which was to be taken up in virtually every annual report in the inter-war years also.

In the early years of intermediate schooling, effective learning in scripture was associated above all with accurate knowledge of set biblical texts. Areas for study were drawn from the Old and New Testaments and outlines of Old Testament history. To reach Honours level, pupils had to satisfy examiners in their knowledge of the text of the Greek New Testament.

At Senior level, examination papers required a blend of factual knowledge and analysis. In 1909, for example, candidates were required to answer six questions in two hours on the paper dealing with I Samuel and Amos. The paper blended some straight factual questions – 'Mention the nations subjugated by David, and give a brief account of the subjugation of each. Draw a map showing the extent of his kingdom. Insert important places.' – with others which allowed bright candidates to make an impact – 'What is the meaning of the Hebrew word for prophet? What references to prophets are found in I Samuel? Discuss the significance of the prophetic movement.' On the whole, however, the phrasing of questions encouraged precisely that rote learning which was supposed to be the bane of examiners across the subjects. For example, the 1898 Senior Certificate paper on St Luke included such questions as 'Into what political divisions was the country divided? What native rulers are mentioned, and how were they related to each other?' or 'Special prominence is said to be given in this gospel to prayer? [sic] Give a list of instances proving the truth of this statement.'

It may be that the sense of vulnerability which examiners felt about their subject affected the tone of their reports which, on occasion, could be considerably more complimentary than was the case in so many subjects. In 1899 the majority of the submitted papers were judged to be most encouraging, testifying to careful teaching and painstaking study. In 1900, it was concluded that the subject continued to receive more serious and methodical study from year to year: 'The standard reached was much higher and the quality of the work rendered was better than in previous years.' Pupils were complimented for displaying a range of competencies including 'first hand acquaintance with the narrative as given in the set books', 'aptness and ease in recapitulating it, freed from irrelevance and confusion'.[72]

In the Honours papers examiners praised candidates for their confidence in handling questions relating to the subject-matter, and authorship and structure of the prescribed books, as well as the translation of passages from the Greek text and the New Testament. At this level, pupils were required to show thorough and critical knowledge not only of the contents of the books but also of scholarly biblical criticism. Examiners' reports remained positive:

> serious mistakes or confusions, meagre and disjointed answers and irrelevant information, though far from being altogether absent, were by no means prominent features of the work ... on the whole the work was good. The pupils showed a sound knowledge of the leading facts and ideas contained in the portions of Scripture studied, and their answers, for the most part, were clearly stated and methodical.[73]

On the other hand, examples abound of similar criticisms of performance in the scripture examinations to those in other subjects. In 1900, for example, in all the stages the work was done in too general a fashion. The main outlines were usually given very correctly, but were not given with any fullness of detail. Precision, clearness, and correct sequence in matters of detail were lacking in the majority of answers. In 1911, candidates' 'unfamiliarity with the texts revealed itself in the appearance of strange forms of proper names, which were learned imperfectly by the ear, such as Lazareth, a frequent form for Lazarus, and Dacus for Dorcas'.[74]

To the modern eye the sophistication expected by some of the specialist examiners from pupils coming to terms with a multi-subject curriculum is remarkable. For example, in 1912 Junior stage pupils were accused of a variety of confusions including: 'the idolatries of Ephesus, Athens and Corinth were likewise attributed to the Jews'.[75] At the Senior stage in 1914, there was 'not much comprehension of Hebrew history as an organic unity. The moral and religious ideas that guided and determined its movements were very little realised.'[76]

While historical perspective was lacking, so was knowledge of the geography of the Bible. In 1911, there was concern at Senior and Junior stages about:

> ...the almost total neglect of the geography of Scripture. The excellence of the greater part of the work was marred by this defect in all but two schools ... it was said, for instance, that the eunuch went daily from Ethiopia to Jerusalem to worship, and that Philip met him at Joppa and baptised him immediately in Jordan. Pupils cannot understand the history with such perverted ideas of the geography it presupposes.[77]

A rather more significant criticism was that pupils were not always able to appreciate the spiritual significance of their work. In their report on the Senior stage in 1913, for example, the examiners reported that 'attention needs to be paid above all to impressing upon the pupils' minds the spiritual significance of the narrative study. Many are unable to discriminate between 'a parable' and 'a miracle'.[78]

However, the recurrence once again of the generic criticisms of irrelevance and rote learning, and lack of critical acumen, are the most revealing because, as the examples from the examination papers have shown, at least some of the responsibility in this regard must lie with the examiners. Any sample of the kind of criticism made gives ample impression of the tone of many of the reports. For example in 1906, in answer to a question asking for the chief lessons of a parable, several pupils thought it sufficient simply to narrate the parable. Another common delusion was the supposition that a 'correct and comprehensive account of a person's career would pass for an estimate of his character'.[79] In 1910, in the report on the Senior examination, the examiner recorded that 'memory work was generally done much better than that which required the understanding of ideas and historical situations'.[80]

Examiners in scripture were keen to encourage teachers and pupils in Welsh-speaking areas to study the subject through the medium of Welsh and to answer questions in the language, which they were allowed to do from 1902. Very few candidates did so. In 1904, for example, only one candidate answered in Welsh, to the regret of the examiner: 'it would be well if this permission were more generally utilized, for there can be no doubt that, for a large proportion of the pupils, a sound knowledge of Scripture in the Welsh version would be a far more useful equipment'.[81] By 1906 there was no increase in numbers of pupils answering questions in the Welsh language. This prompted the examiner to note that 'it is astonishing that in those parts of the Principality in which Welsh is the language of home and Church, and in which consequently children obtain their first lessons in Scripture in the Welsh language, teachers do not elect to build on the foundations already securely laid'.[82] Successive examiners, usually, like Principal Thomas Lewis of Brecon Memorial College and Principal Thomas Rees of the Independent College at Bangor, eminent academics drawn from the theological colleges, realized the educational absurdity of pupils ignoring the Welsh language. But by 1913:

> only three pupils wrote their answers in Welsh . . . a remark made in last year's report may be repeated here; 'Pupils from Welsh districts write their answers in English at a disadvantage . . . but they are at a still greater disadvantage when they write their answers in Welsh, if the teaching has been in English.' The remedy would be to teach Scripture by means of the Welsh language, and when that is done, examination papers should also be set in Welsh.[83]

In summary, in this period the general thrust of examiners' reports in scripture repeatedly argued that improvements in the subject depended upon an emphasis on biblical geography, the use of the Welsh language for instruction and examination, better acquaintance with modern methods of biblical study, and the study of the New Testament in Greek.

Mathematics

For centuries, mathematics has been accorded a central place in the school curriculum, viewed as an essential part of a rounded and complete education. Mathematics has always been regarded as a means of promoting mental discipline by developing an understanding of a language of symbols and diagrams which, it is believed, provides a means of strengthening the powers of reasoning and developing accuracy of thinking.

This emphasis on the centrality of mathematics to the development of a capacity for abstract reasoning, rather than its utilitarian value for commercial purposes, dominated the approach to the subject throughout most of the nineteenth and early twentieth centuries. Victorian grammar schools accorded a greater status to geometry and algebra than to arithmetic. The teaching of geometry was based on Euclid, a sequence of theorems given a central role in the mathematics syllabus because of the belief that the power of reasoning developed by its study could be transferred to other spheres. Arithmetic was regarded as a lower branch of mathematics, more appropriate for elementary school pupils because of its more utilitarian nature. This approach was modified somewhat during the twentieth century, which witnessed attempts to highlight the practical value of mathematics and develop more practical learning experiences alongside the more abstract aspects of the subject.

At the beginning of the twentieth century significant efforts were made to reform the mathematics syllabus. There was a growing awareness of the need to relate mathematics to the demands of science and technology, a need for practical utility being increasingly advocated by the closing decade of the nineteenth century. The debate was of particular importance in Wales where the Welsh Intermediate and Technical Education Act stressed the importance of a close connection between the school curriculum and the national economy. The impetus for change came from individuals led by John Perry. In an address to the British Association Conference in Glasgow in 1901, Perry voiced his concern about the academic nature of the mathematics syllabus and advocated its replacement by a broader scheme of practical mathematics. His comments prompted the establishment of a committee, chaired by A. R. Forsyth, consisting of representatives from scientific, technical and military as well as mathematical circles, which attempted to reconsider the aims and methods of teaching the subject. A number of pioneering textbooks were produced which emphasized experimental and observational skills. The

Civil Service examination schedules were revised and, later, modifications made in the subjects studied by candidates sitting both the Oxford and Cambridge, and the London Examination Board examinations. Nevertheless, the traditional approach remained central to the study of mathematics, notably at the University of Cambridge and in the majority of public schools. Perry's textbook, *Elementary Practical Mathematics,* was severely criticized on mathematical grounds and, by 1914, the movement for reform appeared to be in retreat.

In the early years of the new century, examiners maintained that the emphasis in all studies of mathematics should be on ensuring that pupils were able to understand and apply basic principles and be trained to apply reason to the problems set before them. Matters of mathematical principle, it was maintained, could only be derived from experience of working out examples. Pupils should be taught the relevance of each step in a mathematical problem and trained to apply themselves systematically, setting out each step in their calculations logically and concisely. Examiners maintained the need for the subject to be taught in a way in which practical illustrations were given a central place, with mathematical instruments and log tables being used on a regular basis. Moreover, it was stated that, although the effective teaching of the subject meant that its constituent parts had to be learned individually, pupils should nevertheless be able to recognize that each branch of mathematics belonged to the same whole.

At this time, the teaching of arithmetic concentrated on numeration, notation, resolution of numbers into their prime factors, vulgar and decimal fractions, multiplication, division, averages, ratio, proportion, square roots, percentage profit and loss, simple and compound interest and mensuration. There was an alternative syllabus in commercial arithmetic in which pupils studied the principles of accounts, trade and cash discount, banking, stocks and shares, gross and net profits and calculation of expenses to turnover. The examiners' comments included some praise for the way in which arithmetic was taught in Welsh schools during the years before the First World War. In a number of instances pupils were commended for their ability to demonstrate intelligence and independent thought in their answers and form a mental idea of what each answer should be.

Nevertheless, examiners found that, on the whole, a rather less encouraging picture emerged from a general review of the work submitted by candidates in examinations. In 1909 it was noted that the work of many candidates displayed a lack of intelligence, and evidence of rote learning as opposed to genuine understanding, with few pupils able to demonstrate the ability to reason. Many pupils had not grasped the fundamental principles, rules and operations of mathematics. In addition, many submitted inaccurate work or used unsuitable or laborious methods. In 1906 it was noted that many pupils did not understand the meaning of terms such as percentage, brokerage, discount and significant figures, while the significance of the decimal point was often misunderstood. In 1903 examiners observed that many candidates had not understood prime factors while, in 1905, examiners regretted that mental arithmetic had been neglected, with the result that few candidates were able to check their answers. The examiners maintained:

> Pupils who had been trained in Mental Arithmetic would not have made the absurd mistakes which were only too frequent – such for example as that which found the cost of a few hundred tons of coal to be several thousand pounds, or that which estimated the number of miles in five hundred kilometres as anything from a small fraction of a mile to billions of miles, or that which concluded that a contractor would have to employ an additional 900,000 men in order to get a wall finished in the number of days he had contracted for, or that which found that several hours or even days would be required to walk across a field of a few acres. Such mistakes as these, when Arithmetic is properly and successfully taught in the schools of Wales, the instincts of the pupils being as they are so largely practical, will be almost non-existent.[84]

In 1903 the examiner stated that pupils' knowledge of the skills of mensuration were also weak. Many candidates had confused the perimeter of a square with its area, there was a want of accuracy, and many failed to select appropriate methods.

SACRIFICE OR OPPORTUNITY? 1896–1918

The study of algebra during these years included explanation of symbols and notation, substitutions, the removal and insertion of brackets, positive and negative quantities, simple, simultaneous and quadratic equations, and the application of linear graphs to the solution of problems and equations, ratio and proportion. Pupils were expected to demonstrate a sound knowledge of the principles of algebra, coupled with the power to work accurately and be able to reason logically with algebraic symbols. Initially, the examiners drew attention to the weakness of the subject in schools. In 1898 they noted that the standard of the work was not satisfactory, many pupils having considerable difficulty in dealing with brackets and submitting inaccurate work which they had not been able to verify mentally. The following year it was noted that a number of pupils had great difficulty in manipulating by a negative quantity and had only a vague notion of the theory of quadratic equations. Many pupils showed weaknesses in dealing with fractions and quadratic equations, and at all levels work was marred by carelessness and inaccuracy.

In geometry, pupils were expected to be able to show mastery of theoretical aspects, including designated Euclidean theorems, as well as practical geometry which embodied a range of constructions, such as perpendiculars to a straight line, triangles, quadrilaterals, tangents to a circle and parallels to a straight line. They were expected to know the forms of a cube, rectangular block, sphere, cylinder, wedge, pyramid and cone. In 1899 examiners commended the standard of the work. Teaching appeared to have achieved a desirable balance between the theory and practice of geometry, although examiners continued to emphasize the need for pupils to have experience of practical work in the subject. Too many pupils, it was noted in 1902, relied on memory rather than understanding.

Overall, performance in mathematics deteriorated during the war years, with a very noticeable decline in the standard of work in algebra and geometry at the Junior stage. This was attributed to problems confronting many schools as qualified male teachers joined the armed forces, leaving teaching in the hands of less-qualified colleagues. Nevertheless, over the period as a whole, the general picture was of standards improving gradually in all schools, with examiners commending pupils who were able to demonstrate a thorough knowledge of elementary rules and principles, coupled with the ability to apply that knowledge.

Science subjects

The science subjects provided the most obvious potential points of contact beyond the academic world to the wider economic and social community. Agriculture and the extractive industries, particularly coal, were the staples of the Welsh economy. Both required increasingly complex scientific and technological underpinning if they were to increase their productivity, efficiency and safety. Beyond that, any development in secondary industries, such as chemicals, so lacking in the Welsh economy, would require scientific and technical education and training of a high order. The original curriculum blueprint for the Welsh intermediate schools certainly envisaged links between the education to be provided and such aspects of the Welsh economy. In practice, in the early years particularly, science subjects were of less significance than the arts, and schools struggled to teach the sciences efficiently because of lack of laboratory facilities and equipment.

Teachers of the science subjects, if they had laboratories at all, usually had to operate with sub-standard facilities and equipment. They also had to cope with different theories about the approach to teaching their subject. Under the influence of H. E. Armstrong, fashionable theories of science teaching had swung towards the notion of a discovery learning approach by means of experimental work in the laboratory which involved observation, reasoning and communication – thus developing those faculties by means of a scientific education. However, a government-appointed committee under the chairmanship of Sir J. J. Thomson, in its 1918 report *Natural Science in Education*, argued that laboratory-based discovery methods had sometimes gone too far, with didactic and demonstration methods needed as well.

The committee need not have worried about practice in the schools of Wales.

From the start, science teaching was characterized by a subject-based approach, dominated by chemistry, physics (which became the most important of the science subjects in the Welsh intermediate schools) and botany until the latter was superseded in the 1930s by biology, which then became an increasingly significant subject for both boys and girls. Indeed, even within the subjects, there was something of a hierarchy. In Wales, physics was initially less important than chemistry because it was not recognized by the University of Wales for matriculation purposes until 1903. From the earliest days, too, gender differences within the sciences were evident, with chemistry being regarded as an appropriate subject for boys and botany for girls. For example, throughout the period dealt with in this chapter, and indeed until 1935, botany was the only science subject taught at Carmarthen Girls' School.

There were subtler distinctions underpinning this general gender pattern. Chemistry was regarded as a high-status subject, with botany enjoying a reputation more for providing useful information than the disciplined rigour of chemistry and physics. The approach to the teaching of science across the individual subjects was academic, dominated by the demands of the universities and reinforced by examiners who were drawn almost invariably from the staff of the University of Wales. This 'pure science' approach was regarded as wholly superior to anything which smacked of technical education, closely linked in the minds of academics and parents with low-status vocational education.

Physics

The study of physics during the early years of the twentieth century was divided into two separate areas. At the Higher stage, pupils focused primarily on mechanical aspects, while at Senior level they studied sound, heat, electricity and magnetism, as well as aspects of the propagation of light, statics, dynamics and hydrostatics. Initially, the content was taught without much practical work, with the main emphasis on factual recall, although candidates were also required to show some ability to explain, predict and apply concepts and theories to new situations. Increasingly, however, examiners were highlighting the need for more laboratory practice, arguing that pupils should be taught in a way which led them to understand the fundamental ideas of physics. This meant that pupils should rely less on memory and 'cramming'. Gradually, the provision of laboratory facilities improved so that, by 1911, examiners noted that in several schools where physics had been neglected, significant improvements had been secured both in the quality of the teaching and the achievements of pupils. Progress was, however, very slow. In 1916 T. Campbell James referred to the fact that many pupils continued to be expected to commit notes to memory without being taught to address the question at hand:

> For in whole classes one sometimes found answers all alike to a pattern, differing only in minor details. In some cases also, lengthy descriptions of apparatus were found without an accompanying diagram, and, in consequence of this, pupils often, through lack of time, paid scant attention to the really important parts of the questions.[85]

One of the greatest weaknesses was the inaccuracy evident in answers. In 1911 it was noted that many pupils had described 'an utterly impossible' means of finding the density of mercury. Examiners complained that many candidates confused the different units of measurement, included careless descriptions of experimental methods, and showed a want of accuracy and precision. Inappropriate use was made of specific terminology: for instance the words 'force', 'pressure' and 'power' were regularly confused. Examiners eagerly sought evidence of individuality and independent thought in pupils' answers, together with a grasp of the unity of the subject. In 1918 it was stated:

> The chief criticism concerning the work in general is that the teaching in many schools does not present the subject in its present day aspect. Subjects of fundamental importance, such as the ionic dissociation theory and the law of Mass Action, were often dealt with in a detached and superficial manner instead of being made the basis of the pupils' conceptions of chemical reaction and

change. It is to be feared that this is largely due to the use of textbooks which, though of recent issue, are really out of date.[86]

Chemistry

The syllabus adopted the academic approach of university chemistry departments, with no effort to base it on the needs of local industry or Welsh society, even though, as we have seen, such an approach had been advocated by the architects of intermediate education in Wales. CWB syllabuses were modelled on those of the English examination boards, which were subject to university control. These syllabuses emphasized the need for pupils to gain abstract subject knowledge of a broad range of topics, although inorganic chemistry was given the closest attention. Pupils were expected to master material such as the properties of common substances, the oxidation of metals and the experimental study of atmospheric air. Most of the questions set in the theoretical papers targeted knowledge, recall of factual information, chemical terminology and experimental techniques, procedures and methods.

In the early part of the century, examiners emphasized the need for pupils to demonstrate sound theoretical knowledge, the ability to reason, the capacity to arrange ideas in a relevant way and an effective grasp of experimental knowledge. As early as 1901 examiners expressed confidence that the subject was receiving due attention in schools and it was noted that the majority of schools had been provided with appropriate laboratory facilities. They also noted an improvement in the quality of teaching. In 1904 it was stated that:

> In many respects the work done was considerably in advance of anything hitherto accomplished. Not only increased knowledge but greater accuracy and interest in the subject were generally shown, and the answers gave evidence of larger practical experience. Perfection has not by any means been reached, but there has been progress and it ought to continue.[87]

In 1907 examiners assessed the development of chemistry in Welsh schools as a notable achievement. In 1909 they concluded that chemistry teaching was highly effective in most schools, with increasing numbers of pupils being entered for examination, and standards of attainment continuing to rise. Nevertheless, examiners also used the opportunities provided in their annual reports to make suggestions as to how the teaching of the subject could be improved. It was stressed that pupils needed to have experience of performing experiments under laboratory conditions and to develop the power of investigation and accurate observation. Examiners also contended that some aspects of practical work needed to be improved, particularly in terms of greater individual cleanliness, accuracy and attention to detail in practical work. They insisted that the theoretical aspect of the subject should be given careful consideration:

> The paper work was not as good as that of last year, although the practical work was somewhat better. Much weakness was again shown in chemical theory. Avogadro's hypothesis was imperfectly grasped; the difference between atomic and molecular weight was not clearly understood, expressions such as 'atomic weight of compound' being frequent; the relevance of carbon was not appreciated; and the question on ionic dissociation was almost invariably done badly. In the last case pupils chose illustrative examples of far too complicated a nature.[88]

At the Higher stage, examiners insisted that attention should be given to the philosophical side of the subject and noted that pupils should understand that chemistry was a living, developing discipline. Despite the general satisfaction expressed by the examiners, numerous defects in the achievements of pupils were noted, raising questions about the quality of the teaching. In 1911 it was noted that questions on organic chemistry generated better responses than those on inorganic chemistry, and this suggested to examiners that the inorganic side had been neglected. Moreover, it was observed that there was considerable variation in the quality of the work submitted by different schools. In some, candidates appeared to have been taught concepts that were clearly out-of-date. Many pupils included irrelevant detail in their answers and were evidently confused about different substances. Many had great difficulty in tackling numerical problems: for instance, the failure of some candidates to appreciate the meaning of 'equivalent' led them to make serious errors. Moreover, some work was plagued by the problem of inaccurate diagrams and poor illustrations.

The First World War proved to be both a boon and a blow to the subject. Schools suffered as good, qualified chemistry teachers were called up for military service; yet, at the same time, the subject moved on to benefit from new areas of scientific discovery.

Botany

As late as 1919 botany was offered as an examination subject in only 52 of the 101 Welsh intermediate schools, though this compared favourably with the 46 schools offering physics.[89] As was the case with other science subjects, candidates taking the examination in botany were expected to demonstrate a thorough knowledge of both theoretical and practical aspects.

During the early years of the twentieth century, examiners continually emphasized the need for accuracy and detailed observation, as well as knowledge based on actual observation and study of plants. Examiners were keen to foster an extensive knowledge of the native habitats of the different plants, encouraging teachers to provide pupils with experience of appropriate fieldwork and to generate a spirit of enquiry. Their comments included commendation for the way in which the subject was taught in some schools. In 1914, J. Lloyd Williams[90] went so far as to claim that:

> This year, again, it affords one much pleasure to be able to report that the teaching of Botany is in an exceedingly satisfactory condition. Indeed, with regard to some of the Schools, it is difficult to see how it could be improved upon.[91]

Nevertheless, examiners observed that there were significant differences in the standards achieved in individual schools, a point they attributed to differences in the quality of the teaching. Some candidates produced vague answers, full of irrelevant material, with unsatisfactory diagrams and illustrations. Too many teachers, it was claimed, clearly relied on dictated notes as their only method of teaching and examiners noted that it was obvious that, in some instances, pupils had been taught to draw without ever having seen specimens of the plants, even though they were available in the locality. Lloyd Williams wrote in 1911:

> Incredible as it may seem, there are still teachers to be found who encourage their pupils to draw imaginary representations of objects . . . they are neither artistic nor scientific – they do positive injury to the child by cultivating habits of slipshod inaccuracy.[92]

Candidates often misunderstood basic procedures such as wind pollination and, in some instances, gave examples of the dispersal of seeds to illustrate the process. Few pupils knew the meaning of 'biennials' and 'perennials' and referred to potatoes and carrots as 'annuals'. The practice of entering girls for botany and boys for chemistry was criticized on the grounds that the neglect of chemistry meant that some girls were unfamiliar with the aspects of chemistry which were essential for the study of botany.

Conclusion

Two decades or so after the majority of the Welsh intermediate schools came into existence, to be joined after 1902 by municipal secondary schools, the Welsh secondary sector had assumed a distinctive pattern. It was not a pattern envisaged by the Aberdare Committee nor by those who drafted the 1889 Act. Headmasters and headmistresses in Wales aspired to the status symbols associated with prestigious English grammar schools – school uniform, Saturday-morning games, House systems, academic dress and, above all, the imprimatur of examination success. This success was to be measured by achievement in the examinations of the CWB which, by 1918, had generally assumed a pattern of School and Higher Certificates.

The technical and commercial education envisaged in the 1889 Act was originally catered for by CWB examinations but, with so few candidates, withered away. The core curriculum of the day was that set by the requirements of university matriculation and consisted of the central arts and pure science subjects. Although school examinations in Wales were not administered by the universities, as they were in England, the pattern in Wales could not be different given the parental, professional and social pressures on contemporary education. In Wales, as elsewhere, CWB examiners were normally drawn from the ranks of university teachers. We have seen from their reports the kind of expectations they had of a highly academic curriculum mediated through mainly graduate teachers to a minority of the age range. These examiners expected academic excellence, but made few concessions to the strains that this imposed. It is obvious from their reports that the dictation of notes across the subjects was a staple method of teaching. It is easy to see how this links with Edwards's castigations of the malign influence of the examination system in his 'wooden headed' Report. Yet the examiners took no account of the constraints on teachers who had to impart masses of knowledge for examination purposes without the technical aids with which we are now familiar, and the pressures of time which we still know all too well. Another theme permeating their science reports is the lack of laboratory and practical work. Here again there seems to be no concession to the primitive laboratory conditions and the lack of equipment which relative poverty imposed on Welsh secondary schools.

In retrospect, it is easy to appreciate how the examination system dominated the thinking of teachers and administrators, and led to the strengths and weaknesses associated with the burgeoning Welsh secondary school sector. These were schools for academic achievers, irrespective of social background, whose prospects in life were transformed by their secondary education. Routines could be dominated by dictation of notes and rote learning; but the schools could also be inspirational. And, despite the examination system, these institutions had time for cultural activities, school plays, Saturday-morning games which produced some outstanding sporting performers, and a status within the community which the schools, pupils and staff of the twenty-first century can only envy. It was a tribute to their rapid consolidation that they withstood the massive disruption of staff change brought about by the First World War with relatively little effect on the level of achievement.

References

1. Wynford Davies, *The Curriculum and Organisation of the County Intermediate Schools 1880–1926* (Cardiff, 1989), p. 253.
2. Gareth Elwyn Jones, *Controls and Conflicts in Welsh Secondary Education 1889–1944* (Cardiff, 1982), ch.1 passim.
3. J. R. Webster, 'The place of secondary education in Welsh society 1800–1918', unpublished Ph.D thesis, (University of Wales, 1959), passim.
4. Quoted in W. Harrison, *Greenhill School Tenby 1896–1964: An Educational and Social History* (Cardiff, 1979), pp. 24–5.
5. Harrison, pp. 24–5.
6. Jones, p. 11.
7. W. Gareth Evans, *An Elected National Body for Wales, the Centenary of the Central Welsh Board* (Cardiff, 1997).
8. For the early curriculum of the intermediate schools see Davies, pp. 82ff.
9. The literature relating to R. L. Morant, Permanent Secretary of the Board of Education 1903–11, and his involvement in the Education Act 1902 and subsequent Board of Education policy, is substantial. A short biography is included in R. Aldrich and P. Gordon, *Dictionary of British Educationists* (London. 1989), pp. 173–5; a lengthier biography, by G. K. Fry, appears in the *New Dictionary of National Biography* (OUP, 2004).
10. Welsh Department of the Board of Education, *Regulations in Force for Welsh Secondary Schools*, 1907.
11. For the story of this conflict see Evans, ch.1 and Jones, pp. 24ff.
12. Evans, provides all the necessary background information. For information and regulations relating to Central Welsh Board examinations see appendices 1–4, pp. 212–7, in Jones. For information on numbers of schools offering pupils for examination in individual subjects see Davies, table 10, p. 253.
13. *Manchester Guardian*, quoted in L. W. Evans, *Studies in Welsh Education* (Cardiff 1974), p. 292.
14. See, for example, G. Perrie Williams, *Welsh Education in Sunlight and Shadow* (London, 1918).
15. 'Nationalist', possibly T. Matthews, of Llandybie, *The Failure of the Central Welsh Board* (Cardiff, 1912), pp. 3–15.
16. Quoted in Wynne Lloyd, 'O. M. Edwards' in *Pioneers of Welsh Education*, four lectures published by the Faculty of Education, University College of Swansea (Swansea, 1962), p. 97.
17. (Sir) John Morris-Jones was head of the department of Welsh in the University College of North Wales, Bangor from 1889, and Professor from 1894.
18. W. J. Gruffydd became Professor of Welsh at the University College of South Wales and Monmouthshire, Cardiff. He and Jones were among the most eminent academic authorities on the Welsh language.

19 *Central Welsh Board Today and Tomorrow in Welsh Education* (Cardiff, 1916), pp. 11–3.
20 A. C. Impey, 'The Development of State-provided Secondary Education in Cardiff 1870–1939', unpublished M.Ed. thesis (University of Wales, 1973), p. 56.
21 CWB, *General Report*, 1907–08, pp. 6–10.
22 *Report of the Consultative Committee on Examinations in Secondary Schools*, Cd 6004 (London, HMSO, 1911).
23 *Report of the Consultative Committee on Examinations in Secondary Schools*, p. 132.
24 See Olive Banks, *Parity and Prestige in English Secondary Education* (London, 1955), p. 68.
25 *Report of the Consultative Committee on Secondary Education with Special Reference to Grammar Schools and Technical High Schools* (Spens Report) (London, HMSO, 1938), pp. 79–81.
26 Examples of CWB examination papers in Welsh, English grammar, English literature, Latin, Greek, French, history, geography, scripture, arithmetic, algebra, euclid physics, theoretical chemistry, botany, and domestic economy are included as appendix B, pp. 99–114, in Evans.
27 CWB, *Report on the Inspection and Examination of County Schools*, 1903.
28 CWB, *Report on the Inspection and Examination of County Schools*, 1909.
29 CWB, *Report on the Inspection and Examination of County Schools*, 1913.
30 CWB, *Report on the Inspection and Examination of County Schools*, 1898.
31 CWB, *Report on the Inspection and Examination of County Schools*, 1918, p. 40.
32 CWB, *Report on the Inspection and Examination of County Schools*, 1898.
33 CWB, *Report on the Inspection and Examination of County Schools*, 1903. At Beaumaris in 1906, examiners concluded that several pupils were weak in analysis and the 'power of expression and style' were poor. At Machynlleth the verdict was that most pupils were unable to express themselves coherently or grammatically in English.
34 CWB, *Report on the Inspection and Examination of County Schools*, 1904.
35 CWB, *Report on the Inspection and Examination of County Schools*, 1903, p. 69.
36 Thomas Powel was Professor of Celtic at Cardiff.
37 CWB, *Report on the Inspection and Examination of County Schools*, 1909.
38 CWB, *Report on the Inspection and Examination of County Schools*, 1909, pp. 79–80.
39 CWB, *Report on the Inspection and Examination of County Schools*, 1902, p. 69.
40 *Modern Studies (Report of the Committee on the Study of Modern*

Languages in the Educational System of Great Britain) (Leathes Report) (London, HMSO, 1918).
41 *Curriculum and Examinations in Secondary Schools. Report of the Committee of the Secondary School Examinations Council appointed by the President of the Board of Education in 1941* (Norwood Report), (London, HMSO, 1943), p. 114.
42 Leathes Report, para 196.
43 CWB, *Report on the Inspection and Examination of County Schools*, 1905, p. 55.
44 CWB, *Report on the Inspection and Examination of County Schools*, 1914, p. 70.
45 CWB, *Report on the Inspection and Examination of County Schools*, 1908, p. 82.
46 Frederick Spencer was Professor of Modern Languages at Bangor.
47 CWB, *Report on the Inspection and Examination of County Schools*, 1900, p. 56; 1901, p. 64.
48 CWB, *Report on the Inspection and Examination of County Schools*, 1912, p. 76.
49 *Times Educational Supplement*, 2 January 1912.
50 *County Schools Review*, 1911, p. 218.
51 CWB, *Report on the Inspection and Examination of County Schools*, 1914, p. 33.
52 CWB, *Report on the Inspection and Examination of County Schools*, 1916, p. 157.
53 J. Mortimer Angus was Professor of Latin, later Registrar, at Aberystwyth.
54 CWB, *Report on the Inspection and Examination of County Schools*, 1905, p. 46.
55 This period witnessed the launch of journals such as *The Geographical Journal* and *The Geographical Teacher* and textbooks such as *The Senior Geography*, published for the first time in 1907.
56 Where he was Professor of Geography and Anthropology.
57 CWB, *Report on the Inspection and Examination of County Schools*, 1898, p. 81.
58 CWB, *Report on the Inspection and Examination of County Schools*, 1899 p. 79.
59 CWB, *Report on the Inspection and Examination of County Schools*, 1906.
60 J. E. Lloyd, *A History of Wales from the earliest times to the Edwardian Conquest Volumes 1 and 2* (London, 1911).
61 O. M. Edwards's *Wales* was published in London, in 1901. It was published in a second edition with a chapter on 'Modern Wales' by Edward Edwards in 1925. The title of the series, *Nations*, is significant.
62 Ernest Hughes became Professor of History at the University College of Swansea.
63 CWB, *Report on the Inspection and Examination of County Schools*, 1913, p. 45.

64 CWB, *Report on the Inspection and Examination of County Schools*, 1914, pp. 72–7.
65 CWB, *Report on the Inspection and Examination of County Schools*, 1899, p. 28.
66 CWB, *Report on the Inspection and Examination of County Schools*, 1899, p. 79.
67 Education Act 1870, s 14(2).
68 Hansard, vol. 115, col. 1118.
69 CWB, *Report on the Inspection and Examination of County Schools*, 1913.
70 CWB, *Report on the Inspection and Examination of County Schools*, 1917.
71 CWB, *Report on the Inspection and Examination of County Schools*, 1919.
72 CWB, *Report on the Inspection and Examination of County Schools*, 1900.
73 CWB, *Report on the Inspection and Examination of County Schools*, 1904.
74 CWB, *Report on the Inspection and Examination of County Schools*, 1911, pp. 24, 38.
75 CWB, *Report on the Inspection and Examination of County Schools*, 1912, p. 39.
76 CWB, *Report on the Inspection and Examination of County Schools*, 1914, p. 35.
77 CWB, *Report on the Inspection and Examination of County Schools*, 1911, p. 38.
78 CWB, *Report on the Inspection and Examination of County Schools*, 1913, p. 22.
79 CWB, *Report on the Inspection and Examination of County Schools*, 1906, p. 27.
80 CWB, *Report on the Inspection and Examination of County Schools*, 1910, p. 36.
81 CWB, *Report on the Inspection and Examination of County Schools*, 1904.
82 CWB, *Report on the Inspection and Examination of County Schools*, 1906, p. 28.
83 CWB, *Report on the Inspection and Examination of County Schools*, 1913.
84 CWB, *Report on the Inspection and Examination of County Schools*, 1905.
85 CWB, *Report on the Inspection and Examination of County Schools*, 1916.
86 CWB, *Report on the Inspection and Examination of County Schools*, 1918.
87 CWB, *Report on the Inspection and Examination of County Schools*, 1904.
88 CWB, *Report on the Inspection and Examination of County Schools*, 1911, p. 91.

[89] Wynford Davies, table 10, p. 254. However, he claims, p. 83, that the subject was taught in all intermediate schools, especially to girls. Part of the explanation is that schools attended only by boys taught chemistry, not botany.
[90] J. Lloyd Williams became Professor of Botany at Aberystwyth.
[91] CWB, *Report on the Inspection and Examination of County Schools*, 1914, p. 94.
[92] CWB, *Report on the Inspection and Examination of County Schools*, 1911, p. 95.

Chapter 2
A Means of Escape 1918–1949

Introduction

In the nineteenth and twentieth centuries, wars have been something of a catalyst for social change, not least in the provision of education. While this has emanated in both twentieth-century wars partly from a conviction that social benefits such as education should be more freely and fairly available, such altruism has been tempered with the notion that the system of education in England and Wales has been practically deficient and has placed the welfare of the country at risk.

During the First World War, for example, many political and military leaders in Britain, among them David Lloyd George, became sharply critical of the education system in England and Wales. They believed that it focused too much on the classical tradition, with the result that British industry had lost its vitality during the Edwardian period. Forceful demands for the expansion of secondary and higher education were articulated and it was emphasized that much more attention should be given to science, technology and industry. Whether these widespread perceptions had any validity is debatable. Present scholarship questions, at least as far as England is concerned, whether Germany's system of education was more technologically and practically effective either in the first decade of the twentieth century or between the wars, and, on the other hand, whether the predominant role of the public schools in English education did detract from the effectiveness of scientific and technical performance. In Wales it is arguable that the situation was different in that secondary industries associated with the heyday of industrialization, such as the chemicals industry, were grossly underdeveloped. But in terms of contemporary debate this mattered little, because no one at the time commented on disparities between England and Wales in these terms. What mattered, then, was perceptions, and certainly by 1916 perceptions at the highest level of government were that education in England and Wales was inferior to that in Germany. The result was action.

With the formation of the Lloyd George coalition government in December 1916, H. A. L. Fisher, an eminent academic deeply interested in the expansion of educational provision, was appointed President of the Board of Education and initiated a detailed investigation of the education system in England and Wales. These enquiries examined issues such as the curriculum, the extent to which children were given the opportunity of obtaining post-elementary schooling, and the status of the teaching profession. In some ways Wales was in a fortunate position. Over one hundred schools had been opened under the provisions of the Welsh Intermediate and Technical Education Act 1889, providing a significant minority of the nation's youth with access to an academic education which was available free of charge to some children and supplemented by the more recent municipal secondary schools. The Central Welsh Board (CWB) organized a system of examination and inspection of the intermediate schools which was, at least in principle, controlled by the nation through elected representatives.

Yet even those most closely associated with the creation of this structure recognized the urgent need to reform important aspects of secondary education in Wales. The number of secondary school places provided in the industrial parts of Wales was not sufficient, relative to the supply in rural areas. Welsh intermediate schools lacked adequate financial resources to develop new work, especially in science, and the provision of non-academic courses was inadequate. The structure of the education system was also a matter of considerable argument. The measure of administrative devolution which had resulted from the creation of the Welsh Department of the Board of Education in 1907 had failed to satisfy those who advocated greater autonomy for Wales, and the CWB joined prominent political leaders in demanding that a National Council be established to exercise control over Welsh education. The Board of Education, and Alfred

Davies, the Permanent Secretary to the Welsh Department, remained utterly opposed to the notion, arguing that constitutional, financial and administrative factors meant that the idea was impractical.[1] At the same time, powerful voices within the Board of Education maintained that a separate education policy for Wales was neither desirable nor necessary and regarded many of the distinctive characteristics within the Welsh system as anomalies which should be removed.[2]

Higher Education in Wales was also examined in detail by a Royal Commission, appointed in 1917, chaired by Lord Haldane, the former Lord Chancellor, who had a deep commitment to the notion of civic universities and their role in adult education.[3] The Commission heard detailed criticism of the conservative approach adopted by the University of Wales, especially its failure to acknowledge the importance of science, technology, and social and economic subjects.

The government became convinced of the need for a radical approach to remedy the weaknesses evident within the education system. The Education Act 1918 introduced measures to reform the way in which central government assisted local authorities by introducing a system of percentage grants, whereby a fixed proportion of expenditure in education was met by central government.[4] A new salary structure and pension arrangements for secondary school teachers were established. The number of state scholarships for university students and free places in secondary schools were increased and the government was also favourably disposed to the notion that some pupils should be provided with allowances to meet their maintenance costs.[5] The 1918 Act also introduced part-time instruction for those aged 14–19 who were in employment, although the provision was not enacted.[6] These reforms were greeted eagerly by progressive opinion in Wales. The *Welsh Outlook*'s editorial 'Notes of the month' viewed the proposals as a crucial step in the development of Welsh education and a means of overcoming serious weaknesses within the system.[7]

However, many facets of Fisher's vision, whilst reflected in the Education Act 1918, were not realized. The planned increase in the number of free places in secondary schools was delayed and, although the total number increased gradually until 1931, some officials at the Treasury considered that charging for secondary education was a relatively easy way of reducing public expenditure. On the other hand, the fees issue was regarded by several leading figures in Welsh education as a test of their commitment to enhancing educational opportunity. Even after the severe reductions in expenditure introduced as a result of the *Report of the Committee on National Expenditure*, many Welsh local education authorities (LEAs) sought to use their discretion to relieve parents of the burden of paying towards their children's education.[8] The figures for the industrial counties indicate the importance attached to the fees issue. In 1937–38 a total of 7,525 pupils were enrolled in intermediate schools in Glamorgan. Nearly a fifth (18.7 per cent) enjoyed partial exemption from fees while 5,060 (67.2 per cent) were totally exempt. This meant that 85.9 per cent of those attending the county's intermediate schools were relieved of having to pay all or some fees. In Monmouthshire only 2 of the 1,981 intermediate school pupils were partially exempt, but 1,359 were totally exempt, giving relief to 68.7 per cent of pupils.[9]

The inter-war years also witnessed continuing arguments over examinations policy and curricular issues.[10] As we have seen in Chapter 1, the Welsh intermediate schools and the CWB had been criticized by the Board of Education's Welsh Department, notably its Chief Inspector, O. M. Edwards, for adopting a myopic view of education that emphasized the primacy of academic subjects and was driven by the requirements of examinations and assessment. During the period 1918–38 the CWB continued to justify its policies on the grounds that they enjoyed the support of the majority of Welsh parents, and that few people in Wales believed that commercial or vocational courses should be developed at the expense of the academic in secondary schools.

Nevertheless the CWB recognized that the structure of its examinations would have to be revised. Before the First World War four sets of examinations had been developed which assessed pupils at Junior, Senior, Scholarship and Honours levels. The Junior examination, taken by pupils aged fourteen, generated considerable debate. Many commentators considered it to be unnecessary and argued that Welsh pupils were assessed too early in their secondary school experience.

On the other hand, defenders of the examination argued that it served a valuable purpose in ensuring that the large number of children who left school before the age of sixteen had the opportunity to obtain a certificate, and many believed that it should be retained until the question of 'early leaving' had been addressed. These arguments were, however, to little avail, and after 1924 the Junior and Senior examinations were replaced by a single School Certificate examination. This was to be taken by pupils who had studied at a secondary school for four years. The examination regulations established five groups of subjects, as shown in Table 1.[11]

TABLE 1

Group 1	Group 2	Group 3	Group 4	Group 5
Scripture knowledge	Latin	mathematics	music theory	woodwork
English language and literature	Greek	mechanics	music practical	metalwork
Welsh language and literature	Welsh	chemistry	drama	woodwork and metalwork
History	French	physics 1 (mechanics, heat and light)		needlework and garment construction
Geography	German	physics 2 (mechanics, magnetism and electricity)		cookery
	Spanish	geography		laundrywork
	Italian	botany		book-keeping
		biology		shorthand
		geology		
		agriculture		
		metallurgy		
		domestic science		

Each candidate had to be entered for five subjects, of which four had to be selected from groups 1, 2 and 3, including at least one from each group. The selection from group 1 had to include either Welsh or English. Candidates were then entered for a fifth subject from any group. To achieve a School Certificate a candidate had to pass in each subject from groups 1–3, although a slight deficiency in one group could be compensated for by a very good performance in another group. Candidates who achieved a pass with credit in five subjects were deemed to have matriculated. The regulations stipulated that a candidate taking Welsh language and literature instead of English language and literature would be expected to demonstrate a command of English in history, geography, or scripture knowledge in a separate English paper. Those candidates who failed to achieve a pass in each subject left school with no formal qualifications. In 1926 a sixth group was added, consisting of agriculture, metallurgy and domestic science, which allowed the alleviation of congestion in group 3.

These changes to the structure of the examination system were accompanied by a gradual expansion in the number of pupils who received a secondary education, achieved by extending existing schools and opening new LEA secondary schools. In 1919 there were 118 secondary schools in Wales, including the 100 Welsh intermediate schools, which together provided accommodation for 23,697 pupils.[12] By 1938 the number of schools had increased to 154, and the number on roll had increased to 45,385.[13] The expansion in the number of school places was reflected by the increases in the number of candidates entered for the CWB's examinations, and, significantly, most of the municipal secondary schools established by the LEAs entered candidates for the Board's examinations.

A MEANS OF ESCAPE 1918–1949

TABLE 2

Number of schools entering candidates		Number of candidates					
Year	Number entered from		School Certificate			Higher School Certificate		
	Welsh intermediate schools	Other secondary schools	Examined	Passed	% Pass	Examined	Passed	% Pass
1926	101	18	4285	2960	69.1	501	289	57.7
1927	101	21	4591	3082	67.1	539	357	66.2
1928	101	26	4906	3351	68.3	585	390	66.7
1929	102	28	5299	3735	70.5	591	391	66.2
1930	102	29	5724	3942	68.7	676	447	66.1
1931	102	33	6207	4222	68.0	803	522	65.0
1932	102	35	6724	4522	67.3	947	621	65.6
1933	102	38	7198	4823	67.0	1116	707	63.4
1934	102	38	7012	4843	69.2	1124	724	64.6

These figures also show a growth in the number of Welsh children who left school with the formal qualification of a School Certificate. The total number who passed rose from 2,960 in 1926 to 4,843 in 1934, even though the percentage of those who obtained a School Certificate remained similar throughout this period, suggesting that the increase occurred because of the opportunities which were made available, not as a result of any reduction in standards.

Yet the rise in numbers who passed through secondary schools cannot disguise the fact that many able Welsh children who secured a place at secondary schools were prevented from completing their education because of social and economic factors. Of 97 girls who entered Llanelli Girls' Grammar School in September 1927, only 64 were entered for examination in July 1932. Of these, 38 left with a School Certificate, fewer than 40 per cent of the number who entered the school five years earlier.

Statistics of the school leaving age for 1937–38 give an interesting comparison between the position in Wales and the average situation in England and Wales. The percentage of pupils who left school aged between fourteen and sixteen was higher in Wales than the average for England and Wales, and fewer Welsh pupils left aged between sixteen and seventeen, the age at which they would have sat the School Certificate examination. However, a higher than average percentage of pupils left school after the age of seventeen.

TABLE 3

	Boys						Girls					
	Total	14–15	15–16	16–17	17–18	18+	Total	14–15	15–16	16–17	17–18	18+
Wales	4716	12.7	18.4	25.7	22.4	20.8	4328	12.6	19.2	29.7	21.9	16.6
England and Wales	43228	7.3	17.7	43.1	19.3	12.6	38168	9.0	17.9	42.6	17.1	13.4

A further indication of the differences between the education system in Wales and in England is provided by a survey undertaken in 1938 of the destination of secondary school pupils. Significantly fewer Welsh pupils entered occupations such as the Civil Service, banking and insurance and more of them became teachers, nurses or worked in industry or agriculture. A large number of girls stayed at home, and a higher percentage of Welsh girls entered various forms of domestic work.

TABLE 4

	Wales	Wales	England and Wales	England and Wales
		%		%
Clerical	1147	12.7	14676	18.0
Entered other educational institutes	909	10.0	9494	11.7
Remained at home	753	8.3	4330	5.3
Left – no reason	738	8.2	8601	10.6
Distributive trades	735	8.1	3918	4.8
Skilled trades	657	7.3	6264	7.6
Entered university or university training departments	588	6.5	4225	5.2
Entered training colleges	493	5.5	3749	4.6

	Wales	Wales	England and Wales	England and Wales
		%		%
Civil Service or local government	348	3.8	5359	6.6
Nursing	342	3.8	1708	2.1
Other professions	316	3.5	3407	4.2
Other reasons (e.g. ill-health, death)	310	3.4	2375	2.9
Army, Navy, Air Force, Police	273	3.0	1837	2.3
Agriculture	242	2.7	1344	1.7
Industry	226	2.5	719	0.9
Other commercial occupations	185	2.0	2288	2.8
Domestic work	178	2.0	644	0.8
Post Office	163	1.8	1217	1.5
Became pupil teachers etc	159	1.8	951	1.2
Banking or insurance	120	1.3	2818	3.5
Transport	69	0.8	360	0.4
Entered public elementary schools or other secondary school	66	0.7	831	1.0
Miscellaneous	27	0.3	281	0.3

Experience of secondary education was often essential for individuals as they entered the employment market. A survey undertaken by Archie Lush on behalf of the South Wales and Monmouthshire Council of Social Service indicated that fewer of those who had received secondary education were likely to be unemployed for a prolonged period.[14] What is also clear is that many of those who gained a place in Welsh secondary schools had no option but to leave after a few years, without a formal qualification, due to family circumstances and the effect of economic depression. Despite the endeavours of LEAs to extend educational opportunities, social and economic obstacles regularly proved insurmountable, even for parents who were committed to ensuring their children benefited from a secondary education.

Some support for a radical reassessment of what should be the aims of Welsh secondary schools was evident. A number of prominent Welsh educationists advanced arguments similar to those articulated by O.M.Edwards during the first decades of the twentieth century. For instance, Frederic Evans, the County Inspector of Schools for west Glamorgan, maintained in an article in *Welsh Outlook* that there was ample provision for academic education and that what was required was a focus on aesthetic and physical aspects of learning. In his opinion, schools should consider means by which the personality of the individual child could be cultivated far more effectively than in the past.[15] Similarly, Edmund P. Jones argued that the influence of examinations was undermining worthy notions of education. Significantly, he did not blame the CWB's regulations, but rather the way their policies were influenced by the national Examinations Council and the pressure put on the Board by society in general:

> as long as the Central Welsh Board examinations are under the control of the Examination Council, and as long as the public make a fetish of the matriculation certificate there must be a constant danger of over-pressure, especially in the case of girls. It will also be impossible for the teacher to give to those subjects which do not come within the purview of matriculation that place in the curriculum which he considers their due.[16]

These concerns are reflected in evidence to the Consultative Committee on Education during its investigation of the educational opportunities provided for adolescents in England and Wales. For instance, some teachers' organizations maintained that the regulations concerning what should be taught were far too prescriptive and prevented the development of any innovative methods or approaches. The Welsh branch of the Incorporated Association of Assistant Masters in Secondary Schools believed that there should be more room for a free and creative approach to education and that examination performance should not be regarded as the sole objective of secondary education.[17] At the same time, the need of the school curriculum in Wales to reflect the nation's distinctive characteristics was highlighted. The Association of Assistant Mistresses in Secondary Schools' Joint Committee for Wales believed that more attention should be paid to the history of Wales and that the geography syllabus should focus more on studies of the Welsh environment, as a means of developing a sense of nationhood among Welsh children.[18] The need for a greater emphasis on practical work as a means of generating interest among pupils to whom books did not appeal was also emphasized,[19] and it was held that more room should be allowed to enable pupils to enjoy music, art and open-air activities.[20] R. E. Owen, headteacher of Welshpool Intermediate School for Boys, held similar views. He believed that schools in rural Wales should develop an approach which nurtured an awareness of the richness of rural life and an appreciation of the value of the countryside:

> To my mind it is imperatively necessary for the further development of the welfare of the countryside that much more should be done than at present in all Rural Schools, whether Secondary or Primary, to foster a more intense appreciation of and Respect for its pursuits, and to anticipate, by means of specially devised schemes of study, the concrete future avocation of the countryside pupil.[21]

He maintained that all rural secondary schools should follow the example set at Welshpool by ensuring that the literary texts studied by pupils reflected the experience of the countryside and that the history syllabus allowed room to consider rural life, for instance basing lessons on the Piers Plowman series.[22]

The anglicized ethos of many secondary schools in Wales was a matter referred to regularly by those keen to see a distinctive form of Welsh education,[23] and the attitudes of both the education authorities and many headteachers had been criticized.[24] These concerns were highlighted after the Board of Education appointed a Departmental Committee to consider the issue, which reported in 1927. The Report, *The Welsh Language in Education and Life*, provided a detailed account of the emergence of Welsh education and the rich variety of the cultural and religious activities conducted through the medium of the language. At the same time it noted the decline of Welsh as a spoken language in many parts of Wales, especially in the industrial areas. The education system came under scrutiny, with detailed analysis of the extent to which Welsh was used and taught in teacher training colleges and by the University of Wales. It was found that the number of candidates entered for Welsh in the School Certificate examination had increased during the years immediately after the First World War and that most Welsh LEAs recognized the importance of the language. However, it was acknowledged that few local authorities had developed their language policies to the extent that schools were compelled to give priority to the Welsh language. Little use was made of the language outside Welsh lessons. The teaching of the subject suffered because many of those who taught it were not specialists and many lacked appropriate resources.[25] It was maintained that too many pupils were denied the opportunity for self-expression because of the failure to develop the native tongue.[26]

The CWB did not ignore criticisms of its policies, either in terms of the Welsh language or of the curriculum. During the 1920s it played a leading role in the development of science courses involving experiences of rural areas and it encouraged schools to devote greater attention to music and physical education.[27] Its leaders, notably William Saunders, William George and Joseph Jones, were keenly aware of the contribution the education system had to make to the preservation of the Welsh language and culture and they were also particularly anxious to develop a more autonomous structure for administering education in Wales. The tension between the Board of Education's Welsh Department and the CWB eased considerably after (Sir) Percy Watkins, a former clerk to the CWB, succeeded Sir Alfred Davies as Permanent Secretary in 1925 and this led to a more constructive dialogue between the two bodies.[28] Nevertheless, the CWB proved slow to react to arguments in favour of curricular reform. To some extent this attitude could be attributed to the fact that considerable power lay in the hands of individual LEAs and Welsh headteachers, some of whom were reluctant to abandon their schools' traditional emphasis on academic subjects, and an ethos based on the classical English tradition of schooling.

Many of them vigorously refuted allegations that the secondary school curriculum was too concerned with providing a narrow, academic instruction.[29]

Moreover, to many minds, the purpose of the Welsh secondary school was to provide its pupils with opportunities akin to those presented to the privileged classes in England and Scotland and they viewed education as a means of enabling a small number of individuals to achieve distinction in a particular field. This was an attitude shared by a substantial body of Welsh parents and members of LEAs, many of whom wanted Welsh pupils to be given access to a broad academic curriculum, free of the influence of industry and commerce, which opened pupils' minds to horizons far beyond the local community or even Wales. Significantly, the Labour Party's emphasis was on extending access to the existing form of secondary schooling and, with notable exceptions, the main focus of the party's education policy concerned issues such as maintenance grants, tuition fees, school transport, finance and other practical issues rather than curricular matters. The need for reform was acknowledged by the Spens Committee's report of 1938[30] which highlighted the need for a thorough reconsideration of the aims and methods of secondary schools in England and Wales, issues central to the discussions which led to the Education Act of 1944.

English

During the years immediately before the First World War, voices continued to be raised which questioned the methods and aims of English teachers. The syllabus was criticized for reflecting too closely the approach adopted in teaching Latin and Greek[31] and prominent figures within Welsh education, notably Edwards, maintained that such an approach was in dire need of reform. These ideas were voiced more forcefully in the inter-war years. Commentators commented adversely on the way in which grammar, composition and literature were taught separately in many schools and claimed that the study of literature often meant little more than consideration of questions of a factual, biographical and historical nature. An increasing number of commentators maintained that a broader and more liberal approach should be taken, placing a greater emphasis on self-expression and creativity. The extent to which grammar should be viewed as the cornerstone of English teaching was also a matter of debate. The humanistic role of literature was emphasized. Pupils, it was maintained, should be given the opportunity to explore and develop a personal response to the literature they studied.

The Newbolt Report of 1921[32] considered these issues and sought to balance an emphasis on traditional methods of teaching the subject with arguments for reform. It expressed doubts about the inclusion of Old and Middle English in the syllabus, criticized the abstract way in which grammar was taught and wanted to see English freed from its classical pedagogical mould. At the same time, it emphasized the importance of pupils gaining a thorough knowledge of English grammar through formal essay construction and textual study. Despite the influence of the movement for reform, the traditional approach continued to dominate during the inter-war years. There were few changes to the pattern of the School Certificate examinations in English, and textbooks with an emphasis on grammar composition continued to be relied upon in the majority of schools. This approach was also staunchly defended within the teaching profession itself. For example, in 1932 the Association of Assistant Mistresses stressed the need for the study of the subject to provide the same discipline as the study of Latin and Greek. The study of grammar was considered essential and reservations were expressed about any move to a greater emphasis on self-expression.

Examiners in this period regularly drew attention to the quality of the teaching of English in Welsh secondary schools. Their reports commended instances where essays displayed the characteristics of careful planning, coherence and logical arrangement, as well as correct spelling and punctuation. Teachers were advised to devote attention to teaching pupils to write essays and to be set frequent timed papers, to discuss topical questions in class and to construct blackboard summaries of outline answers. Moreover, correct spelling and the avoidance of slang and Americanisms were considered essential. Examiners noted that essay writing was obviously very difficult for some pupils, with formless, irrelevant and disorderly arrangement, and lack of coordination, being perennial problems.

The ability to write a clear and accurate précis also continued to be an important element of work of quality in the School Certificate examination. Schools were urged to ensure that pupils had constant practice in this art, to teach them how to extract the essential meaning from each separate section and to reconstitute the material into a satisfactory new form.

The debate about the extent to which formal English grammar should be taught in schools was reflected in examiners' reports. It was conceded that grammar should not necessarily be taught as an end in itself but should be viewed as a means of enabling pupils to write clear and correct English. In teaching grammar, teachers were advised to ensure that all grammatical facts were arrived at by 'induction'. Observation of the actual practice of the language through the study of numerous examples, rather than mere rote-work, was seen as the basis of effective grammar teaching, as it would overcome the tendency for definitions to be committed to memory but not understood. In 1929, it was forcefully stated that bad spelling remained a problem at the School Certificate stage. At the same level in 1930, nearly every case of poor work was characterized by bad spelling and often semi-legible handwriting, while in 1934 it was stated that almost half the candidates continued to write grammatically incorrect English.

Errors of idiom were commonplace and were sometimes attributed to confusion between the Welsh and English languages. This prompted a debate about the effect of bilingualism. In 1918 one examiner concluded:

> This year again there was ample proof that poor expression was not the result of Welsh pupils' difficulty in handling English, and it seems clear that teachers in Welsh Intermediate Schools should not believe that their difficulties in teaching good English style are greater owing to Welsh influence than the difficulties of their colleagues in English schools. There are possibly sporadic cases of

pupils who think in Welsh, who translate their Welsh idioms literally, but the vast mass of errors is of the type common to bad English all over England.[33]

Similar sentiments were expressed the following year. Examiners noted that candidates from schools in isolated Welsh-speaking districts often submitted work of a very high standard, and invariably the poorest results were in those schools where English was taught in 'a soulless, uninspired fashion'. Similarly, in 1921 it was argued that:

> The most striking fact which emerges in this year's examination is the wide difference in the work of the schools. In some, the answers reveal careful, intelligent, and thorough teaching, producing good work which it is a pleasure to examine; in others the answers are poor, the style is slip-shod, the vocabulary restricted, the matter meagre, and there is a general lack of attention to accuracy of detail. This difference is not to be traced entirely to bilingual difficulties, for many of the schools in the Welsh districts give excellent results. It appears to be due to lack of knowledge and enthusiasm in the teaching. Too often, also, pupils are entered who are not up to the standard of the examination. The result is a tendency to set down anything, provided an attempt is made to answer the question. Such work is unreal and can but lead to careless and inaccurate habits.[34]

In 1932 the examiner returned to this theme, recognizing that the influence of Welsh on the thought process did not affect the performance of pupils in English. He concluded that:

> On the whole, it certainly appears that schools containing a majority of Welsh-speaking pupils *do* have somewhat greater difficulties than others, but many of these very schools have shown that such difficulties can be and have been very successfully overcome.[35]

The unintelligent use of clichés and memorized notes in answers to questions requiring explanation and knowledge of context suggested that 'talk about books and authors is often undertaken before thorough mastery of the books themselves', leading to 'gross misquotations and excruciating violations of metre'.[36] Examiners complained of an excessive attention to critical commentaries which, in some instances, had clearly been studied more closely than the texts themselves:

> They were even better known than the works on which they were based, though not infrequently the way in which they were quoted showed that they had not been properly understood. This was especially noticeable in the answers on *Hamlet*, in which the theories of Coleridge, Goethe, and Professor Bradley were often reproduced in garbled form and without any acknowledgement of their sources.[37]

Welsh

Throughout this period examiners emphasized the need for the status of Welsh as an academic subject to be recognized. Examiners argued that this meant devoting adequate time and resources to the subject and appointing teachers who were specialists in the language. The argument, propagated forcefully by W. J. Gruffydd before the First World War, was reiterated in the inter-war period. In 1920, examiners noted that there was a tendency on the part of some school governors and headteachers to consider Welsh to be a subsidiary subject which could be taught by non-specialists. Some examiners maintained that each school should have an honours graduate in Welsh on the staff.

After 1918 the use of English in examining the Welsh language declined as the academic status of the language was steadily reinforced, dictionaries became more readily available and attitudes towards its teaching became more enlightened. Questions on grammar were set in Welsh and a number of textbooks were produced, suitable for use by school pupils, which explained the rules of grammar. Nevertheless, the standard of understanding shown was a matter of concern for examiners. T. H. Parry-Williams[38] noted that pupils needed to be trained to give more complete explanations and that greater attention should be given to skills in parsing, etymology and the laws of mutation. In 1928 and 1929 G. J. Williams[39] noted that there was a danger that grammar was being neglected in some schools. In 1931 the examiner at

School Certificate level warned of a tendency for some pupils to emphasize style at the expense of grammar, while throughout the 1930s it was noted that in some schools, notably those in Welsh-speaking areas, there was a clear impression that the mechanics of the language did not receive sufficient attention.

Competence in translation was also deemed a key attribute. Pupils were urged to note that translation was not merely a matter of substituting the word in one language for another mechanically but that style and idiom also had to be taken into consideration. Examiners complained of mistakes involving the tenses of verbs, and of many candidates' grasp of Welsh vocabulary being inadequate. Pupils were often unable to provide the Welsh equivalents of common words such as swallows, hazel, hawthorn and nightingale, while the impersonal forms of verbs gave great difficulty. In 1936 Thomas Parry[40] noted:

> In the unseen pieces they were too careless with the syntax of English. Sometimes sentences were syntactically imperfect, and there were other unmistakable signs that the candidates had not read over their translations. But the surprising thing was that candidates who could write a good essay in correct and idiomatic Welsh, wrote sheer nonsense when they attempted to translate from English. They had never realised that it is the translator's duty to convey through the medium of one language what has already been conveyed through the medium of another, and that the new language very often requires an entirely different arrangement of words and phrases for the purpose. In this respect translating was a better test of the candidates' ability and resources than writing an original essay.[41]

The standard of Welsh composition was also a matter of concern. In 1918 Ifor Williams[42] observed that some candidates disregarded the need for punctuation and correct spelling while, in 1923, Parry-Williams stated that examples of good Welsh prose produced in the examination were rare. The influence of English idioms on Welsh composition was also noted and the use of colloquialisms criticized. According to D. Gwenallt Jones:[43]

> the pupils, by all means, should refrain from writing dialectal forms such as 'fferam', 'dwgyd', 'buais', 'gyda nhw', 'llefydd', 'ellith', 'eis', 'es', 'dyfn', 'yr ydan ni', 'disymwyth', 'a bywient', 'clywes', 'taw',

'tu fas', 'yn trial', etc. Grammar deals with the language of the nation, not the language of the parish. Grammar was the mother of the arts in the schools of the Welsh poets.[44]

Writing about the Higher examination in 1932, G. J. Williams emphasized the need to encourage pupils to read a broad range of Welsh literature as a means of enhancing their vocabulary and increasing their familiarity with correct forms of the language.

The greater attention to Welsh literature evident from 1914 was accompanied by an extension of the opportunity for pupils to answer literary questions in Welsh. Candidates were expected to write logically developed, well-illustrated answers which showed an awareness of the context of the period in which the literature was set and the ability to undertake appropriate literary criticism. At the Higher level it was expected that candidates be able to display a personal literary taste. Answers to the questions set on Welsh literature were often marred by candidates confining their reading to the set books, with the result that they were unable to place the text in its correct historical and social context. For instance, in 1933 the examiner noted that few candidates understood the events described by Edwards in *Cartrefi Cymru* or had any idea of the incidents and places to which he referred in *Clych Atgof*. Many pupils included irrelevant material and quotations in their answers, paying little regard to the actual requirements of a question. In 1937 the examiner maintained that the aim of all literary study should be to 'develop a taste for fine literature, and a love of everything artistic'. Yet it was observed that many answers lacked initiative and originality.

French

During the inter-war years the examination of French continued to focus on the skills of translation. Examiners emphasized the need for accuracy and sound knowledge of the written language and for candidates to be trained in grammar and composition. Pupils were criticized for submitting work which was inaccurate and demonstrated lack of sufficient vocabulary. Examining at the Senior stage, Fynes-Clinton[45] noted:

> Too many did not realise that the supreme criterion of a good translation is that it should make sense, and some rendered simple French idioms and expressions in words which they would not dream of using in ordinary life.[46]

At the Higher level, in 1922 it was noted that many candidates chose to paraphrase instead of translate, and gave an 'excessively free rendering of the French'. Moreover, there was evidence of carelessness as well as a lack of knowledge of basic French vocabulary and grammar. Schools were reminded of 'the valuable mental discipline' which was seen as an essential part of the study of modern languages, and candidates were expected to know and understand basic constructions, verbs and tenses. Examiners emphasized the need to undertake the necessary grammatical groundwork and to ensure that pupils had a secure and definite understanding of French grammar before they proceeded to more detailed study.

The examination schedules pertaining to French literature highlighted the need for candidates to comment on style and the composition of set books, as well as demonstrating an awareness of the social and political background to the texts studied. Examiners found that problems in applying learned information remained. Although candidates were often able to recall a considerable body of material, they could not select what was appropriate to answer particular questions and attempted to write all they knew about a particular author or book. There were many candidates who could not use quotations properly.

Standards of oral French were under increased scrutiny during the inter-war years. Examiners highlighted the need for accuracy and correct pronunciation in the spoken language. They noted that, generally, the standard of oral French was satisfactory but there remained a tendency among some teachers to attempt to teach pupils to answer questions which were likely to be asked in the examination rather than to cultivate pupils' general proficiency.

The number of candidates entered for the Direct Method alternative examination declined during the inter-war years and by 1939 only six schools entered pupils to be examined in this way. For the majority of pupils in Wales, French continued to be taught and assessed in the traditional form.

Both Fynes-Clinton and Mary Williams[47] noted that French conversation was, on the whole, satisfactory, that pupils were able to understand what was said to them and that their replies were often fluent and correct. Nevertheless, some candidates had difficulty in expressing themselves without considerable hesitation and few were able to use idiomatic expressions. Mistakes in pronunciation were also observed. The consonants 'c' and 'p' were over-emphasized, especially by pupils from schools in north Wales, and the quality of the reading was noticeably lower than the standard achieved by most pupils in French conversation. In 1928 Prof Barbier[48] wrote:

> On the whole, I have the impression that the confidence of the pupils is not developed quite as much as one would expect it to be at this stage. The candidates were often shy of expressing their ideas.[49]

Examiners maintained that the introduction of new techniques, most notably the use of radio and gramophone records, would lead to an improvement in the standard of oral French. In 1925 Morgan Watkin[50] wrote:

> If teachers want their pupils to learn to speak French well, they must use French more freely as a medium in their teaching, and must, among other things, acquaint them with some simple system of *Lecture expliquée*. The provision of a gramophone with a good supply of French records would be a great help to acquiring familiarity with the spoken tongue.[51]

In addition, examiners commended those schools which had been able to arrange exchange visits to France or had benefited from the services of a French assistant, which had resulted in pupils being given direct experience in hearing the language spoken naturally.

During the 1940s, examiners reiterated concerns about the standard of much of the work presented for examination. For example, in 1942 the examiner noted that the translation of the verse passage was 'thoroughly unsatisfactory' and that pupils clearly lacked adequate vocabulary. He believed that pupils appeared not to have had sufficient training in the art of translation, some candidates producing absurd translations of fairly basic French. The standard of French composition continued to cause concern. Many candidates were reported to have difficulties in writing even a few words of French without making some mistakes, with carelessness in the use of tenses a particularly prevalent feature.

Teachers were urged to make strenuous efforts to enlarge pupils' vocabulary and to ensure they understood fully the exact meaning of each word. At School Certificate level in particular, examiners complained that little attention was paid to oral French, pupils' performance indicating that they had been taught a few sentences in the months immediately before the examination with the result that the standard of conversation was in general below that of reading.

The quality of learning in French literature was also uneven. In 1942 the examiner commented that too many pupils appeared to rely on notes provided by teachers, their work suggesting that they had never made a detailed study of the texts themselves. Candidates continued to produce irrelevant and imprecise answers, with many unable to quote accurately from the set texts.

Latin

In 1921 the view was reiterated that a study of Latin and Greek should remain a central feature of the school curriculum. Although the Board of Education relaxed curricular prescription for secondary schools after 1926, the status of Latin as an academic subject remained firmly established in grammar schools during the inter-war years. Nevertheless, widespread dissatisfaction concerning the nature of Latin at School Certificate level continued to be expressed and many commentators maintained the need to devote more attention to classical literature and ancient history. The Spens Report of 1938 advocated awakening interest in Roman life, achievements and history[52] and placing less emphasis on the study of grammar and syntax.[53] However, the Norwood Report of 1943 acknowledged the doubts about the relevance of teaching Classics[54] and, increasingly, inspectors noted that only a few pupils appeared to have gained any advantage from their study of Latin.

Examiners continued to comment upon the varying quality of work produced in examination papers. In 1916 they criticized the striking difference in the quality of the work submitted by different centres, attributing it to the lack of interest and energy shown by some teachers. Nevertheless, examiners also noted that schools appeared to be committed to retaining Latin as a key element in the school curriculum, as was evident from the rising numbers being entered for the examination throughout the 1920s. Significantly, in 1929 the examiner observed that increased numbers of candidates had not led to a deterioration in the quality of the work, attributing this to the fact that the methods adopted by the teachers had improved.

Examiners continued to emphasize the need for candidates to be given a thorough grounding in the elements of Latin grammar, maintaining that 'until the functions of accidence and elementary syntax are securely laid, the superstructure of set books and unseen translation is bound to be unsound'. Questions requiring explanation of the format of Latin sentences were amongst the most searching on the grammar paper at the Higher level, requiring independent thought and judgement. Success in translation was claimed to be directly proportional to good work in grammar, with pupils being expected to know the functions of words and being able to parse sentences correctly. Nevertheless, examiners saw evidence that basic rules of grammar had not been understood. Many candidates submitted vague generalizations about grammatical phenomena: they displayed ignorance of the meaning of many ordinary words, with parsing often weak and based on guesswork. At the Senior stage in 1929 many pupils lost marks because of their failure to recognize and understand common syntactical usage. Examiners deduced that many pupils were unwilling to face the drudgery of learning grammar and cultivating the habit of accuracy.

Unprepared translation was seen as a crucial test of pupils' mastery of Latin grammar. Pupils were expected to show evidence of their own powers of thought and judgement and to pay attention to construction, meaning and elementary principles of grammar. Work submitted often fell short of this standard. Incoherent passages were sometimes produced and many candidates were found to possess insufficient vocabulary or knowledge of syntax to deal with the passage set. Some examinees confused words with similar sounds, and few were able to parse every case form mentally, to keep the thread of each clause distinct and to extract a reasonable sense from the set passage. Many candidates lost marks because of indifference to tenses, failure to analyse and parse each sentence, and deficient vocabulary.

Examiners drew attention to evidence that translation of prepared passages had been memorized, arguing that effective translation involved the correct handling of ideas as well as words. Candidates were expected to be able to know the meaning and value of each word and phrase. In addition, examiners maintained that poor spelling of English words was unacceptable.

In answers to questions on the subject-matter of the set books, examiners rewarded work which demonstrated recall and used relevant knowledge, as well as the ability to formulate sound judgement. They sought evidence that the set books had been studied with care and intelligence and that appropriate use was made of pertinent and concise quotations. Nevertheless, many candidates experienced great difficulty in addressing the needs of specific questions and many included irrelevant detail. There was also evidence that some candidates repeated statements gleaned from textbooks and had not made a detailed reading of the set books.

By the 1940s, examiners were still emphasizing the need for greater accuracy and understanding of the rules of Latin grammar. Pupils were expected to be able to discuss Latin sentences and to illustrate points of Latin syntax. In 1946 the examiner noted:

> It was almost always possible, after marking the first two or three grammar questions, to estimate accurately what the candidate was likely to do in the rest of the paper. In no case did a candidate who

failed in grammar make any success of the other sections: in almost every case candidates who answered the grammar questions correctly, or nearly so, did creditably in the rest of the paper.[55]

The need for closer attention to be paid to Latin grammar was again emphasized in examiners' comments about Latin composition. Writers of Latin prose were advised to consider the value of retranslating as an instrument of self-criticism and it was noted that grammatical inaccuracies and an undue predilection for the English idiom detracted from the quality of many compositions.

The practice of learning translations of prepared passages continued to vex the examiners. In 1940 it was declared that this was of no value to the pupils nor to Latin as an academic study. It was noted in 1942 that around 10 per cent of those candidates taking passages from Virgil and 20 per cent taking those from Caesar omitted words or even entire phrases. In 1946 it was stated that rarely did it appear that a translation was entirely the product of a candidate's own work:

> Translation seemed almost everywhere to have been learnt by heart – and, be it said, thoroughly well learnt by very many candidates. Often there would appear phraseology peculiar to a whole set, occasionally indeed very peculiar and sometimes too free, not to say flowery.[56]

Candidates were urged to analyse each sentence and identify constructions before attempting to translate – not jump to conclusions but rather to pay close attention to each word. Moreover, they were encouraged to adopt an appropriate style and to express themselves in good English, as many of the mistakes suggested that it was the pupils' English vocabulary and grammar that was at fault.

Geography

In the political climate which existed after the First World War, examiners such as Prof Fleure were acutely aware of the need for the study of geography to contribute to the generation of better international understanding. He maintained that its study should entail detailed examination of specific regions of the world, set in a broader, global context. Pupils should be able to make comparisons between these regions in order to spread a vision of the world and to develop an attitude of mind that fostered tolerant and constructive discussion of global problems.

A fresh approach to geography was reflected in the new Higher and School Certificate examinations introduced in 1923. Pupils pursuing the Higher course sat two written papers, together with a practical examination. Paper I was devoted to physical geography which included climatology, vegetation regions, mathematical geography and map projections. Paper II examined human geography, including sections on economic and historical geography, a study of a major natural region, and an analysis of topographic maps and weather charts. Candidates attempting the School Certificate examination were expected to know and understand ordnance survey maps, the relief and drainage of the British Isles and the climate, vegetation and landforms of various regions of the world. At both Higher and School Certificate levels, examiners sought to emphasize the need for candidates to show their understanding and ability to work as geographers, rather than simply to regurgitate memorized facts. Thus, candidates were expected to be able to select relevant material and to apply principles they had understood to the questions set. As Fleure noted in 1930, the primary aim was for candidates to be able to demonstrate an 'amplitude of thought rather than plenitude of information'.[57]

In addition, examiners constantly emphasized the importance of practical work. Pupils were expected to be able to interpret maps, understand special distinctions and be able to present information in graphic form through sketch maps and diagrams. The limited and inadequate nature of the facilities available for geography teachers was a matter of remark in the examiners' reports. The use of maps, lantern slides and the introduction of practical fieldwork were advocated, and examiners insisted that such work could only be undertaken if classrooms were equipped with the appropriate apparatus. They suggested the creation of geography laboratories where it would be possible to undertake detailed map work. In 1918 the examiner complained that in many schools geography was taught by people with no specialist training in the subject and that the time allocated to it was inadequate. Even so, during the 1920s examiners noticed a slow improvement in the quality of teaching, attributing it to the impetus given to the subject in the universities and the fact that more specialist teachers were now being appointed to schools throughout Wales. In 1923 the examiners maintained that the quality of the work at the schools in which pupils were taught to read and use maps correctly was excellent and commended the teaching and learning in schools where there was evidence of practical work, maintaining methodical records and field work.

Nevertheless, the performance of many candidates in geography continued to be of concern to the examiners. They regularly came to the conclusion that too many pupils were taught by dictated notes which they failed to understand. Some pupils wrote 'wild statements', prompting the conclusion that the work undertaken in almost one third of Welsh schools was unsatisfactory. Pupils continually failed to select relevant factual details; there was an inability to make connections between different aspects of the course; too many pupils were content to record their knowledge instead of applying what they knew, leading to 'flagrant irrelevance' in many answers. Poor map work and candidates' inability to use geographical terms correctly were further sources of concern. For instance, in the Higher examination in 1920, many candidates were unclear as to the meaning of 'mean annual temperature' and 'annual range of average temperature'. At School Certificate level in 1930, the examiner noted ignorance of terms such as 'temperate forests', 'climatic', 'products', 'natural resources', 'localized' and 'relief'.

During the Second World War and the years immediately afterwards, examiners continued to highlight the need for candidates to demonstrate a thorough understanding of the principles of geography as well as of the detailed factual knowledge required in the subject. The emphasis on studying Wales and its localities was also reaffirmed. For instance, in 1945 E. G. Bowen,[58] one of Wales's outstanding geographers and most effective popularizers of the subject, was convinced that knowledge of the homeland was 'axiomatic to all geographers'[59] and he strongly urged teachers to give pupils the opportunity to undertake practical exercises in studying land formations, climatic patterns and mapping so that they understood that geography was primarily a description and interpretation of the landscape.

The comparatively weaker performance of girls in geography examinations also attracted regular comment from examiners during the first half of the twentieth century. As early as 1913, Fleure had referred to the suggestion that girls were under-performing and were noticeably poor at map work. The issue was again a matter of concern for examiners during the inter-war period. In 1921 and 1922 it was noted that the total average mark for girls in the Higher examinations was 5 per cent and 6 per cent less respectively than for boys. This led to the advocacy of experiments in effective teaching methods for girls in order to make geography more appealing to them.[60] Fleure believed that more effective cross-curricular links with domestic economy would contribute to the broadening of girls' outlook. He called for the enrichment of school libraries and the establishment of 'current events' clubs to promote 'an intelligent foundation of knowledge especially in international affairs'.

History

During the inter-war years, the history syllabus continued to focus on developing an awareness of the sequence of the main stages of British history. Pupils were taught a chronological diet of political and constitutional history, although this was gradually broadened in an effort to ensure that pupils also gained an understanding of social, religious and economic development. It also encompassed an awareness of the relationship between the various nations within the British Isles, interaction with the European continent and the growth of the British Empire. Powerful voices were raised demanding greater recognition for Welsh history in the school syllabus. A variety of commentators contended that the history of Wales was relegated to the status of a 'footnote' and accused the

CWB of failing to take proper account of comments by its own examiners.

In addition to concern about the neglect of Welsh history, examiners noted that the medieval period received little attention in many schools. Only thirty-seven pupils sat the medieval history examination in 1945, while few of those who were examined in other periods had an adequate understanding of the medieval background. According to A. H. Dodd[61] it was essential that pupils understood the general pattern of medieval civilization in order to comprehend the significance and meaning of later periods:

> The Reformation and the Wars of Religion are hopelessly misconceived by those who know nothing of the medieval Church; the geographical discoveries lose their point for pupils brought up to imagine that before Columbus everyone thought the world was flat; and some appreciation of the idea of the medieval Empire is essential if one is to make sense of contrasting concepts like the national state or enlightened despotism.[62]

Dodd also expressed concern that modern history continued to be regarded as 'past politics' in many schools.

Examiners emphasized that factual knowledge in itself was not sufficient, especially at the Higher level. In 1927 the examiner for the School Certificate paper urged teachers to insist that examinees should avoid including irrelevant, descriptive material in their answers. In 1929, Dodd noted that many answers were replete with irrelevant material, with candidates unable to use it appropriately. This fault was also observed by William Rees[63] who regretted that even at the Higher level 'the knowledge displayed by the candidates far exceeded their ability to use it'. Examiners commented that a large number of pupils appeared to have little understanding of chronology, the sequence of events or causation.

Teachers were also reminded of the need to ensure that pupils were aware of the fruits of historical debates and changing emphases in interpretation. They were urged to read and make use of the scholarly writing of recognized historians, including contemporary authors. What examiners found suggested that many teachers used outdated and often second-rate textbooks. In 1920 examiners complained that the practice led to 'erroneous views' of key periods in history and that:

> Small text-books of the pot-boiler type are frequently quoted by name as final authorities and long memorised passages from fourth-rate reactors are given as definitive statements.[64]

The failure of some teachers to make sufficient use of maps and wall charts was also highlighted by the examiners. According to Dodd, an atlas should be given a central place in every history lesson. Rees commented:

> The use of a historical atlas or of wall-maps is indispensable to the study of political, and especially diplomatic history. Such work can have no meaning without the physical background.[65]

Despite such advice, many candidates continued to show a marked weakness in geographical knowledge, both in relation to the geography of the British Isles and of continental Europe.

The style and language adopted by many candidates was also a matter of regular comment by history examiners. Dodd maintained that candidates needed to be trained to think about the structure of their answers before committing pen to paper. Rees argued that clarity and precision of thought were essential for effective writing in history. Teachers were reminded that history was a 'literary subject' and that success owed much to the ability of candidates to express their thoughts clearly. They were urged to ensure that pupils were given sufficient practice in writing essays and that they were trained to select appropriate material. In 1937, Rees wrote:

> A well-constructed answer even if it reveals less adequate knowledge is to be preferred to a half-digested medley of facts. No candidate at the Higher Certificate stage should have failed to acquire a certain standard of orderliness in presenting his case. Each question should be regarded as a problem to be elucidated rather than as a peg upon which to hang the greatest possible number of facts. Many pupils seem still to labour under the impression that history is a subject in which memory alone counts.[66]

Serious errors in the use of terminology and quotations were also highlighted. In 1927 examiners referred to the tendency of many candidates to misquote. Stock phrases appeared year after year. Teachers were reminded that terms such as 'assizes', 'circuit', 'palatinate', 'state', and 'constitution' had to be explained to pupils – the evidence of examination papers indicated it was not done adequately. According to Dodd:

> Too many candidates failed to realise that a 'conciliar' movement has to do with councils, that a tax is not 'issued' and that neither a king nor a minister 'passes' a law ... and much confusion was shown in the use of words like 'policy' and 'system' (the overworking of which generally indicates an unreal and mechanical view of history), 'state', 'sovereignty', 'liberty,' and 'democratic'. This last word [democratic] was used in various scripts as the antithesis of monarchical, arbitrary, intolerant, conservative, despotic, and even Armenian. 'Freedom' ... came off even worse: in almost every answer it was interpreted as the equivalent, in some vague fashion, of 'reform'.[67]

Scripture

The teaching of religious education (or scripture as it continued to be called until the 1980s) in maintained schools was an issue of intense controversy during the nineteenth century, and drew the attention of religious, political and educational leaders. Gradually, the views of those who urged that some form of non-denominational religious education should be introduced by the schools prevailed. By the second decade of the twentieth century it was being argued that the decline of the Sunday schools meant that the subject had to be taken much more seriously and that the spiritual element of education needed to be viewed as one of the crucial tests of a national system. At the end of the First World War it was noted that:

> When the moral and spiritual factors should certainly be more emphasised than lightly regarded in our national system of education, is it not advisable to make a more general use of the Scriptures unto this end?[68]

Examiners expressed disquiet about the lack of interest in the subject in Welsh secondary schools, summed up by the Revd Principal Joseph Jones[69] who noted in 1921 that:

> I must share the surprise of my predecessor that only half the County Schools or even less take up Scripture Knowledge for the Board's Examination. There may be difficulties – they always exist when subjects are optional – in arranging this, but in a country noted for its loyalty to the Bible and at a time when the state of religious knowledge in schools is generally deplored, further effort should be made to overcome them.[70]

The Hadow Report of 1926 argued that the 'truths of religion' and their bearing on human life and thought should be brought home to pupils[71] and that the teaching of religious knowledge developed an important sensitivity among pupils. LEAs in England gradually adopted religious teaching as an integral part of the education system and in the 1930s there were signs that religious instruction was being taken more seriously, prompting the Board of Education to turn its attention to the task of developing an appropriate and acceptable syllabus.

Examiners continued to emphasize factual knowledge of Biblical texts as the key element in religious instruction and pupils were expected to provide clear explanations of textual and historical issues. They drew attention to the high standards achieved by many pupils, attributing this to diligent study and painstaking preparation. Pupils at the Higher level were commended for their knowledge of Biblical history and skill at translation. At the School Certificate stage it was noted that parts of the syllabus, notably the Book of Samuel and early Christian history, had been mastered by a significant number of candidates.

Nevertheless, examiners also had reason to complain about the standard of work submitted by weaker candidates. Many gave superficial, confused and irrelevant answers: candidates' knowledge of the terminology of the subject was often inadequate and there was a suspicion on the part of the examiners that, because of its low status, the subject had not been taught properly, with the result that knowledge of the Scriptures gleaned on the hearth or in the Sunday schools was relied upon as the basis for pupils' answers. In 1926 they maintained that teachers had to recognize that the School Certificate examination required more from candidates than the knowledge required in Sunday school examinations. In 1933 examiners noted that many candidates continued to rely on general Biblical knowledge without having made a serious study of the texts prescribed. There were some candidates at the Higher level who found great difficulty in translating from the Greek texts. Lack of knowledge of geography continued to hamper many candidates. For example, in 1919 it was observed that some candidates appeared to be unaware that Zion was in Jerusalem and few had any notion where Cyrna was situated, while Ramah was unknown.

More fundamentally for a subject whose protagonists were keen to champion its status as an academic discipline, candidates were unaware of recent scholarly study, a point stressed by Joseph Jones who noted that research into authorship, dates, sources and literary structure should be studied and understood. This message was repeated by examiners throughout the inter-war years as Biblical scholarship adopted an increasingly 'scientific' approach. It was expected that candidates would be able to discuss the critical problems bearing upon their study of Biblical texts, and teachers were encouraged to adopt a modernist approach to their teaching. There was some evidence that the scholarly approach urged upon schools during this period was influencing teaching in Welsh secondary schools. In 1928 the examiner noted that some of the candidates at the Higher School Certificate level were able to discuss intelligently the uniqueness of the Book of Revelation and could point to the chief features of the class of literature to which it belonged. Similarly, it was noted that revisionist expositions concerning 'I Samuel' were familiar to many candidates.

During the 1940s examiners continued to emphasize the need for candidates to show a thorough knowledge of the facts and the texts to provide them with the basis upon which more scholarly study could later be undertaken. Candidates were expected to show evidence of careful study and mastery of the pivotal points of Biblical history and to be able to quote accurately from the Scriptures. Examiners continued to report serious weaknesses in the quality of the work submitted by many candidates, especially at the School Certificate level. These included vague and irrelevant answers, carelessness, confusion of facts and inadequate textual knowledge. At Higher level they complained that some candidates lacked a sound grounding in the Greek language, that translations were often inaccurate or did not display evidence of literary criticism or reflection. Nevertheless, a number of candidates did produce work of a good quality at this level. In 1949 it was stated:

> The general standard of the work of the 23 candidates from 11 schools offering the subject at this advanced stage was higher than it has been in previous years. The best script in this paper could not easily be surpassed ... The translations of, and comments on, the Greek text in both papers were always good and often of real excellence. The very high quality of the best work in this examination reflected the greatest credit upon the quality and range of the teaching.[72]

Mathematics

During the First World War, the need for reform of the mathematics curriculum was acknowledged by many politicians and business leaders concerned about a loss of momentum in scientific and technical innovation. In the inter-war period, new approaches to mathematics, aimed primarily at less academic pupils and reflecting the influence of studies in educational psychology and the importance of activity, experience, and pupil interest, were developed. The Hadow Report, published in 1926,[73] emphasized the need for the arithmetic syllabus to focus to a greater extent on the practical applications of mathematical principles as a means of overcoming the distaste for the subject apparent among many pupils. Similarly, in geometry, the Report advocated the introduction of more practical experimental work and training in deductive processes and logical thinking. These sentiments were echoed in the Spens Report, published in 1938,[74] which maintained that reform was long overdue, and reiterated the need for greater attention to be paid to the utility of mathematical ideas in real life. The Norwood Report of 1943,[75] noted that previous recommendations for change had had little impact, and the traditional theoretical approach predominated, although this latest report did acknowledge that there was a greater unity in mathematical courses and that some irrelevant material had been removed.

Examiners were concerned at the standard of much of the work they assessed during the First World War and pointed to deterioration in the quality of work in algebra and geometry at the Junior stage. This they attributed to the problems confronting schools as qualified teachers were called to active service, leaving teaching in the hands of less-qualified colleagues. After the war, however, examiners noted a slow improvement, although progress in the girls' schools in 1920, for example, was less noticeable than in the boys' schools.

In arithmetic, teachers were urged to try to develop their pupils' mental awareness and analytical powers and insist on work which was careful and accurate. Candidates needed to be trained to use the power of mental arithmetic to check their answers and to be able to select appropriate methods of calculation. A number of weaknesses in the work submitted were highlighted. The quality of work involving skills of mensuration was notably poor: there were regular instances of confusion, for example between a foot and a square foot, and many pupils had no understanding of the difference between area and volume. Even questions based on practical situations, for instance on commercial transactions, were said to be treated in an abstract form and few candidates used common sense in approaching them.

In algebra, pupils were expected to demonstrate a firm grasp of the principles and methods of the subject, attempt questions accurately, apply principles in order to solve a variety of problems, think clearly and demonstrate understanding as well as knowledge of algebraic operations. Examiners noted that the quality of the work submitted was on the whole good and was improving each year. There was evidence that pupils had grasped the fundamental principles of the subject and that a greater emphasis was being placed on the need for candidates to arrange their work appropriately and be able to verify their results accurately. Even so, examiners highlighted significant weaknesses in many aspects of the work submitted. In a number of schools its quality fell far below the standard expected and there was a considerable difference in the standard attained by individual candidates. Weaknesses included the failure of many candidates to work out a preliminary rough estimate of results in logarithmic work, errors and inaccuracies in the use of brackets, and uncertainty about characteristics and rules. Some candidates were confused between addition and multiplication and had difficulty in using algebraic fractions. More failed to appreciate the meaning of symbols, with the result that they sometimes came up with absurd answers. There was considerable uncertainty evident in answers to some elementary operations.

During these years examiners continued to emphasize the need for pupils to demonstrate a theoretical understanding of geometry, competence in its practical application, and the ability to use mathematical instruments accurately. Pupils were expected to know the meaning of definitions and be able to trace the relationship of propositions to each other. In 1919 the examiner at the Senior level emphasized the need for candidates to show that ideas had been mastered as well as learned. In the 1920s examiners commended those pupils who had obviously been taught using modern methods whereby propositions and their geometrical principles had been tackled and their significance highlighted by illustrative calculations, constructions and riders. Nevertheless, considerable dissatisfaction was voiced about pupils' performance during these years. Pupils were poor at constructing figures from given data: there was a marked absence of geometrical 'instinct' whereby candidates were able to sense the essential points of a problem or theorem, and realize when it had been solved or proved. Many answers were inaccurate.

Despite some improvements in the 1930s it remained the case that geometry was the weakest part of the mathematics examination. Pupils regularly failed to provide proofs that were concise and logical; there was confusion in mastering the congruency of triangles, and weaknesses in answering theoretical riders.

In this period, trigonometry remained an optional part of the mathematics syllabus. In general, examiners expressed satisfaction with the standard of the work produced, yet there were also shortcomings. Many candidates submitted work which was below the standard expected and there was evidence that insufficient time had been given to the subject. Pupils from certain schools were considerably below the standard required. In many scripts, examiners found a lack of basic knowledge and an inability to apply general principles to practical illustrations.

At the Higher level the number of candidates examined in this period was comparatively small. The majority pursued a combined course in pure and applied mathematics, although a minority pursued more detailed separate courses. During the inter-war years, examiners noted that the quality of the work was, on the whole, gratifying. It was reported that pupils demonstrated a good grasp of the principles of the subject. Nevertheless, there were aspects of pupils' performance which caused concern to many examiners. In 1922 it was observed that aspects of the work lacked conciseness and appropriate arrangement. Riders in the algebra and geometry questions on the pure mathematics paper were not satisfactory while, in applied mathematics, the methods used in applying principles to examples were reported to be tedious and indirect, as candidates appeared to be too reliant upon rules and formulae without being able to demonstrate a proper appreciation of their derivation or implication.

In the Second World War, candidates attempting the School Certificate examination in mathematics continued to sit papers in arithmetic, algebra and geometry, with trigonometry remaining optional. Examiners noted that the general standard of the work submitted in arithmetic was high, though specific weaknesses – indiscriminate use of logarithms and a failure to make rough checks to ensure accuracy – remained. Moreover, too much essential work was left in rough on blotting paper or scrap paper. By the immediate post-war years it was clear that standards in work in arithmetic were being maintained, and examiners praised the greater accuracy evident in the work of many pupils. Shortcomings, such as the failure of some candidates to comprehend the phrase 'to three significant figures' or the tendency to use long calculations instead of logarithms, remained evident.

In algebra the standard was reported to be fairly consistent, although the perennial faults of inadequate checking, use of wrong methods and failure to show all relevant workings, continued. The standard was maintained after the Second World War, with nearly all candidates showing a good knowledge of algebraic processes, although some lacked the ability to carry the steps forward to a successful conclusion.

Examiners noted instances where enunciations had been stated carelessly or incorrectly, coupled with poor drawing and a tendency to misread questions. The inadequate quality of the work in this aspect of mathematics was a matter of concern to examiners after the Second World War. Examiners noted evidence of more learning by rote, disappointing rider work and a continued tendency on the part of many candidates to misread the questions set.

Examiners' reports also included suggestions as to how the teaching of the subject could be improved. They maintained that teachers should not teach geometry as an isolated series of topics but seek to develop a view of the subject as a real and complete science:

> I feel confident that if all schools adopted the group method of development we would hear less of the uselessness of geometry. Practically all general weaknesses to which attention is drawn by the examiners can be traced to a lack of '*grip*' of general principles – a grip which can only be obtained by grouping propositions and applications. One examiner states. 'The answers to the questions suggest, and this is also the *general impression of the whole paper*, that too little attention is paid to general principles and too much to isolated facts. While pupils can work a simple exercise on a definite theorem they fail to tackle a general question and to choose out the appropriate facts and then apply them'. Another says, 'The most permanent impression left on the examiner was the indifferent work done on those parts of the paper which involved practical constructions and numerical calculations. It was evident that a very big percentage of the candidates had little experience of such exercises.' Fundamentally these weaknesses show the non-grouping of principles and the development of a *partial* science by disjointed steps leading to knowledge which is not convincing.[76]

Science subjects

The Report of the Thomson Committee in 1918[77] not only raised the matter of the balance between the acquisition of factual information and discovery methods in the teaching and learning of science, as we saw in the last chapter, but also that of the balance between general science study and that of individual subjects. Schools were criticized for concentrating on the training of future specialists in a narrow field of science – predominantly chemistry and physics for boys and botany for girls – and neglecting the majority of pupils who needed a good general understanding of science. The thrust of the argument was that all secondary schools should introduce pupils to salient facts about the life of plants and animals, and scientific study should acquaint pupils with broad outlines of scientific principles in order to train their minds and develop their powers of interpreting evidence. In the inter-war period there was increasing official support for the teaching of general science. The Hadow Report of 1926[78] emphasized the need to highlight the practical application of science to everyday life. Nevertheless, in these years, chemistry and physics remained the dominant science subjects in Welsh secondary schools and science remained primarily a male study. Biology became increasingly important as an examination subject not only for boys but also for girls in the 1930s, replacing botany.

Even in the relatively conservative atmosphere of secondary education in Wales there were, then, those who criticized the restrictions of scientific education, arguing that pupils' scientific training may have been carried out on the narrowest of lines and be insufficient to meet contemporary ideals of a liberal education. Thus the School Certificate in science should include some knowledge of physics, chemistry and biology. This should be guaranteed by means of an obligatory general science paper, followed by optional additional papers in physics, chemistry and biology. There were also criticisms of the syllabus content of individual subjects, particularly in physics and chemistry, being geared towards the needs of the small minority, about 5 per cent, of pupils who intended to proceed to the Higher Certificate course in the science subjects or to a university course. By the end of the period covered in this chapter there had been some broadening of the syllabuses, but the general structure of single science courses remained in place.

Physics

Examiners' reports for the inter-war period suggest that the deficiencies identified before and during the First World War remained. They emphasized the need for candidates to be able to demonstrate understanding of the fundamental principles of the subject and apply them to particular problems. They continued to refer to evidence that practical experimental work was neglected. In 1921 it was stated:

> Knowledge was of a 'bookish' character and indicated that the pupils had not themselves carried out the experiments they were attempting to describe.[79]

Practical work was often 'inaccurate' and candidates lacked the ability to determine what experimental methods were appropriate under different circumstances. At the same time, many candidates had failed to state fundamental principles and clearly did not grasp the theory of the experiments they had carried out. Many were unable to apply definitions and deal with the important features of a question, showing lack of clear ideas about the essentials of conduction, convection, radiation and balance. In addition, candidates often suffered from their failure to gain a basic factual knowledge. For instance in 1921 it was stated that Hooke's Law was not thoroughly known; there was a lack of precision in making graphs; diagrams were often of a poor quality; and there were many arithmetical slips, often due to the fact that candidates did not show arithmetical workings. Examiners continued to stress the need for better illustrations and more precise workings. They also noted that the standard of work on magnetism and electricity was often poor, especially where candidates were required to answer questions which were not covered in their textbooks.

There were also more positive messages. In 1930 it was stated that some schools had covered all aspects of the syllabus and the way in which the subject had been taught as a complete whole had cultivated a broad view of the subject. The following year examiners noted the way in which:

> ... some pupils had demonstrated a good general knowledge of the subject, in addition to the more specialised knowledge of the branches detailed in the syllabus ... A variety of methods for instance of measuring high temperature, some quite novel, were submitted by some of the candidates. It is encouraging to find this proof of the wider outlook taken in some schools. Furthermore the candidates showed that they were able to apply the knowledge gained to good purpose, as, for example, in the last question in the second paper where they were given a number of materials to verify physical laws with which they were acquainted. Several candidates displayed initiative and resourcefulness in the answers they submitted to this question ... It is in the laboratory that the pupil gets to close grips with the subject and its difficulties and it is probable that many pupils derive more instruction of permanent value from the laboratory than they do from the classroom.[80]

Chemistry

The emphasis on the importance of practical work was reflected in the comments of those who examined chemistry during the inter-war years. Teachers were urged to cultivate a sense of discovery by ensuring that pupils' learning was based on experimental work wherever possible, and to reduce their reliance on blackboard drawings of apparatus and verbal descriptions of methods and processes. The reports indicate that the advice was not taken on board. Teaching staff were reminded that it was 'absolutely essential' that they base their teaching on practical work carried out in the laboratory. At the Higher level, it was maintained that practical work should not degenerate into mere routine but that pupils should understand the reason for every process carried out, and should be able to write the equation for every reaction performed on the basis of understanding, not memory.

Examiners noted that there were numerous instances where pupils had been able to grasp the fundamentals of the subject and that the standard of the work in general was maintained year on year. Many candidates demonstrated clear conceptions of the meaning of chemical equations, together with knowledge of the facts and principles of chemistry. Nevertheless, examiners drew attention to problems which continued to undermine pupils' performance in schools. They detected that candidates were attempting to describe experiments they had not performed. In a few cases it was clear that different experiments had been allocated to various pupils in a class, but all pupils had entered them in their books as if they had done the work. Calculations were often clumsy and incorrect, and candidates tended to attempt to bring in knowledge of a large number of equations and tables which had been learned but not understood. Moreover, some candidates wasted their time drawing unnecessary diagrams and descriptions of apparatus instead of describing the experimental work they were required to do. Examiners highlighted instances of the basic phraseology of chemistry being neglected. They pointed to the indiscriminate use of the word 'substance' and 'combustible', and the tendency of some candidates to use formulae instead of names in the descriptive parts of their answers.

Similar criticisms were repeated throughout the inter-war years, suggesting that little notice had been taken of previous reports. For instance, in 1938 the examiners noted that certain words were still consistently misused or misunderstood, and vague phraseology suggested that the principles of the subject were still not being grasped.

The teaching of the subject was inevitably affected by severe shortages of apparatus and experimental materials during the Second World War. This had a particular impact on the standard of practical work. Even so, it was stated that much of the work presented reached a good standard and that in most cases a satisfactory knowledge of laboratory methods had been attained. It was observed that the best candidates at Higher level attained excellent standards. Many pupils had obviously carried out or observed experiments at first hand. However, perennial deficiencies continued to be noted. Diagrams were not always properly used or labelled; there was carelessness in the writing of equations; some pupils were unable to record what was observed and done;

theoretical principles had not been understood; and there was a tendency to divorce the theoretical from the practical.

Botany, biology and zoology

During the inter-war years, examiners saw a gradual improvement in the quality of the work submitted in botany, a factor which was attributed to the gradual improvement in the quality of the facilities enjoyed by teachers. In 1918 examiners noted that the work was satisfactory at all levels except at the Senior stage. Later, they noted that the style and quality of the drawings had improved considerably and that candidates showed a better understanding of technical terms. The number of 'absurd' or 'impossible' answers had decreased, while more pupils demonstrated originality and independent judgement in their answers. Examiners were, however, concerned that too many pupils continued to rely on the power of factual recall and many had clearly not received adequate experience of practical work. In 1924, the following was observed:

> It is obvious that a short investigation done well is of far greater value than a long account of a subject treated more or less theoretically. Thus, in the case of the subject of the anatomy of water-plants, it would be much more valuable to make a thorough practical study of one plant than to treat at great length the general ecology of hydrophytes. The independent work must be an investigation and not a theoretical treatise.[81]

Examination methods changed at this time. Greater emphasis was placed on testing practical and experimental skills, and an element of oral examination was introduced which gave examiners the opportunity to explore the depth of pupils' knowledge of the subject. Examiners thus diagnosed the extent to which enthusiasm and interest had been generated and found it easier to identify which schools relied on teaching from textbooks. Nevertheless, perennial deficiencies continued to be highlighted. In 1932 Lily Newton[82] complained that the standard of the practical work undertaken in many schools remained unsatisfactory. She reminded schools that it was more important for candidates to be able to identify tissues under a microscope than to recite a complete list of tissues, learned by heart. Many pupils had clearly been taught disparate facts but were unable to make a connection between them or to differentiate between relevant and irrelevant information. There was a lack of linkage between experiments and the laws which experiments had been intended to illustrate. Many pupils were unfamiliar with outdoor botany and few could deal effectively with comparative questions.

During these years, examiners were on the whole complimentary about both botany and zoology. Their reports indicated that an appropriate balance had been achieved between the subjects and that the syllabuses had been covered appropriately in most schools, although there was a tendency to emphasize botany at the expense of zoology at the Higher stage. Despite some positive aspects, candidates at School Certificate level were found to be unacquainted with such concepts as the 'living organism', and were not sufficiently aware of the basics of the subject. For instance, many had difficulty in explaining 'respiration' and were unfamiliar with the simple chemistry of the atmosphere. Although some of the most glaring deficiencies were addressed by about 1920, it was noted that the general standard attained by candidates in the biology examination was lower than that achieved by candidates who sat separate papers in biology and zoology. This was attributed to the fact that many teachers continued to teach biology as two subjects rather than one:

> The standard of work shown by the candidates in this year's examination does not reveal any improvement over that of last year. The fact still remains that the standard of attainment of the Biology candidates falls below that of the candidates taking Botany and Zoology as separate subjects. This appears to be true of candidates sitting for this examination and is the experience of other examining bodies also, and the reasons for this discrepancy are a cause of concern to examiners and authorities alike. It may be that the greater amount of time spent by the candidates taking Botany and Zoology as separate subjects in dealing with animals and plants gives them greater measure of maturity and experience, and this cannot be attained by the pure biologists. It is certainly true that they do not reach, on their reduced syllabus, the standard

of dissection and of observation which the Botanists and Zoologists show. They fall into more errors in fundamentals. Various criticisms of the syllabus have been received which suggest that it is difficult to bring these fundamentals within its scope. Possibly the new syllabus will give a new impetus to the study of Biology and result in work of equal standard to that done on Botany and Zoology.[83]

Moreover, it was emphasized that too many teachers continued to rely on ensuring their pupils memorized a series of facts based on the available textbook rather than understanding what had been taught. This report, like so many, concluded with the enduring refrain common to most examiners across the subjects in this period.

The inter-war years were a time of significant change for the natural sciences. Throughout the 1930s an increasing number of schools introduced biology instead of botany, even though there was continuing controversy over the syllabus to be studied. Biology, unlike botany, was widely regarded as a serious scientific subject which had a disciplinary rigour to match that of physics and chemistry.

Conclusion

The formal examination system in Welsh secondary schools changed little as the world was revolutionized around them in the three decades following the end of the First World War. The major change in the Wales of this period was little short of cataclysmic. The economic disasters of the 1920s and 1930s left industrial communities reeling. The outbreak of war in 1939 brought economic relief but at a terrible cost in human and material destruction. At the end of the Second World War it became apparent that the war itself was the catalyst of a social revolution which found expression in the election result of 1945 and the socialist measures which were to follow.

Each of these phases had its impact on the secondary school system. Strains on schools increased as numbers expanded rapidly. The system of segregated schooling for the minority who passed the scholarship examination, substantial as that might be in Wales compared with England, remained.

As the realization grew that elementary education for the remainder was wholly inadequate, pressures accumulated in Wales, sometimes for practical reasons, sometimes for ideological, for a multilateral school solution. All such pressures were brusquely rebuffed by the Board of Education. Two minority Labour governments, themselves ideologically divided on the matter of common secondary schools, were able to change little.

With the outbreak of war in 1939 came the inevitable disruption caused particularly by evacuation, damage to school buildings and the call-up of male staff. As usual, the teachers who remained – including those women who normally had to relinquish their posts on marriage – performed heroics and the pupils of Wales were prepared for their examinations as regularly and almost as thoroughly as previously.

The Education Act 1944 cautiously caught something of the spirit of social change which was to result in electoral victory for the Labour Party in 1945. It replaced the principle of fee-paying in state secondary education with that of free schooling. What it did not bring was the multilateral or comprehensive secondary education which some influential figures in the Labour Party now endorsed. The 1944 Act did not stipulate the kind of secondary education which was to be offered, but senior civil servants, in alliance with the majority in the Labour Party who saw the grammar schools as providing the best opportunity for bright working-class pupils, ensured that the local authorities produced development plans for reorganization which preserved a segregated system of schooling. Wales became a country of grammar and secondary modern schools. Few exceptions, whether in the form of bilateral or multilateral schools, were approved. By 1949, the system envisaged by the Education Act 1944 was being implemented, although all-age schools were phased out only years later. The grammar schools, as they were now known, had once more settled into equilibrium after the upheavals of the war.

It was an equilibrium in which those who taught in the Welsh county intermediate schools before the war were very much at home. Organizational changes impacted lightly on day-to-day routines. In 1949 the CWB gave way to the Welsh Joint Education Committee which had no inspection function. Nevertheless, it took over as the national examining body for the secondary schools of Wales. The 11 plus examination remained firmly in place. Changes to the examination system were on the way, to come into force in 1951, when the School and Higher Certificates were replaced by the General Certificate of Education at O level and A level. Nevertheless, there was no sea-change in form and content of examinations, merely the gradual evolution characteristic of previous decades.

It is remarkable that the secondary school system of Wales remained one of the constants throughout all upheavals. Formal examination qualifications, tried and tested, and traditionally administered, became even more important as their economic value in the 'locust years' was so much to be treasured. Early leaving blighted the educational opportunities of a multitude of intelligent pupils in these years, as did the inability of many pupils to capitalize on the award of School Certificates by taking up places in higher education. Boys and girls alike were forced by economic circumstance to take training college rather than university places, or to surrender either to become family breadwinners. Nevertheless, the examination successes provided by the Welsh secondary school system assumed a personal and communal value which, arguably, was never more significant.

References

[1] Public Record Office (PRO), ED24/205.
[2] For example, initially there had been opposition to the development of post-matriculation courses in Welsh schools. It was led by O. M. Edwards, who remained convinced that the age of entry to university should be seventeen and that advanced courses were not required in intermediate and secondary schools. Moreover, the fact that pupils entered secondary schools in Wales at the age of twelve, and not eleven, caused immense difficulties at a time when the Board of Education sought to standardize policy across England and Wales.
[3] (Viscount) Haldane had played a leading role in the development of

the London School of Economics and was deeply interested in extending opportunities for working class education for children and adult learners.
4   PRO, ED24/205.
5   *Parliamentary Papers*, 1920, XV.
6   National Library of Wales, Thomas Jones MSS.
7   *Welsh Outlook*, IV (1917), p. 301.
8   *Parliamentary Papers*, 1930–1 (Cmd. 3920) XVI.
9   CWB, *Annual Report*, 1937–8.
10 A compromise solution to the question of inspection of schools by the Department and the Board was achieved in 1922.
11 Gareth Elwyn Jones, *Controls and Conflicts in Welsh Secondary Education* (Cardiff, 1981), p. 81.
12 *Parliamentary Papers*, 1920, XV.
13 *Parliamentary Papers*, 1938–9, X.
14 A. J. Lush, *The Young Adult: Being a Report Prepared in Co-operation with Young Men in Cardiff, Newport and Pontypridd, under the Auspices of the Carnegie United Kingdom Trust* (Cardiff, 1941), p. 16.
15 Frederic Evans, 'Secondary education for all – the meaning of re-organisation', *Welsh Outlook*, XVII (1930).
16 Edmund D. Jones, 'Examinations in Wales', *Welsh Outlook*, XIX (1932), pp. 152–3.
17 PRO, ED10/148.
18 PRO, ED10/148.
19 PRO, ED10/148.
20 PRO, ED12/452.
21 PRO, ED10/147.
22 PRO, ED10/147. Similarly, Frederic Evans, while acknowledging that children in rural schools should enjoy access to the same general curriculum as their counterparts in other areas, insisted that the local environment should be used intelligently. See Frederic Evans, 'The Problem of the Rural School', *Welsh Outlook*, XV (1928), pp. 125–7.
23 *Yr Herald Cymraeg*, 23 March 1920.
24 *Yr Herald Cymraeg*, 15 April 1924, 17 June 1924; *Y Cymro*, 6 April 1921, 28 August 1929; *Western Mail*, 21 July 1921, 17 October 1923, 7 July 1921.
25 PRO, ED10/148.
26 PRO, ED10/148.
27 CWB, *Annual Report*, 1925–30.
28 Percy E. Watkins, *A Welshman Remembers: An Autobiography by Sir Percy E. Watkins LLD* (Cardiff, 1944), pp. 124–6.
29 PRO, ED12/452; ED10/147; ED10/147; ED24/205.
30 *Report of the Consultative Committee on Secondary Education with Special Reference to Grammar Schools* (Spens Report) (London, HMSO, 1938).
31 Board of Education Circular 753.

32 *The Teaching of English in England* (Newbolt Report) (London, HMSO, 1921).
33 CWB, *Report on the Inspection and Examination of County Schools*, 1919, p. 46.
34 CWB, *Report on the Inspection and Examination of County Schools*, 1921, p. 31.
35 CWB, *Report on the Inspection and Examination of County Schools*, 1932, p. 16.
36 CWB, *Report on the Inspection and Examination of County Schools*, 1925, p. 38.
37 CWB, *Report on the Inspection and Examination of County Schools*, 1926, p. 32.
38 (Sir) Thomas Parry-Williams became Professor of Welsh at Aberystwyth.
39 Professor of Welsh in University College of South Wales and Monmouthshire, Cardiff.
40 (Sir) Thomas Parry became Principal of the University College of Wales, Aberystwyth.
41 CWB, *Report on the Inspection and Examination of County Schools*, 1936, p. 58.
42 (Sir) Ifor Williams succeeded Sir John Morris-Jones as Professor of Welsh Language and Literature at Bangor.
43 Aberystwyth academic and one of the most famous of twentieth-century Welsh poets.
44 CWB, *Report on the Inspection and Examination of County Schools*, 1930
45 O. H. Fynes-Clinton was appointed Professor of French and Romance Languages at University College of North Wales, Bangor in 1903.
46 CWB, *Report on the Inspection and Examination of County Schools*, 1921, p. 58.
47 Mary Williams became Professor of French at University College Swansea.
48 André Barbier was Professor of French at the University College of Wales, Aberystwyth.
49 CWB, *Report on the Inspection and Examination of County Schools*, 1928
50 A former stonemason, he became Professor of French and Romance philology in Cardiff.
51 CWB, *Report on the Inspection and Examination of County Schools*, 1939, p. 72.
52 Spens Report.
53 Spens Report, p. 229.
54 *Curriculum and Examinations in Secondary Schools: Report of the Committee of the Secondary School Examinations Council appointed by the President of the Board of Education in 1941* (Norwood Report) (London, HMSO, 1943), p. 119.

55 CWB, *Report on the Inspection and Examination of County Schools*, 1946, p. 36.
56 CWB, *Report on the Inspection and Examination of County Schools*, 1944, p. 33.
57 CWB, *Report on the Inspection and Examination of County Schools*, 1930
58 E. G. Bowen became Professor of Geography at the University College of Wales, Aberystwyth.
59 CWB, *Report on the Inspection and Examination of County Schools*, 1945, p. 92.
60 CWB, *Report on the Inspection and Examination of County Schools*, 1919, p. 104.
61 A. H. Dodd became Professor of History at the University College of North Wales, Bangor.
62 Central Welsh Board, *Report on the Inspection and Examination of County Schools*, 1945.
63 William Rees became Professor of Welsh History at the University College of South Wales and Monmouthshire, Cardiff.
64 CWB, *Report on the Inspection and Examination of County Schools*, 1920; see also 1925, p. 44; 1927, p. 44; 1929, p. 45.
65 CWB, *Report on the Inspection and Examination of County Schools*, 1937, p. 25.
66 CWB, *Report on the Inspection and Examination of County Schools*, 1937, p. 21.
67 CWB, *Report on the Inspection and Examination of County Schools*, 1929, p. 46.
68 CWB, *Report on the Inspection and Examination of County Schools*, 1919, p. 55.
69 Principal of Memorial College, Brecon.
70 CWB, *Report on the Inspection and Examination of County Schools*, 1921.
71 *The Education of the Adolescent*, (Hadow Report) (London, HMSO, 1926) p. 189.
72 CWB, *Report on the Inspection and Examination of County Schools*, 1949, p. 3.
73 Hadow Report.
74 Spens Report.
75 Norwood Report.
76 CWB, *Report on the Inspection and Examination of County Schools*, 1922, p. 74.
77 *Natural Science in Education* (London, HMSO, 1918).
78 Hadow Report.
79 CWB, *Report on the Inspection and Examination of County Schools*, 1921.
80 CWB, *Report on the Inspection and Examination of County Schools*, 1931.
81 CWB, *Report on the Inspection and Examination of County Schools*, 1924.

82 Lily Newton became in turn Professor of Botany, Vice Principal and Acting Principal of the University College of Wales, Aberystwyth.
83 CWB, *Report on the Inspection and Examination of County Schools*, 1949.

Chapter 3
Continuity in Change 1949–1970

Introduction

We saw at the end of the previous chapter that forces for change in the secondary school system had become irresistible during the war. In 1938 the Spens Report[1] had recommended major modifications to the education system in England and Wales, concluding that the curriculum pursued in secondary/grammar schools focused too heavily on academic subjects and that children were subjected to a surfeit of formal examinations. Spens maintained that there was a need to reduce the emphasis on acquiring factual knowledge, and recommended that much stronger links be developed between schools and the communities they served. The document suggested a range of options, including the establishment of common schools for pupils aged 11–13, although it fell short of recommending the creation of a common school to serve all pupils after the age of eleven. Yet, at that time, the government rejected major change.

With the closing stages of the Second World War, however, came the Education Act 1944 which would transform educational structures in England and Wales; and, by 1949, the extent of that transformation was evident, as we saw in the previous chapter. From the outset it was obvious that this legislation would have far-reaching consequences for education in Wales. First, it became clear that the new Ministry of Education did not believe that the Central Welsh Board (CWB) should continue to play a role in the nation's education system. A number of reasons accounted for this: the Board's financial position had always been precarious; there were many powerful voices who believed it should be replaced by a body with a wider remit and a more modern outlook,[2] and it was widely recognized that the issue of dual control in Welsh secondary education – involving the CWB and the Welsh Department of the Board of Education – had to be addressed in view of the proposals to expand post-elementary education.[3] The leaders of the CWB made strenuous efforts to convince the government that a new body was not required and that, if it was given new responsibilities, the Board could continue to serve the needs of Welsh education. These views did not convince R. A. Butler, President of the Board of Education in the wartime coalition government, nor his Labour successors, Ministers of Education Ellen Wilkinson and George Tomlinson, who were convinced that a new body should be established which would serve the needs of all secondary schools, untrammelled by an association with the past, particularly the system of dual control.[4] As a result, in 1948 the Welsh Joint Education Committee (WJEC) was constituted and, from 1 April 1949, assumed responsibility for all the functions previously exercised by the CWB, the Advisory Council for Technical Education in Wales, the Welsh Academic Board of Technology and the South Wales Mining Committee.

The Education Act 1944 did not propose a restructuring of the local education authorities (LEAs), although Part III authorities, which administered elementary education in some urban areas, were abolished. The LEAs were retained despite the fact that they varied immensely in size and resources and the extent to which they were able to effect economies of scale. It was believed that the question of the capacity of LEAs could be addressed to some extent by joint working through the WJEC, for example in areas such as the development of technical education[5] and schooling for children with special needs.[6] The WJEC, based mainly on local authority representation, rapidly emerged as a forum for the development of educational policy in Wales and played a major role in disseminating information, identifying areas which needed reform and urging LEAs, either individually or in partnership with others, to develop new services. An administrative model emerged whereby one LEA was given responsibility as the lead authority, supported by all or some other LEAs in Wales. The 1950s saw immense expansion as special schools for deaf, blind, partially sighted and other children were established.[7] The schools museums service was enhanced in cooperation with the National Museum of Wales,[8] as was the provision of radio programmes for schools with the help of the BBC. The WJEC also took responsibility for the National Youth Orchestra of Wales.[9]

Further impetus to the process of reform was provided by the Central Advisory Council for Education (Wales) (CACE(W)), appointed in 1944. As was the case with its counterpart in England, this was a body of individuals appointed by the Minister of Education to act as a forum for the detailed consideration of education policy. The work undertaken by the Council indicates clearly the extent to which its members were convinced of the need to recognize distinctive characteristics within the education system in Wales, while at the same time ensuring that Welsh schools kept abreast of developments in education in other parts of the United Kingdom and further afield. Several members were convinced that Welsh grammar schools were out of touch with modern needs and that their methods needed to change radically, given that their mission was no longer to educate a small number of children with an exceptional gift for academic subjects.[10] Their views also suggested that, in common with many others in post-war Britain, they believed that there was a need to free schools from restrictive curricular straitjackets. For example, (Dame) Olive Wheeler[11] believed schools should seek to promote a love of knowledge for its own sake and enable individuals to mature in a social context as well as intellectually, by giving teachers more freedom to select what to teach according to their own philosophy of life.[12] Saunders Lewis[13] argued that the education system was too focused on fulfilling the narrow demands of the industrialized society which had emerged during the nineteenth century and he questioned the value of the amount of examining and testing which was a central feature of that inheritance.

One of the Council's main functions was its role in investigating and commenting upon the school curriculum. It supported the view that history should be taught as a means of fostering understanding of the complex problems of the modern world and that less emphasis should be placed on developing a facility for factual recall.[14] It supported the notion of a more integrated approach to geography and history[15] and came to a consensus in favour of making greater use of the local environment in teaching both subjects.[16]

Considerable attention was devoted to considering science and mathematics. Here again there was an acknowledged need for reform in the aims and methods of teaching in order to encourage pupils who studied science to develop an awareness of the physical environment and an understanding of processes by arousing their interest and curiosity.[17] CACE(W) recognized the need to develop an enhanced sense of inquiry among children: teachers were urged to undertake practical work which would engender a feeling of excitement and capture the pioneering spirit which was an essential part of scientific work.[18] At the same time it was emphasized that courses should be relevant to the everyday experiences of a child.[19]

The need for schools to provide a broader cultural foundation for children and young people by developing an appreciation of culture and art was also a feature of the Council's deliberations. It devoted considerable attention to this aspect of the curriculum through its investigation of arts and crafts in the schools of Wales.[20] According to one commentator, it was incomprehensible that:

> ... a race of men living in a romantic country amongst noble hills and lovely villages, a race with a stirring history behind it, a strong poetic strain and a great natural gift for song, should so far have made no remarkable contribution to the art of the world.[21]

The CACE(W) was in favour of broadening the range of learning enjoyed by pupils at secondary school by encouraging an appreciation of architecture, the environment, the health and nature of society and the problems confronting different groups in the modern world.[22]

Similarly, the CACE(W)'s Technical Education sub-committee, chaired by Dr Idris Jones,[23] emphasized the need to restore respect for manual skills and practical work. Jones argued that the Depression of the 1920s and 1930s, with its concomitant unemployment, had led Welsh educationists to go even further than their predecessors in highlighting the need to equip school pupils for white collar work. Jones's thinking was evident in the recommendation that manual instruction should be given a central role in the curriculum of every child.[24] However, the sub-committee was not enamoured of the suggestion that Welsh schools should focus more on vocational education. It warned that pupils should not specialize in any one industrial field but should, instead, pursue a broad curriculum, including training in the use of machines.

The Education Act 1944, and the debates which influenced it, meant that the structure, aims and ethos of the School Certificate examination were subjected to rigorous scrutiny. A growing consensus emerged in favour of a radical revision of the system, although examination bodies differed in their response to the challenges. Surprisingly, in view of its previous conservatism, the CWB[25] acknowledged the need for a thorough consideration of the new methods of assessment at a time when others, notably the Oxford and Cambridge Board, objected to the 'abolition' of the School Certificate and the Higher Certificate. Opposition to change was voiced in Wales, notably by representatives of the University of Wales who were concerned that its role in the examinations structure would be diminished.[26]

The consensus for reform soon translated into practical change in the grammar schools' external examination system. In 1951, a General Certificate of Education (GCE) examination replaced the School Certificate and Higher Certificate examinations. The new examination had three levels, Ordinary (O), Advanced (A) and Scholarship, the first intended to be approximately equivalent to the old School Certificate. Unlike its predecessor, however, which required simultaneous passes in subjects chosen from various groups, a certificate could be awarded for a pass in just one subject. Furthermore, differentiating grades of pass, credit and distinction, were replaced by a pass/fail system, the certificate merely recording each success. State scholarships to university, dating from 1921, which had traditionally been awarded on the results of the Higher School Certificate examination, were now to be based on performance in special scholarship papers. Scholarship candidates were deemed to give promise of gaining a first or upper second class honours university degree, while others who did not seem to possess such exceptional ability, but nevertheless showed promise of being able to benefit from a university education, were eligible for LEA awards.

In 1955 an autumn supplementary examination was introduced in certain subjects at O level, candidates being able to retake those subjects they had failed in the summer examinations. New subjects were introduced from time to time to meet the needs of technical schools and institutions of further education, while there were changes, too, in the arrangements for examinations in Welsh. In 1953 an additional O level examination was introduced for candidates who had gained their knowledge of Welsh by studying it at school, followed in 1961 by an A level examination for the same pupils. By 1969 Welsh language papers were provided in history, geography, music, scripture, art, French, Latin, metalwork, cookery, dressmaking and domestic subjects.

In the wake of the Education Act 1944, secondary education in Wales was slowly reorganized. By 1961, 52 per cent of secondary school pupils in Wales were in secondary modern schools, 34 per cent in grammar schools and 11 per cent in comprehensive schools, with some 3 per cent of senior pupils still in all-age schools. The secondary modern school not only lacked pedigree but also any external formal assessment tool of the kind provided by the GCE. The curriculum was much less academic than that of the grammar school, concentrating, especially with the less able pupils, on English, mathematics and handicrafts. Civil servants and politicians planned things this way.

When introduced in 1951, entry to GCE O level examinations was limited to candidates who were at least sixteen years of age in the September of that academic year, that is beyond the school leaving age, in an attempt to preserve the elitism of the sixth form. With the school leaving age set at fifteen from 1947, secondary modern pupils were intended to be barred from the examination. In 1952 this regulation was removed, candidates below the age of sixteen being allowed to take the examination, but exceptionally, and only at the discretion of the headteacher, who had to be of the opinion that such candidates were virtually guaranteed to obtain a pass.

In practice, some secondary modern schools were able to enter their ablest pupils for the O level examination, but it was an academic examination unsuitable for the great majority. Following the report of the Beloe Committee,[27] the Minister of Education in July 1961 accepted the proposal of the Secondary Schools Council for the introduction of a new school examination, designed for pupils of a lower level of ability than those for whom the GCE examinations were considered suitable, which should be largely under the control of teachers. In Wales, the WJEC became the examination body for the Certificate of Secondary Education (CSE), and set up a CSE Committee which had a majority of serving teachers. The first examinations, with assessment of course work playing an integral part in several subjects, were held in 1965, numbers of candidates multiplying rapidly.

The task of overseeing the reform of the examinations system occupied much of the attention of the WJEC during the first years of its existence. Particular problems were experienced in developing the A level syllabus (the equivalent of the former Higher Certificate course), not least because of the attitude of some representatives of the University of Wales.[28] After lengthy discussions a compromise was reached whereby a Joint Academic Advisory Committee was established to oversee the A level examinations. It would include representatives of the University of Wales and would be responsible for recommending syllabuses and names of examiners, although the final authority in these matters was vested in the WJEC.[29]

English

After the Second World War the teaching of English was influenced by the continuing debate about the nature of the subject. Academics and teachers considered issues such as the extent to which English teaching should emphasize formal grammar, and whether free expression and creativity should be encouraged. The syllabuses and examination papers of this period suggest the movement for change exerted little influence in Wales. The A level English syllabus confirmed the need for pupils to become familiar with the classical texts of English literature and little attempt was made to include more contemporary works discussing twentieth-century social issues. In 1954 it was asserted that memorizing Chaucer's descriptions, Hamlet's soliloquies or Keats's odes was essential, the rewards of doing so lasting a lifetime.

Many 1950s candidates at A level were penalized for their inability to write satisfactorily. Their poverty-stricken vocabulary was attributed partly to a very narrow range of reading, partly to the tendency of some candidates to indulge in highly coloured 'journalese' and use of jargon. Later, in 1963, it was asserted that 'the concern of examiners in English language is with the candidates' powers of expression and not with their attitudes to life, their problems and their morals'.[30]

In the literature section of A level, examiners complained that memorized notes were regularly unloaded in the examination room. For instance, candidates in 1954 were chastized for using the hallmarked phrases and ideas of critics such as T. S. Eliot, David Cecil and C. S. Lewis as if they were their own original thoughts. There was often little evidence of individual reaction to the texts. Essays continued to betray a lack of planning and purpose, and an inability to deal with the precise point at issue in the question. In 1956 the A level report epitomised the difficulties of the period:

> Many candidates were unable to express themselves correctly or adequately. They mis-spelt common words, omitted all punctuation except commas, and went wrong on 'either . . . or', 'only', 'shall' and 'will', and so on; they confused similar-sounding words (for example, 'credible' and 'credulous') wherever possible, freely used vulgarisms and slang, and managed their time so badly that they had to write the last answer in note form or with abbreviations such as '18th cent', or 'Shak'. Generally their vocabulary and powers of expression were quite inadequate to their purposes, though it must be admitted that a few had made it their business 'to hunt more after words than matter', with equally distressing results . . . The candidates' main weakness, however, lay in their matter.

Often they incurred heavy penalties by mis-reading one or other of the questions. Then, in their answers, many could do no more than summarise the story of the book, or, at best, write character sketches, when that was possible. Their knowledge of the historical background of the books they chose was very thin, and only a small number of candidates could grasp a literary work imaginatively as a work of art, and relate it to a wider awareness of life.[31]

Examiners continued to emphasize the qualities of the traditional English syllabus. The study of English literature, it was maintained, required thoughtful consideration of issues such as the extent to which Lady Macbeth was the 'perfect wife' to Macbeth, how far pride was essential to a great man and whether Chaucer was tolerant of the Pardoner's frailties. Quality of learning in English at A level required a competent understanding of the text, awareness of the differing crafts and skills of various writers drawn from many periods of history, and an appreciation of the relationship between an author and the age in which he lived. Such learning, it was maintained, imposed considerable demands on a pupil's intellect and sharpened powers of critical analysis.

School Certificate examinations in English continued to test pupils' proficiency in essay-writing, comprehension, grammar and sentence analysis. The English language examination paper for July 1948 required pupils to write an essay of between 500 and 600 words on one of six topics – 'The schoolboy or schoolgirl in fiction', 'The best film I have ever seen' (where pupils were required to give an account of its plot, the actors and the photography, for example, and say why they had chosen it), 'A school speech day', 'Mirrors', 'People I dislike' and 'The attractions which Wales offers the tourist'. Pupils were also required to précis a study of the origins of the game of chess, demonstrate the meaning of prefixes derived from Latin and punctuate a letter of application for a secretarial post. None of these tasks would be out of place in years to come.

Traditional standards were still being emphasized by examiners of O level English during the 1950s and 1960s. Correctness and careful choice of words, together with competence in paragraphing and sentence construction were taken to be essential hallmarks of good essays. Teachers and pupils were regularly reminded that an essay had to have a form and should be characterised by careful punctuation, paragraphing and grammatical accuracy, while planning and organizing material were essential hallmarks. The need for competent précis writing, sentence analysis and vocabulary were also insisted upon. In writing a précis pupils were expected to grasp the essentials and write coherent, readable accounts in their own words of the salient points of the original passage.

Welsh

Examiners of Welsh at this time also highlighted the lack of attention to formal grammar. At A level, they noted a lack of knowledge of the basics of grammatical structures, reporting that many candidates had not understood what they had been taught. Poor spelling and unacceptable modes of expression, coupled with English idioms, were a matter of frequent comment. Candidates were reported to be uncertain as to what form a verb should take in the past tense and made errors in mutations. Problems were also experienced with composition. In 1963 T. Arwyn Watkins observed that many candidates had taken advantage of the essay question to present well-planned and closely argued essays which were well-written in correct, grammatical Welsh. Nevertheless, other candidates gave the appearance of having devoted little time to the question, the work betraying an ignorance of the basics of the language. In 1966 it was stated:

> It was felt that the conception and discussion were very frequently extremely elementary considering that the applicants were on average eighteen years old. Of course, there were exceptions; there were some good essays – but they were few; there were perhaps more than half a dozen of which it could be said that they were a pleasure to read. We also had the impression that many of the applicants wrote in a slapdash manner, as if the result of the examination was of no importance or interest to them ... As might be expected, this immaturity was reflected in the style and the language. Some scripts were full of orthographical and grammatical errors of all kinds, some of them simple spelling mistakes that would not be expected from a ten year old child ... We could not

but come to the conclusion that some children did not read any Welsh (apart possibly for one reading of their set books). Incorrect spelling in Welsh is becoming quite a problem. But what can be done? Rules and standards certainly cannot be relaxed, allowing all to spell as they wish. That undoubtedly would be the beginning of the end for literary Welsh. It must be reiterated that the only answer is plenty of reading and plenty of writing practice – bearing in mind that we have an excellent guide in the *Orthography Book (Llyfr yr Orgraff)*.[32]

Examiners noted that few candidates were able to show complete mastery of the language and that their vocabulary was often very limited. Teachers were urged to redouble their efforts to ensure that pupils read a wide range of modern Welsh literature as a means of preparing themselves for the examination.

The quality of the work on literary criticism was also of concern to the examiners. In 1951 they observed that many answers gave the impression of being based solely on memorized notes, with the result that they lacked spontaneity and originality. In 1952 the examiners commented:

> Despite last year's report, reviews and critical articles continue to provide the content of many scripts. The effort to think, to feel, and to imagine in precise response to the words of an author is alien to the habits of an increasing number of candidates. Their answers are loaded with abstractions, and pretentiousness is a common feature. The candidate who discovered that Christian Stoicism had not damaged the versification of an *englyn* exemplifies the kind of study that is being substituted for the discipline of literature.[33]

O level examiners in Welsh continued to reiterate traditional values, maintaining that pupils should be able to produce well-written, well-prepared essays, free from colloquialism, using correct and appropriate vocabulary. In the précis and translation exercises, examiners felt there was room for a considerable improvement in the standard of written Welsh. They pointed to weaknesses in sentence construction and an ignorance of grammar, reflected in mistakes in the use of mutations and grammatical forms.

In 1955 D. M. Ellis and J. I. Evans observed that very few candidates were able to write polished Welsh, even though the best candidates regularly produced excellent work. Examiners commented that too many candidates used colloquial Welsh instead of literary Welsh in their compositions. The consequences were illustrated by G. M. Ashton in 1964:

> And this brings us to a subject which I believe must soon be faced anew, which is what is correct Welsh? We took a very broad and generous view of the subject, and accepted oral forms, as long as they were expressed correctly on paper. We fear that the day is approaching when we will look at a phrase such as 'Mae arna' i eisiau' as an antiquarian curio; when we will rejoice in seeing 'Rwy'n eisiau'; and when we shall not be horrified when we come across 'Rwyf eisiau'. We are not so naïve that we do not recognize that forms such as these occur in the spoken language. We hold that they are adulterations, and we do not see any good reason why a healthy and robust phrase such as 'Mae arna' i eisiau' ('eisio', 'eisia', 'eisie') cannot be used. This construction is certainly not unknown to the children.[34]

The quality of work in the literature papers also varied. Although examiners regularly referred to the quality of some scripts which discussed topics with maturity and in correct and idiomatic Welsh, and indicated that the set texts had been read thoroughly and with pleasure, this was by no means true of all work submitted. For example, in 1953 the examiners noted that although some candidates were able to quote entire poems, many were unable to discuss their literary values to a satisfactory standard. One of the main weaknesses was the lack of thought and planning before candidates set pen to paper, and many candidates suffered because of poor style and expression.

French

The examiners who marked A level French during the 1950s were not impressed with much of what they saw. The first report on the new examination highlighted serious deficiencies in the standard of the work submitted. Many candidates were careless and failed to demonstrate evidence of original thought. They also failed to show the kind of interest expected of candidates at this level, and grammatical errors indicated a failure to appreciate the importance of the basics.

Examiners concluded that A level candidates lacked sufficient knowledge of French vocabulary and idiom, and teachers needed to devote considerable attention to extending these pupil skills. Unseen translations were considered to be unsatisfactory. Candidates were reminded of the need to pay due attention to every word in both original and translation, and to ensure that the translation conveyed the meaning, as well as the words, of the original. In composition, candidates at A level were criticized for failing to produce answers which addressed the particular requirements of the question, while few were able to provide the examiners with a fluent and correct essay which expressed ideas in a lively and personal way.

The quality of answers to the literature papers also caused concern. Pupils were said to be prone to regurgitate ill-understood passages based on textbooks and teachers' notes: their work did not provide evidence of personal analysis or criticism. In 1966 it was concluded that:

> In many schools the techniques of literary commentary, as applied to *prose* passages, are either not taught or are inadequately taught. The prime fault was paraphrasing – only too frequently the 'commentary' on subject-matter was a mere translation (and, in many cases, a mistranslation) of the passage. Candidates should be trained more thoroughly not to paraphrase but to discuss the effects and aims of the passage and to relate it, where relevant, to other parts of the work.[35]

During the early 1950s, there was a considerable increase in the number of candidates entered for examination in French and, to a lesser extent, in German, a reflection of the growing importance attached to modern languages in the school system after the Second World War. The introduction of the GCE examination in 1951 did not result in any marked changes in the expectations of the examiners. The new examination tested candidates' proficiency in grammar and translation and the emphasis remained on the written form of the language.

Examiners expressed concern about the quality of many translations, including the way in which some candidates expressed themselves in incorrect and ungrammatical English.

Many candidates were reported to have been careless in their reading of the texts and made serious blunders even when translating simple words and phrases. Pupils translating passages into French were said to have little regard for the need for grammatical accuracy and had little grasp of tenses and verb forms.

Latin

The introduction of GCE examinations coincided with a growing concern that the number of candidates being entered for examination in O level Latin was in decline. However, there was no compromise over approaches to the teaching and examination of the subject. Candidates were still expected to produce accurate work based on a thorough knowledge of Latin grammar. The importance of translation continued to be stressed and examiners like Prof M. W. Clarke warned that the emphasis on studying Latin literature should not detract from the need for candidates to be able to demonstrate their proficiency in translating both prepared and unprepared passages. The concern that many passages were being learned by rote was again expressed and it was noted that too often candidates submitted inaccurate translations from which words were omitted. Examiners complained that some candidates' knowledge of Latin vocabulary meant they had no option but to leave blank spaces as they had not understood the meaning of the passage sufficiently. In 1963 the examiner observed that:

> During my lifetime there has been a great change in the emphasis of Latin studies from grammar and syntax for their own sake to their use as instruments to enable the student to translate the works of Latin authors. The application of their knowledge to the unravelling of a Latin sentence that has not previously been explained in my opinion provides the best test of the ability of candidates.[36]

Examiners of Latin papers regularly complained about the quality of the work which they saw. They concluded that many answers were based on passages memorized from textbooks on Latin literature which often bore little relation to the demands of the question. Many candidates failed to make appropriate use of quotations and, in many instances, the Latin quoted was irrelevant. In 1967 it was contended:

> The essays were, as in previous years, an unsatisfactory exercise. Most candidates are so ill-equipped on many counts – principally either in material or in the technique of literary criticism – as to have little opportunity to demonstrate ability.[37]

Geography

The introduction of the new GCE examinations led to a revision of the geography syllabus, intended to achieve a better balance between physical and human elements. The O level syllabus demanded more attention be given to the study of landforms and the principles of physical geography. Questions based on photographs were introduced from 1954 as a means of highlighting the 'reality' of the geographical study of people and places, and these required considerable detailed knowledge. In addition, examiners regularly emphasized the need for pupils to show an understanding of geographical principles which could be applied to diverse regions in the study of world geography. Examiners were not impressed by much of what they read. Pupils were reported to be too ready to provide vague, uncertain, over-generalised, inaccurate and irrelevant answers which suggested that many of them relied on memory rather than on thought. Map work remained a cause for concern, knowledge of geographical definitions was said to be weak, and examiners complained that many candidates seemed to be ignorant of basic geographical terminology.

History

Examiners in history made pointed criticisms of much of the work which they encountered during the 1950s and 1960s. They insisted that what was required was quality rather than mere quantity of knowledge, arguing that candidates should strive to produce answers that were relevant to the questions set and demonstrated understanding of the historical situation to which questions referred. The way the subject was taught came in for criticism. Examiners concluded that some schools relied on a limited range of textbooks and did not provide pupils with access to pioneering works of historical research which revised long-held interpretations of history. Examiners insisted that pupils at A level should be introduced to stimulating works such as R. W. Southern's *The Making of the Middle Ages*, Max Beloff's *Age of Absolutism*, and to the works of Mattingley, Plumb, Namier, Mowat, Pelling and Mack Smith.

Stylistic weaknesses were highlighted by successive examiners. Spelling and grammar were reported to be poor in many instances, and the presentation and style of many candidates' papers left much room for improvement. In 1954 it was noted:

> Spelling was very careless. Words such as *aggressive*, *bankrupt*, *comparative*, *monasteries*, *paid*, *possession*, *Huguenots*, *Mazarin*, *Mediterranean*, *Philip*, *Richelieu*, and *Scheldt*, were frequently spelt wrongly. Punctuation varied from the non-existent to the erratic. Many candidates failed to arrange their work in an interesting, orderly fashion, and set down a mass of fact, half-fact, and fancy, with little regard to syntax and grammar.[38]

Followers of Calvin were habitually referred to as Calvins, and terms such as 'domestic politics', 'mercantilism' and 'democratic' were often misused.

It was clear that the history of Wales did not receive the attention it deserved and that topics continued to be discussed naïvely and insubstantially. Moreover, examiners regretted that many teachers tended to teach Welsh history as an entity apart from mainstream history and treated it in a detached and fragmentary manner. Examiners maintained that history needed to be viewed as an organic whole and should be taught in a way which enabled pupils to gain awareness of parallel movements in England and Wales.

During the early 1950s some improvements were noticed, especially in answers to questions on modern Wales, but work on medieval Wales continued to be unsatisfactory. According to A. H. Dodd, many teachers blamed the poor standard of

Welsh history on the lack of suitable textbooks. He maintained, however, that recent initiatives meant that this argument was no longer valid and that the increase in available reading material should have led to more satisfactory performance in examinations.

Scripture

Throughout the 1950s there was a general feeling that standards in scripture were improving and that it was beginning to be treated as a serious academic subject. In 1956 more than one hundred candidates sat the A level paper and the standards achieved were warmly applauded by the examiners. They commended work on the Old Testament, although continuing to emphasize the need to encompass contemporary scholarship in the teaching. Even so, by the mid-1960s, examiners were concerned that the improvement in quality detected in previous years was being reversed, not least because of the increased number of candidates who were attempting the examination. Persistent faults included irrelevance and a failure to evaluate information, coupled with confusion about details and a lack of a historical grounding.

The validity of scripture as a subject continued to be a matter of comment. In 1950 the Revd Bleddyn J. Roberts noted that the evidence of both the numbers of candidates and the quality of some of the scripts suggested the subject should be taken more seriously. He maintained that its status in schools was low and urged conscious effort to enhance its standing as a GCE subject. Examiners complained that too many candidates appeared to be content with reproducing the facts required to answer a particular question instead of attempting to delve more deeply into the meaning.[39] They also complained that in some schools doctrinal teaching appeared to have been given at the expense of studying the texts themselves and, although some candidates were able to make reference to critical works, their answers lacked a thorough grounding in theories and texts. By 1967 examiners observed that there had been an increase in the number of good quality papers and there was evidence of more intelligent interpretation, discussion and critical comment than in previous years. Throughout this period the number of candidates sitting the examination through the medium of Welsh increased and, overall, the quality of their work was commended by the examiners.

Mathematics

In mathematics, the introduction of the GCE examination did not lead to any significant changes in the syllabus. Examiners continued to apply the same rigorous standards in testing candidates in pure and applied mathematics at A level. In 1953 and 1954 examiners commended the general standard of the work, noting that a significant number of candidates had demonstrated the ability to grasp the principles of the subject. Nevertheless, it was also felt that performance in applied mathematics was frequently below the standard reached in pure mathematics, not least because of the problems derived from a lack of precision and poor presentation. The criticisms were even more frequent in judgements on performance in the more challenging separate papers in applied and pure mathematics. In 1957 candidates were criticized for failing to explain and establish formulae, with the result that they were unable to use them convincingly. In 1959 it was felt that some candidates were clearly out of their depth, and many of the good candidates spoiled their work through poor presentation. There were frequent instances where terms such as 'reaction', 'tension' and 'resilience' had been misused, and of confusion between significant figures and decimal places. Examiners noted the incidence of rote learning which led some candidates to include irrelevant material. Many spoiled their work by failing to include detailed numerical checks or explain essential steps. It was emphasized that good work at A level involved a grasp of fundamental principles and the ability to apply knowledge appropriately rather than to memorize formulae.

O level candidates continued to sit separate examination papers in arithmetic, algebra and geometry. In the judgement of the examiners, the work remained at an acceptable standard even though it was acknowledged that the examination proved very difficult for some. Examiners maintained the need for accuracy and for candidates to be able to apply what they had learned. There was some indication that their advice was being heeded. By 1957 examiners drew encouragement from the fact that there was less evidence of rote learning and that more candidates showed an understanding of the subject.

In arithmetic, examiners commended work which was accurate and clearly presented. They noted that many candidates were able to use logarithms appropriately and that more of them included 'rough work' in the books provided. They observed, however, that some candidates experienced difficulties in undertaking tasks in which they were required to select an appropriate method. There was a general inability to give answers correctly to three significant figures and many candidates had worked laboriously with decimals, often spoiling their work by errors of simple calculation. By the 1960s examiners observed that pupils' performance had improved considerably. For example, more candidates demonstrated a greater awareness of the correct methods to apply. However, inaccurate work continued to mar performance, and failure to show 'workings' caused difficulty for many.

Standards in algebra were also commended. Candidates were congratulated for presenting clear and neatly written scripts which displayed a clear understanding of algebraic methods. Nevertheless, examiners also drew attention to the problems arising from examinees not reading questions properly or where important work had been relegated to rough paper. Signs had been confused and many mistakes were made over the use of brackets.

Performance in geometry was more varied. Examiners felt that many candidates showed a lack of understanding of the fundamentals of geometric reasoning. In 1962 much of the work indicated that candidates possessed only superficial knowledge of the topic, with careless lettering and poor expression spoiling many scripts. Examiners complained that there was insufficient coordination of geometry with other branches of mathematics. Weaknesses identified included careless drawings, theorems devalued, the omission of data, and misuse of terms such as 'obtuse' and 'reflex'. Similarly, in trigonometry, examiners noted some confusion in the use of large and small letters, carelessness in the use of tables and errors in elementary arithmetic. In 1960 it was said that this was the weakest part of the curriculum and that candidates were prone to use tedious and inappropriate methods resulting in their work being often marred by inaccuracies.

Science subjects

In 1949 the Welsh Department of the Ministry of Education published its report on *The Future of Secondary Education in Wales*. This report, echoing sentiments expressed forcefully in the inter-war years, argued that in the basic curriculum, the study of the separate sciences should be abandoned in favour of a general science course – the content of which should be determined by the principle of interest. It also advocated increasing use of the environment in the teaching of science. Biology still struggled for parity of esteem in the post-war years but the 1940s and the 1950s saw this subject continuing to attract more candidates. By 1959 more pupils sat GCE O level biology than either chemistry or physics. At A level, however, biology remained the poor relation. The nature of the precise intellectual content of the subject continued to be contentious. Higher status as a rigorous laboratory-based experimental science in schools and universities came later in the 1960s and 1970s, influenced by developments in molecular biology and Nuffield Foundation projects.

The transition from the era of the School Certificate to that of the GCE had led to no immediate significant changes in science education. Nevertheless there was increasing questioning of some of the practices underpinning teaching and formal examinations. The emphasis on the acquisition of factual information and the lack of attention to experimental work were particularly highlighted. Syllabuses were criticized for being overloaded with factual content. Examination practices came under fire for demanding the regurgitation of this memorized factual information and providing insufficient emphasis on scientific method.

xamination structures remained relatively unchanged, despite a decade of curriculum development in the 1960s. National projects funded by the Nuffield Foundation and the Schools Council led to major rethinking of science courses and teaching methods. Nuffield projects in chemistry (1966), physics (1966) and biology (1967) echoed ideas voiced decades previously by Armstrong[40] in emphasizing the promotion of understanding and the acquisition of skills by replicating the work of the scientist in the school laboratory. However, the impact of these projects on the schools of Wales and on the examination system was limited in the period covered by this chapter.

Physics

In 1951, the first year of the new GCE O and A level examinations, physics attracted 2,113 candidates at O level and 770 at A level. This compared with 2,525 candidates for O level chemistry, 2,772 for O level biology, 835 for A level chemistry and 202 for A level biology, though the biology figures are complicated in that zoology, not available at O level, attracted 258 at A level.[41]

At O level, pass rates within the sciences, indeed in all those subjects which attracted substantial entries, were uncannily uniform, but reflected a remarkably high wastage rate. The combined success rates for boys and girls in all the major subjects hovered around 60 per cent (58.9 per cent in physics, 59 per cent in chemistry, 54.7 per cent in biology, 59.6 per cent in geography, for example).[42] What is particularly interesting is that physics was a heavily gendered subject, attracting 1,755 entries from boys, 358 from girls. However, the percentage pass rate among boys was 58, while for girls it was 63.4 (this was a trend not apparent in mathematics, chemistry or biology).

The clustering of success rates at around 60 per cent almost certainly indicates that marking policies, despite this being a new kind of examination, were based on success rates over previous years, a feature of examination marking throughout much of its history. These rates doomed 40 per cent of entrants to failure and, if repeated across the subjects, they would be barred from entering the sixth form. Here, then, after the 11 plus examination, was the major hurdle for pupils, another segregating device which eventually channelled only about 3 per cent of the age range to university by the end of this period.

At A level, physics attracted 688 boys but only 82 girls. The reversal in success rates was now dramatic. The pass rate for boys was 62.8 per cent, for girls only 39 per cent. The disparity in success rates is inexplicable and not reflected in any associated subjects. Pure mathematics, for example, produced a success rate of 69.6 per cent among boys, 78.8 per cent among girls; chemistry 65.14 per cent for boys, 57.3 per cent for girls.[43]

The expansion in numbers in Welsh grammar schools in the 1950s is evident in the rate of growth of entries for examinations. By 1960, 3,612 boys were entered for O level physics but the gender imbalance remained, with only 1,006 girl candidates. The success rate among girls was still marginally better.[44] The dramatic increase in the numbers of pupils proceeding to A level courses is also evident by 1960. In that year, physics attracted 1,547 entries, with a success rate of 66.8 per cent. However, there was little change in the gender imbalance. 1,324 of these entries were from boys, only 223 from girls.[45]

In 1965 the CSE examination was available for the first time, tailored specifically to the needs of secondary modern schools. It attracted 478 candidates in physics among boys, 23 from girls. The gender imbalance was thus even more in evidence.

Throughout the 1950s and 1960s physics reflected the tendency evident in other subjects to emphasize knowledge and understanding of the facts and principles central to the discipline. However, much of the content had remained the same for decades and, particularly in the 1960s, there was a growing demand among educationalists that more attention should be paid to scientific method, developed through practical work. The Nuffield Foundation science projects of the 1960s particularly brought this debate to the fore.

Although the School and Higher Certificates were replaced in 1951, the kinds of criticisms levelled at candidates sitting the new examinations were uncannily similar to those of previous decades. They were accused of inaccurate measurements, elaborate and unnecessary descriptions and weak diagrams. Above all, the criticism of rote learning and consequent irrelevance recurs like some mantra. In 1956, for example, the examiners included this diatribe in their report:

> In definitions and in descriptions of experimental procedure it was clear that many candidates had learned the subject matter by heart rather than sought to understand it . . . it is often all too clear to the examiner that the candidate has neither seen nor performed the experiment he seeks to describe. Candidates should, as a minimum, offer a reasonably sized labelled diagram, a short statement of experimental procedure, a table of results, a graph where this is applicable, and brief deductions to be drawn from the results . . . it is perhaps in making deductions from experimental results that candidates are least successful, but this is not, at the Ordinary level, very surprising.[46]

In 1957 the examiner noted that 'sometimes it was evident that the candidate was really reciting a piece of algebra which had been memorised without any understanding of the physical principles involved'.[47]

In 1951, the replacement of the School Certificate by the O level was paralleled by the demise of the Higher Certificate in favour of the A level, although in physics the format of the Higher/A level examination papers remained the same. The examiner's report for 1951 contains the intriguing comment that:

> The A1 and A2 papers of the present system are somewhat less difficult than the H1 and H2 papers of the former Higher Certificate examination. It had been accordingly anticipated that the work done by this year's candidates would appear better than that of last year's group; but the reverse has unfortunately proved to be the case. Not only is the general level of this year's work distinctly below that of last year, but the number of outstandingly good candidates is less, and the continuing deterioration in standard which has been noted in recent years is disquieting.[48]

The following year the examiner stated that 'the standard continues to be considerably below that of six or eight years ago'.[49]

In 1954, examiners bemoaned the fact that, despite a substantial rise in the number of entries, there had been no increase in the number of good candidates. The examiners themselves adduced the obvious reason for this two years later when, in 1956, they reported that 'it is perhaps significant that the increased entry at A level has been accompanied by an increase in the proportion of very weak candidates'.[50]

In 1958 examiners noted again that 'there was a noticeable increase in the number of very weak candidates. It is difficult to believe that some of these entrants could ever have shown sufficient promise to justify their presentation for examination at this level.'[51] The following year again 'there was a large number of candidates who could not be considered as proper candidates at this stage'.[52] It is difficult to avoid the conclusion that, with examiners tending to serve regularly over many years in most subjects, a preordained standard, carried over from the very small numbers of candidates presented before the war and immediately afterwards, would never have allowed the expanding numbers of the 1950s to be comparable to that earlier elite. It is this kind of mindset that makes comparison over the decades so complicated.

We must also remember that the examiners across the subjects seemed to deem their function to be pointing up weaknesses rather than strengths. Obviously, despite its constant refrain, it was this kind of critical feedback which teachers expected and would wish to have acted upon. The negativity of all those reports we have commented on needs to reflect this perspective. Examiners could also be sympathetic, however, as they were in drawing attention in 1951 to the difficult conditions for practical work in which many physics teachers were 'severely handicapped by overcrowding'. This resulted in it being the 'common practice of using the . . . form classroom'.[53] The examiners commended teachers for what they managed to achieve in such conditions. Nevertheless, examiners had mastered the art of the somewhat patronizing put-down. In 1952 the physics practical examination merited the following observation:

> The prevailing impression is one of competent mediocrity. Most candidates were able to carry out the practical exercises allotted to them, but it was not usual to find an experiment carried out with

the good technique and meticulous attention to detail which betokens good experimental discipline.[54]

This judgement could surely only have been marginally tempered for teachers by the associated remark that 'the condition of the apparatus used for the examination in some schools was poor'.[55] It is perhaps surprising that the examiners did not strike a more sympathetic note in this regard, given the major difficulties of obtaining scientific apparatus in the immediate post-war period. It is significant that, by 1953, the examiners noted an improvement in the supply of laboratory equipment.

Chemistry

Standards in chemistry were often commended. In 1951 the examiner was pleased to find that so many candidates produced direct and clear answers, and that many candidates demonstrated an obvious familiarity with industrial processes. There was evidence of good coordination of theory and practical experience, and appropriate knowledge was shown of both organic and inorganic chemistry. However, even at this stage, candidates displayed an alarming lack of knowledge of aspects of chemistry:

> A high proportion of candidates displayed ignorance of the formulae of common compounds and of equations for well-known simple reactions. This state of affairs can only be ascribed to an indifferent attitude to such matters. The writing of balanced chemical equations and formulae not only forms an integral part of the subject but also carries a fair proportion of marks at examinations and may well decide the success or failure of a candidate. While a reasonably good knowledge of industrial processes was displayed, the reverse was true of reactions which should have been familiar from laboratory practice. There was an evident lack of co-ordination of knowledge gained from laboratory and theory courses.[56]

Chemistry examiners continued to emphasize the need for pupils to gain practical experience of experimental work and to show the ability to apply factual knowledge. They required candidates to be able to draw accurate and well-proportioned diagrams and to ensure that all information was relevant.

Questions which involved simple laboratory practice and routine processes were frequently badly answered. There was an increased tendency to use formulae and symbols instead of the names of elements and compounds, and examiners noted disturbing spelling mistakes in the use of chemical terms and names. Moreover, there were shortcomings in pupils' knowledge and understanding of the quantitative aspects of chemical facts and definitions.

Botany

Following normal practice, the examiner at O level was a university teacher. In 1961, for example, this was Dr John Wilkinson, senior lecturer in botany at the University of Exeter. In that year, the tone of his report was more upbeat than in many subjects:

> Most candidates showed considerable knowledge and reached a good standard in this paper. Some improvement was evident over last year in the quality of illustration, though a minority of candidates are still not convinced that simple annotated drawings are usually more effective than wordy descriptions as answers to questions which do not involve the elucidation of processes.[57]

Why should this be? One possible answer is that botany was exceptional in that most O level candidates took the examination when in the sixth form. The examiner certainly ascribed the overall commendable standard to this fact, and it was a trend which continued. In 1970, for example, the same examiner commented that the standard was higher because of the 'relatively greater proportion of entries from the "lower VIth"'.[58] Yet not all was sweetness and light. In 1965, for example, Dr Wilkinson commented that 'a few of this year's scripts were a pleasure to read. Nevertheless it must be said that a number of answers ... continued to be verbose, vague and loaded with much irrelevant information.'[59]

During this period the A level examinations continued to consist of two papers and a practical examination. In 1961, 393 candidates sat the two A level papers, 54 of these the Scholarship paper.[60] The number of candidates at A level tended to fall off somewhat by the end of this period. For example, by 1969, 338 pupils sat the A level examination, of whom 42 sat the Scholarship paper.[61] Again, examiners accorded with the profile across the subjects. The reporting examiner was Dr Ivor Isaac, at that time senior lecturer in botany at the University College of Swansea, later to be Professor and Vice-principal. His report was characteristic also:

> Very many of the criticisms made in previous years must be repeated. Candidates should realize that they must answer the question asked, and they must be selective with the data at their disposal. It is obvious that most of the examinees have worked hard at accumulating factual knowledge, but they must use it intelligently and show that they understand general principles. It should be emphasized again that diagrams should be drawn to illustrate answers and to *reduce* the amount of written text.[62]

There were regular variations on this theme. In 1963, for example, we are informed by the same examiner that 'answers are still much too verbose – all five questions could have been fully answered in about twenty pages and yet it was not uncommon to find candidates presenting forty or more pages, much of which was quite irrelevant to the question'.[63]

Changes of examiner in 1964 and 1965 made no difference to the nature of the criticisms. The length of answers and the verbosity of candidates once more merited comment: 'it might be well to point out at the outset that the value of an answer is not judged on its length; legibility, neatness, conciseness, and the provision of adequate illustrations, as indicated on the question papers, are also taken into account'.[64]

The examiner's most stringent criticisms were levelled at the practical examination. 'Again one has to report that the practical work as shown in the examination was not good enough. It must be stressed that critical observations, drawing, and interpretation are looked for.'[65] The following year he reiterated this criticism, although he tempered it with the observation that 'the practical note-books and files of candidates from the vast majority of schools were of really first-class quality'.[66] The assumption must be that perennial accusations of spoon-feeding and rote learning underlay this situation. When it came to the unaided situation of the examination, pupils were found lacking in critical observation.

Biology

As with other subjects, the advent of the GCE in 1951 did not substantially change the general structure and format of examination papers either at O level or A level. Again in common with other subjects, examiners tended, particularly at A level, to be senior university teachers. For example, in the early 1960s the examiner for A level biology was Dr Emrys Watkin, senior lecturer in Zoology at the University of Wales, Aberystwyth. He was replaced in 1964 by Dr W. A. L. Evans, senior lecturer in Zoology at the University College of Cardiff. The examiner at O level, however, F. F. Glasspool, came from a teacher-training background as lecturer in Redland College, Bristol. School teachers did occasionally become involved in the examining process. Mrs C. B. Wright, who was head of the botany department in a public school in Derby, examined the human biology paper and D. A. Parry, head of the Biology department in a Kent grammar school, took over as chief examiner of biology O level in 1962. The first appearance in the ranks of biology examiners drawn from teachers in Wales came in 1967 when Mrs May Thomas of Cwrt Sart Secondary School in Neath examined the CSE paper.

The involvement of the University of Wales went far deeper than merely providing virtually all examiners at A level and many at O level across the subjects. For example, in 1963 Dr Watkin noted in his report that:

> a total of 302 candidates from 76 schools completed the examination which followed the usual course of previous years. This total represents a 10 per cent increase over 1962 and is a continuation of a trend which may continue into the future at an accelerated rate if the schools accept the recommendations of the University, to concentrate their teaching at the Advanced Level on Biology rather than on separate Botany and Zoology as a preparation for entry into the university.[67]

It is obvious from subsequent reports that this university advice was increasingly followed.

It is also evident from reports of the examiners that biology examinations were perennially affected by the same kinds of faults as applied across the subject range. At O level in 1960, for example, the examiner reported that:

> A comparison of this year's examination with those of previous years shows that the standard of general presentation has been maintained although there are still faults to which attention has been drawn in the past. The chief of these is the apparent inability to read the questions carefully and to answer them without the inclusion of irrelevant matter. Candidates should realise that in addition to being well informed, they are expected to be able to think clearly and to marshal facts in logical sequence. There was evidence of a great deal of factual knowledge of parts of the syllabus but the biological experience of many candidates was inadequate. This lack of experience showed in questions demanding personal acquaintance with organisms.[68]

In 1962 a new examiner was able to judge that 'standards in general have not changed from previous years but even among the better candidates there is a lack of precise, clear expression. Candidates would do well to read the question carefully and not jump at a single 'clue word' as a result of which they do not answer the question as set.'[69]

Another feature of the examiners' reports at O level was the repetition of the comment, virtually word-for-word, that 'candidates are still being entered who stand little chance of success'.[70] It was in this respect, perhaps, that the credibility gap between examiners and teachers was most pronounced, with little understanding of the pressures under which teachers operated.

At A level the examiner noticed a decline both in the number of entrants and the number of schools entering pupils in the early 1960s, and the substantial reversal in this trend by 1970. The tone of his 1960 report may be gleaned from his comments on a question which was answered by a very high proportion of the candidates, that on respiration and transpiration:

> Many of the answers would have been good at the Ordinary level but something more is expected of Advanced candidates. Many

assumed that only a mammal was implied in the question, others an animal with blood, thus candidates were too much concerned with the mechanism of respiration rather than the general principle ... many assumed that a mammal transpired and so confused sweating with transpiration. Much of the experimental work given was unworthy of Advanced candidates in attention to details, few used manumetric methods. A few candidates even placed live rats in air-tight chambers and allowed them to die.[71]

Another problem which always featured in the sparring match between teachers and examiners was evident in the A level practical examination. In 1960, for example, the examiner noted that:

> ... adverse comment was made at some schools on the setting of a transverse section of a testis or an ovary as a spot in Q. 4 in that these sections are not specifically asked for in the practical section of the syllabus. This is true. A knowledge of the structure of these organs is required in the theory section of the syllabus and all candidates should have been able to deal with these sections in general outline without of necessity dealing with them as detailed histological preparations.[72]

The credibility gap remained.

By the end of this period, despite the sea-change which was slowly taking place in the organization of secondary education, the curricular experiments so evident in primary education in the 1960s and the curriculum projects being financed by the Nuffield Foundation and by the Schools Council, little had changed in the structure or organization of the O and A level examinations. Chief examiners at A level were still drawn from the ranks of university teachers, although a grammar school teacher was now chief examiner at O level. University advice as to which subjects to take to facilitate entry to university had been heeded, so that by 1970, 634 candidates sat A level biology, an increase which cannot be accounted for by expanding sixth form numbers alone. The A level examination still consisted of two papers, each with ten questions from which to choose. The O level paper remained a single paper, with a choice of twenty-two questions. The reporting examiner at O level commented in 1970 that 'criticisms arising from this year's examination have all been made in previous years. Poor spelling and little understanding of the meaning of technical terms were again in evidence'.[73] The A level report was depressingly repetitive, referring to misuse of information, misinterpretation of questions, careless reading of questions, verbosity and aimlessness. It is difficult to see what purpose was served by the repetition of such comments. They obviously had no remedial effect, otherwise presumably the examiners would have noticed. There is never a hint that the questions themselves were in any way to blame. The advent of an additional examination, CSE, had no obvious impact. Teachers may have been hardened against such perennial criticisms, but it seems likely that both examiners and teachers changed little in their mindset in the period up to 1970, with both examinations and teaching methods firmly rooted in the past.

Conclusion

The outstanding feature of examiners' reports during this and earlier periods is the reiteration of similar criticisms from year to year, very similar across all subjects. Essentially, they centre on the tendency among pupils to write answers which were irrelevant and repetitious, their ability to describe but not to analyse, and their habit of regurgitating notes without understanding. Most significant is the regular criticism that many candidates were entered for the examination who, in the opinion of the examiners, stood no chance of success. In most subjects statistics bear this out in that about 60 per cent of candidates were normally successful. We have to remember that, in the period covered in this chapter, most Welsh secondary schools presenting candidates for the A and O level examinations were still grammar schools. The intake to these schools, although more generous than in England, was already severely selective, particularly in the urban areas. The original expectation of the Welsh intermediate schools when they were founded was that they would admit candidates who were capable of successfully completing a four-year course which would result in entry for the School Certificate, equivalent to a group of subjects in the later O level. It is obvious that, by the 1950s and the 1960s, the weeding-out process within these schools came to be dominated, even for the elite who had been successful in the 11 plus examination, by an inability to complete successfully the O level examination.

This situation was itself now being transformed by the gradual change from a Wales of grammar schools to one in which comprehensive schools became the norm. The proportion of secondary school pupils in comprehensive schools increased from some 10 per cent in 1958 to 28.4 per cent in 1965. By 1969, nearly half of all Welsh secondary pupils attended 118 comprehensive schools. To the examiners, standards were being maintained by means of traditional syllabuses and examination formats, together with a pass rate which remained remarkably similar from year to year. Neither the reorganization of secondary education nor the curriculum debates of the 1960s had influenced the process of Welsh secondary education by 1970. In far too many instances rote learning and dictation of notes remained staple methods of instruction and were reflected in the kinds of criticisms made by examiners in their reports.

As we shall see in the next chapter, a relatively staid system of secondary education in Wales was experiencing a major upheaval. The reorganization of secondary education, together with curriculum reform and debate, themselves linked to economic crisis and youth unemployment, fed into a politics of education which became increasingly frenetic in its pace and was to change the educational landscape to an extent that would have been unrecognizable to those who had examined the pupils of Wales in earlier days.

References

[1] *Report of the Consultative Committee on Secondary Education with Special Reference to Grammar Schools* (Spens Report) (London, HMSO, 1938).
[2] Public Record Office (PRO), ED12/812.
[3] PRO, ED12/812.
[4] PRO, ED136/812.
[5] PRO, ED136/472.

6 PRO, ED136/472.
7 *Minutes of the WJEC*, 10 March 1950; *Minutes of the Special Services Sub-Committee*, 19 January 1951.
8 *Minutes of the Local Authorities Sub-Committee*, 26 April 1950.
9 *Minutes of the WJEC*, 8 December 1950; *Minutes of the Administration Sub-Committee*, 19 May 1950. *Minutes of the WJEC*, 12 March 1954; *Minutes of the Welsh Language Sub-Committee*, 9 July 1954, 13 November 1956.
10 PRO, ED136/882.
11 (Dame) Olive Wheeler was Professor of Education at the University College of South Wales and Monmouthshire, Cardiff.
12 PRO, ED136/882.
13 Eminent playwright and Welsh nationalist; his was the most intriguing appointment to the CACE(W), given his pre-war incarceration.
14 PRO, ED136/880.
15 PRO, ED136/879.
16 PRO, ED136/880.
17 PRO, ED136/751.
18 PRO, ED136/751.
19 PRO, ED136/751.
20 PRO, ED136/751.
21 PRO, ED136/751.
22 PRO, ED136/749.
23 Chief scientist for the National Coal Board.
24 PRO, ED136/751; PRO, ED136/880.
25 PRO, ED12/479.
26 *Minutes of the WJEC*, 24 April 1949.
27 *Secondary School Examinations other than GCE* (London, HMSO, 1960).
28 *Minutes of the WJEC*, 1 March 1949, 25 April 1949.
29 *Minutes of the WJEC*, 1 September 1949, 9 February 1950. A further compromise was reached over the continued use of scholarship papers, although the WJEC insisted that decisions on awards should not be based on a candidate's performance in one subject.
30 WJEC, *General Report on the Examinations for the General Certificate of Education*, 1963, p. 3.
31 WJEC, *General Report on the Examinations*, 1956, p. 3.
32 WJEC, *General Report on the Examinations*, 1966, p. 29.
33 WJEC, *General Report on the Examinations*, 1952, p. 19.
34 WJEC, *General Report on the Examinations*, 1964, p. 34, 1968, p. 43.
35 WJEC, *General Report on the Examinations*, 1966, p. 71.
36 WJEC, *General Report on the Examinations*, 1963, p. 52.
37 WJEC, *General Report on the Examinations*, 1967, p. 63.
38 WJEC, *General Report on the Examinations*, 1954, p. 64; the examiner was (Sir) Glanmor Williams, who, in 1957, became Professor of History at the University College of Swansea.
39 WJEC, *General Report on the Examinations*, 1956, p. 76.

40 See Chapter 1, p. 25.
41 WJEC, *General Report on the Examinations*, 1951, p. 3.
42 WJEC, *General Report on the Examinations*, 1951, p. 5.
43 WJEC, *General Report on the Examinations*, 1951, p. 6.
44 WJEC, *General Report on the Examinations*, 1960, p. 6.
45 WJEC, *General Report on the Examinations*, 1960, pp. 3-5.
46 WJEC, *General Report on the Examinations*, 1956.
47 WJEC, *General Report on the Examinations*, 1957.
48 WJEC, *General Report on the Examinations*, 1951.
49 WJEC, *General Report on the Examinations*, 1952.
50 WJEC, *General Report on the Examinations*, 1954.
51 WJEC, *General Report on the Examinations*, 1958.
52 WJEC, *General Report on the Examinations*, 1959.
53 WJEC, *General Report on the Examinations*, 1951.
54 WJEC, *General Report on the Examinations*, 1952.
55 WJEC, *General Report on the Examinations*, 1952.
56 WJEC, *General Report on the Examinations*, 1951.
57 WJEC, *General Report on the Examinations*, 1961, p. 185.
58 WJEC, *General Report on the Examinations*, 1970, p. 274.
59 WJEC, *General Report on the Examinations*, 1965, p. 245.
60 WJEC, *General Report on the Examinations*, 1961, p. 181.
61 WJEC, *General Report on the Examinations*, 1969, p. 264.
62 WJEC, *General Report on the Examinations*, 1961, p. 181.
63 WJEC, *General Report on the Examinations*, 1963, p. 195.
64 WJEC, *General Report on the Examinations*, 1964, p. 228.
65 WJEC, *General Report on the Examinations*, 1961, p. 183.
66 WJEC, *General Report on the Examinations*, 1962, p. 195.
67 WJEC, *General Report on the Examinations*, 1963, p. 201.
68 WJEC, *General Report on the Examinations*, 1960, p. 200.
69 WJEC, *General Report on the Examinations*, 1962, p. 200.
70 WJEC, *General Report on the Examinations*, 1966, p. 242.
71 WJEC, *General Report on the Examinations*, 1960, p. 194.
72 WJEC, *General Report on the Examinations*, 1961, p. 180.
73 WJEC, *General Report on the Examinations*, 1970, p. 280.

Chapter 4
Comprehensive Examinations? 1970–1988

Introduction

> Any new organisation must give the majority of children more opportunities than did the old. I believe that the old social and intellectual stratification of the school system is no longer acceptable to democratic opinion in the 1960s. We must therefore set ourselves a new objective, which is not to deprive the minority of their present educational standard, but to give all our children a more ample opportunity.

Those words, spoken by Anthony Crosland in a speech to representatives of the world of education in January 1966, characterized the hopes and expectations evident during the mid-1960s that the education system of England and Wales was about to be revolutionized for the better. Crosland's period as Secretary of State for Education and Science paved the way for momentous changes in secondary education in both countries. The tripartite system of grammar, technical and secondary modern schools which had developed after 1944 was gradually being replaced by a system of comprehensive schools to which all pupils aged between 11 and 18 were admitted, on the basis of where they lived rather than as a result of a test of intelligence or aptitude.

The ideals which inspired Crosland and other promoters of the comprehensive model were clear. The tripartite system had never been universally accepted. R. A. Butler had promised that each type of school would enjoy parity of esteem.[1] The reality proved rather different. The grammar school continued to be regarded as the institution which promoted excellence, where pupils would be given the best opportunity to pursue an academic curriculum and enjoy the benefits of a privileged education. The organization of those schools was based on a system of rigid streaming and a culture which emphasized success and failure. The secondary modern schools, on the other hand, never achieved an acknowledged status. Their staff included some excellent teachers who were attracted by the opportunity to innovate and develop a new syllabus free from the pressure of examinations. Yet from the beginning their work was hampered by the simple fact that pupils who entered secondary modern schools had failed a test. There was often little focus or incentive within the schools, and staff took the opportunity to enable promising pupils to move to grammar schools.

Furthermore, the tripartite system of secondary education was increasingly regarded as anomalous in a society which emphasized equality of opportunity and the need to expand educational opportunity. Practical issues, such as the unreliability of the evidence provided by a test taken at the age of eleven, were highlighted. The considerable local discretion that the system allowed meant that pupils who had failed the test could still gain admittance to a grammar school at the request of the Director of Education, and there were marked differences in the number of grammar school places available in each area. In Wales, a very high proportion of children in rural areas gained a grammar school place because the demographic trends in their areas had enabled the building of a large number of schools under the Welsh Intermediate and Technical Education Act of 1889. In Merioneth all children of secondary school age attended grammar schools in 1965, yet fewer than half did so in the County Borough of Swansea in the same year. At the same time, shortages of places in some areas meant that children who would have gained a grammar school place in a neighbouring area were denied entry, thereby compounding the sense of inequality and unfairness.[2]

The concept of the comprehensive school was not new in Wales. Pioneering work had been done in Anglesey in the 1950s and other local education authorities (LEAs) had experimented with the idea of multilateral schools. In most parts of Wales, however, education authorities had concentrated on the development of secondary modern schools alongside the existing grammar schools, and very few technical schools had been opened. Thus it was not until the publication of the Department of Education and Science (DES) Circular 10/65 that most LEAs addressed the issue of comprehensive education. The Circular gave them the task of producing schemes to reorganize the entire secondary school system within a relatively short period of time.[3] It was emphasized that a single school receiving pupils from a fixed catchment area could develop a close relationship with the community it served, and it was expected that those who lived in the locality would take pride in the achievements of the school. Of equal importance was the fact the new system would enable LEAs to plan and allocate resources more effectively. Each school catchment area could be analysed to identify particular economic, social and demographic trends, and additional resources targeted to areas which suffered from particular disadvantages.

Despite the conviction with which those committed to reform promoted the ideal of the comprehensive school, the proposals did not gain universal approval. Three issues dominated the debate. First, a large number of parents, governors, LEA members and teachers remained to be convinced that change was desirable. Fears were expressed regarding the size of the proposed new schools. It was claimed that they would not allow pupils to specialize in areas of the curriculum for which they had an aptitude, and many people, while acknowledging the weaknesses of the tripartite system, were reluctant to close grammar schools which had been successful and esteemed for their academic excellence.

Secondly, LEAs were obliged to consider how the existing secondary schools could be arranged in order to provide one school for each area, a task which proved to be immensely difficult. A large proportion of secondary modern schools were housed in unsuitable buildings erected at the end of the nineteenth century, and many were designed to accommodate either boys or girls. A glance at the way in which secondary education was arranged in the County Borough of Swansea gives an indication of the size of the problem. In 1965 Swansea had four grammar schools, two for boys and two for girls, with a total of 3,200 pupils. All four schools were in the centre or the western portion of the borough. Three comprehensive schools, accommodating 2,730 pupils, had been built to the east of the town and there was a small technical school for girls. The remainder of the school accommodation was provided in fifteen secondary modern schools which accommodated a total of 3,900 pupils. Only two had places for more than 400 pupils and four had fewer than 200 places.

This pattern was mirrored throughout the urban parts of Wales and a major programme to build new schools was required in order to implement the new policy.[4] Given the pressure to introduce the comprehensive school model, however, LEAs had little alternative but to adopt temporary arrangements.[5] Schools were set up over two or even three different sites, sometimes miles apart. Timetabling became an immensely difficult and complicated task as teachers and some pupils were required to move between sites and, to add to the difficulties, the sixteen LEAs which managed education in Wales were reorganized into eight authorities based on the new counties in April 1974.[6] The result of these changes was that, from the outset, the new comprehensive schools were handicapped by problems caused by inadequate premises, overcrowding and inappropriate facilities. Despite the best efforts of teachers and the cooperation of pupils, some disruption of education was inevitable and, to some extent, affected performance in examinations.[7]

The third area of change addressed in this period was that of the curriculum and the teaching approaches associated with it. Whereas the objectives of the grammar schools were clear and well-defined, the comprehensive schools had more varied goals and it was recognized by the DES that parents and other commentators would need to be convinced of the merits of the new system:

> Parental expectations may reveal a heavy emphasis upon high academic aspiration and achievement, especially as reflected in external examination success; the school may often have to work hard to convince parents (and in some cases teachers) of the need for a wider interpretation of its role.[8]

Comprehensive schools, which were generally larger than those which had previously existed in Wales, had to provide both academic and non-academic subjects and, from the outset, the DES emphasized that all pupils were to have the opportunity to develop both practical and intellectual capacities by pursuing a broad range of subjects.[9] These laudable aims proved difficult to implement. In most schools the practice was adopted whereby pupils pursued a common curriculum between the ages of eleven and thirteen, even though in some subjects they were divided into streamed classes, according to ability, after the first year of secondary education. At the age of fourteen most pupils chose between academic and non-academic subjects and, while some specialized in science, others focused mainly on the arts. Mixed-ability classes became the exception rather than the rule in the fourth and fifth years and teaching methods changed little.[10] The practice of one teacher being in control of classroom activities continued. Many teachers were totally opposed to any notion that pupils might be allowed to work without supervision and they preferred them to sit in rows, facing the front, rather than the more informal arrangements fashionable among progressive educationists at the time.[11] The conservatism of Welsh teachers proved reassuring to many parents and commentators during this period of transition. Wales did not witness the vociferous debate about pedagogical methods which occurred in England during the 1970s and Welsh teachers were not subjected to the kind of accusations levied against their counterparts in areas like London after the publication of the *Black Papers*.[12] More surprisingly, the curriculum in Wales continued to mirror that of England, even though prominent educationists had been promoting the idea of a distinctive approach throughout the twentieth century.

English

By the mid-1960s the notion that English should focus primarily on linguistic conventions, spelling, grammar and punctuation had been challenged by a large body of opinion which included teachers, academics and other professionals who emphasized the value of self-expression and who sought to reduce the amount of teaching time devoted to formal grammar. Those who took this view were concerned that less able pupils derived little benefit from their studies, and challenged the notion that the study of language should be separate from English literature.[13] It was argued that many of the essay and comprehension questions set in English language examinations were unimaginative, offering few opportunities for pupils to flourish, and that too many obscure questions were set in English literature which gave little encouragement to personal involvement with the subject.[14] The methods adopted to test the General Certificate of Education (GCE) courses appeared increasingly arcane when compared with the new Certificate for Secondary Education (CSE) examination which assessed oral and aural as well as written skills, and included contemporary works alongside traditional texts. Examining boards were urged to reconsider their GCE schedules; many abandoned specific questions on grammar and analysis, although it remained the case that those attempting the examination had to demonstrate their proficiency in the correct use of words, sentence structure and punctuation.

On the whole, the reforms were welcomed but the new structure was targeted by the authors of the *Black Papers*, who cited parental objections and the concerns expressed by employers as evidence that the standard of spoken and written English was in decline. In response to this heated debate the government appointed a committee chaired by the respected historian Prof Alan Bullock to undertake a detailed examination of English in the education system. The committee's report refuted many of the allegations levied against the way in which English was taught and found no evidence that teachers generally were neglecting basic skills.[15] The report emphasized that society had to be realistic in its expectations of school-leavers and rejected the arguments of those who wanted to return to the narrow exercises and tests which had characterized so much of English teaching in the twentieth century.

These views mirrored those of the school Inspectorate. A working paper published in 1977 maintained that a sixteen-year-old:

should be able to write in narrative, descriptive and explanatory forms, to respond personally to an aesthetic experience and to present a point of view or a line of thought on a topic about which he feels he has something of his own to say.[16]

The balance between self-expression and competence in standard English recommended by the Bullock Report was clearly reflected in the Welsh Joint Education Committee's (WJEC) schedules. Candidates at A level were expected to be able to criticize and interpret material and to treat a theme in an orderly way, while at the same time expressing their ideas effectively in writing. Candidates sat two examinations. Paper A1 analysed proficiency in the works of authors such as Chaucer, Shakespeare, Milton, Keats and Wordsworth, where detailed knowledge of the texts was expected. Paper A2 focused on prescribed works of poetry, drama, descriptive prose and novels. Candidates were expected to be informed about the background to the texts and be familiar with the ideas of critical commentators.[17] The examiners found that the work of a small number of those examined revealed a sensitive involvement with the subject and the texts. Yet a large number of answers could only be described as adequate. It was evident from the examination scripts that notes provided by teachers had been used as the basis for answers, with little understanding or any real interest in ideas. Specific areas of the syllabus, notably the work on Chaucer and Browning, and context questions, were highlighted as causes of concern, prompting the examiners to assert in 1977 that:

> we feel strongly that candidates should not be encouraged to venture on to the wilder shores of literary speculation without a proper preliminary engagement with the richness and difficulties of the text itself.[18]

At O level, the number of papers submitted continued to rise as the new comprehensive schools took a conscious decision to enter as many pupils as possible for the examination because of the importance attached by employers to an O level qualification in English. The essence of the format adopted by the WJEC since the introduction of GCE examinations was retained. Candidates spent three hours answering four questions. The first involved writing an essay of between 500 and 600 words. The second tested comprehension of a piece of written material which included an optional question on grammar, vocabulary and punctuation. Thirdly, a piece of written material was to be summarized; and a fourth question asked candidates to compose a letter, speech or other type of communication. In view of the large numbers entered it was inevitable that the overall performance varied: the pass rate continued to increase but nearly a third of all those entered in any year failed to obtain a grade E. In general, however, examiners were impressed with much of what they saw.[19] For example, in 1976 it was noted that the best work was informed, mature and ably expressed, and some essays were inspired by a love of language and facility in its use. In the comprehension section examiners sought to select passages which would be interesting and relevant, extracts being taken from travel writing and articles which had appeared in journals and magazines as well as from literary works. However, few candidates were able to perform as well in comprehension as in the essay. A large number failed to confine answers to the information contained in the passage and much concern was expressed at the standard of grammar and spelling, as well as the use of colloquialism, jargon and slang. This pattern continued to characterize the response to English language examinations in the early 1980s. Examiners commended the way many candidates had responded to the essay question in a lively and interesting way and it was found that comprehension passages had engaged their interest, but grammar and spelling remained unsatisfactory and knowledge of what constituted a logical sentence was often poor.

Meanwhile, CSE English was examined by means of two written papers lasting two-and-a-quarter hours, together with listening comprehension and oral tests. In paper 1, which represented 40 per cent of marks, candidates were required to write an essay and answer comprehension questions which tested their ability to summarize information and discriminate between different opinions. In paper 2 they were presented with previously unseen extracts from works of poetry, prose and drama, the questions being designed to probe understanding and response to what was read. The second section of the paper provided an opportunity to discuss various forms of literature.[20] The listening comprehension test sought to discover to what extent pupils had been able to understand information provided by their teacher, and the oral test included reading, comprehension and informal conversation. Examiners were pleased with the facility demonstrated in the use of spoken English. For instance, in 1971 it was observed that the overall standard was very satisfactory, even though performance in the written paper was more varied. The content of what was produced in the essay question was often laudable and reflected a community spirit, an awareness of controversial issues, and a broad vocabulary. Yet attention was continually drawn to recurring problems such as misrelated participles, errors in punctuation and spelling, and the habitual misuse of capital letters and apostrophes.

The CSE examination was a progressive and carefully planned test of candidates' abilities.[21] Yet it was clear that it was a victim of a culture which derided the aims and the achievements of those who met its challenges, even though a grade 1 at CSE was officially deemed to be of equivalent standard to a pass (grade C) at GCE O level. A substantial number of employers, parents and even some candidates themselves viewed the CSE as an inferior alternative to GCE O level, an examination designed for second-rate candidates who had failed academically. Few appeared to appreciate its merits or to recognize that those who obtained a CSE qualification often produced work of excellent quality. Schools made a deliberate effort to enter as many of their pupils as possible for the O level examination, and under such circumstances it was inevitable that the quality of performance in CSE English deteriorated.

The great majority of candidates entering O level English literature took paper Oa, based on set texts. The course involved a detailed study of one of Shakespeare's plays, an anthology of poetry, a prescribed novel and a play. As well as extended writing on these texts, candidates were expected to identify and comment on 'gobbets' from the set texts. Syllabus Ob had no set texts, assumed a breadth of reading that would allow candidates to answer general questions based on period or genre and included a previously unseen poem. Examiners were impressed by the overall response: the

Shakespeare questions elicited some lively answers and the use of quotations and knowledge of context was commended. Indeed, the main faults identified by examiners occurred because of poor examination technique and problems of expression. Many scripts were illegible, essays had not been planned, spelling and punctuation were poor, and a knowledge of basic literary terms was sometimes lacking.

Coursework, designed to introduce candidates to a broad range of works, was an integral part of the CSE syllabus in English literature. A folio, containing twelve pieces of work, had to be submitted, and could include discussions of works which had been read or critical information about a particular author. During the early 1970s examiners commended the imaginative and original way in which much of the folio work was presented. The overall response was pleasing, many candidates making good use of the opportunity to show evidence of wide reading. For instance, candidates were commended for their response to the work of twentieth-century poets like Wilfred Owen, Ted Hughes and R. S. Thomas. Yet it was also clear that the CSE course had not been taught properly in some schools. Many centres had limited their courses to one reader, one anthology and one play. Folios sometimes betrayed evidence of hurried work completed by individuals who cared little about the need to impress the examiner and many of them simply used the opportunity to produce material on a topic of personal interest.

Welsh

By the late 1960s those who maintained that GCE courses in Welsh overburdened pupils and focused too heavily on grammar and textual analysis had succeeded in persuading the WJEC to reduce some of the content. A revised schedule was produced whereby those studying Welsh at A level sat two papers. There was an opportunity for creative writing in the first paper, which also presented candidates with an unseen literary text for appreciation, while a third question examined knowledge either of a piece of medieval Welsh poetry or a prose work from the seventeenth or eighteenth century. The second paper focused on four books which had been studied as part of the course. Candidates were expected to comment on matters such as the style of writing and literary attributes, while a section on language required comments on the grammatical and linguistic features of a previously unseen passage. Here again the response varied. Those who marked the papers complained of a tendency to summarize the works studied instead of providing appropriate analysis, and questions on the bardic tradition and on style and structure were rarely answered with conviction.

The quality of the essays caused great concern to the examiners. Throughout the 1970s they complained of poor spelling, grammar and syntax and the inclusion of English idioms and phrases. Examiners' reports warned that an emphasis on creativity and self-expression did not mean that basic rules of grammar could be ignored and urged teachers to ensure that their students appreciated the need to acquire a wider vocabulary. Gradually, examiners identified more promising work. In the early 1980s a distinct improvement in the quality of the written language was perceived and it was found that creative work based on personal experience was of a very high standard.[22] Moreover, it was evident that most candidates had read the set texts with interest, although questions on style were rarely answered satisfactorily.

At O level, those attempting the *Iaith Cymru* paper, which was designed for those who were fluent in the language, were required to compose an essay of between 500 and 600 words, and answer questions testing their understanding and ability to summarize a piece of previously unseen written material. They were also expected to produce a factual report or a dialogue, or to present an argument. A question testing knowledge of formal grammar was optional. In common with English language examinations, the quality of the answers became more varied as the number of entrants increased. The standard achieved by those awarded an A grade was often impressive and it was a source of great satisfaction to the examiners that so many sixteen-year-olds could produce such work under examination conditions. It was noted that many had a talent for writing a creative piece of literature reflecting a personal experience or point of view:

> It is a matter for pride that we have promising young writers, who can compose effortlessly, fluently and correctly; who plan meticulously and purposefully; who write in a lively and full way and who express personal experiences very interestingly.[23]

It was also noted that some of those who achieved a creditable grade would have done still better had they applied themselves more fully to the task. Grammatical errors were the most common fault and the extent to which English idioms were used in the examination denied many candidates the grade which they might otherwise have achieved. During the 1980s examiners found that the level of grammatical accuracy declined even further. Problems with mutations, negative forms, misuse of verb forms, poor spelling and limited vocabulary were highlighted, and it was observed that comments on the folio work submitted by pupils contained few remarks about the craft of writing. In 1986 the examiner declared:

> Is it not time, for the sake of linguistic correctness, to return to some practices that were acceptable many years ago and believe again that there was value in understanding the nature of a language derived from the study of a more limited amount of written work than to produce streams of work of no quality for the sake of 'creative writing?' It is only by mastering the nature of a language that its length and depth can be understood.[24]

In Welsh language C1, an examination designed for those for whom Welsh was a second language, candidates were expected to write a composition of between 200 and 250 words and to answer questions on a modern book read as part of the course. They were also required to be able to write a letter or a set of minutes and to show understanding of a piece of poetry, while an oral test judged their skills in reading, understanding and conversation. Examiners found that many of the stories produced in the essay question lacked originality, the standard of spelling was often poor, and grammatical mistakes through misuse of mutations and faulty syntax were rife. During the early 1980s the overall quality had declined further and many scripts were replete with elementary mistakes. The work produced in the oral reading test was generally commended, but the conversations were marred by lack of imagination in selecting topics, errors in mutation and a tendency to use English words and idioms.

Welsh literature was likewise examined on the basis of three papers, for which candidates were entered on the basis of their proficiency in the language. Those pursuing syllabus O1 studied four set texts, including a selection of poetry, drama and a novel, while the O2 and O3 papers concentrated on fewer set texts and placed greater emphasis on oral work. The best response in all three papers was elicited by modern works. Examiners found evidence of thorough preparation, sound textual knowledge and an ability to discuss the issues raised in the literature with maturity and insight. The main deficiencies arose from poor expression and examination technique. As in the case of the language paper, the standard of spelling and grammar was often low. Candidates had not read questions carefully and, as a result, failed to carry out what was required of them. It was evident that closer attention should be given to matters such as style.

The CSE examination was divided into three sections. The first included questions on a selection of Welsh literary works which had been studied as part of the course. The second sought to assess general reading by means of questions on two novels, while the third section focused on poetry. Few candidates reached the required level, however, and many had a limited knowledge of the texts they had studied. Few pupils had been introduced to a broad range of works and a large number showed no interest in what they had studied.

Modern languages

The growing realization of the importance of modern languages in economic and social life was reflected in an increase in the number of candidates entered for examination in these subjects throughout England and Wales during the 1970s and 1980s. French, and to a lesser extent German and Spanish, were no longer regarded as subjects to be studied only by able pupils with an aptitude for modern languages. At the same time, much of the formal grammar work which had characterized the teaching of modern languages was abandoned and replaced by an emphasis on oral proficiency. The target language was much more widely used during lessons and the development of audio-visual aids and language laboratories, supported by the WJEC, paved the way for a new approach.

French

Three written papers and an oral test formed the basis of the examination at A level. Paper A1 required candidates to provide a textual analysis and a critical appreciation of passages selected from the works which they had studied as part of their course. They were required to demonstrate knowledge of the country whose language they studied, including developments in education, government, law, agriculture and industry, and to be familiar with national institutions. In paper A2 candidates were required to translate two pieces of unprepared text into English or Welsh, while in A3 a passage was set for translation into the target language. However, examiners were disappointed with the quality of the work produced by those examined in French during the 1970s. Limited vocabulary and poor spelling, punctuation and syntax were identified as areas of particular concern. Questions on style were rarely answered with conviction and were often beset with misquotations, while those questions which required comment on subject-matter were answered by a summary or approximate translation of the text and irrelevant biographical information about authors. In the oral and aural sections, candidates experienced difficulty with hyphenation and in determining gender, and few displayed genuine fluency in spoken French. Although the quality of work in the language paper improved during the 1980s, both the comprehension and literary appreciation sections continued to be marred by irrelevant material and a failure to answer the question, and basic mistakes such as confusion of gender and poor work with tenses and articles continued to cause concern.

At O level, examiners found the overall performance in French more satisfactory.[25] The quality of the work in free composition was creditable, despite weaknesses in vocabulary and grammar, and particularly promising work was produced in the oral communication and aural understanding sections. Nevertheless some problems recurred. Candidates were found to be too rigid in their written work, partly because in composition they had attempted to translate their thoughts into French and had not been sufficiently confident to employ French idioms and sentence structures.

The CSE examinations in French focused mainly on oral work and this aspect accounted for some 60 per cent of the total marks. Those examined were expected to demonstrate a proficiency in free conversation by giving information both about themselves and about familiar topics such as the weather, school and shopping. The written paper included a short composition and comprehension exercise which throughout the 1970s and 1980s proved the most arduous test. Very few of those examined could compose a sentence in French, and many lacked awareness of basic grammatical features such as the use of the perfect and imperfect tenses, pronouns, conjugations, adjectives and simple idioms.

German

Similar weaknesses to those in French were highlighted by examiners of German. At A level many candidates experienced difficulty in translating passages into German because of deficiencies in vocabulary, together with difficulties with case endings, sentence structure, participles and declensions. It was equally evident that many of those who sat the examination had little interest in, or enthusiasm for, the subject. Examiners found that promising candidates seemed to have found the experience uninspiring and the large proportion of standardized answers on German literature suggested that very few pupils empathized with authors and their ideas.

The quality of oral German varied immensely in different centres. There was a marked reluctance to engage in anything but the most basic conversations, and inaccuracies in pronunciation and intonation abounded.[26] Reports indicate that these issues remained during the 1980s. Indeed, examiners complained that the general standard of grammatical accuracy and the ability to compose syntactically correct German was in decline. Relevant secondary works had not been read and there was little to suggest a deep interest in German culture and society.

At O level, performance was also extremely varied and the overall standard lower than expected. Basic faults were highlighted, notably limited vocabulary and poor command of grammar, sentence structure and syntax, except among the strongest candidates, and the complexities of German gender and case forms, verbs, tenses and the use of prepositions were clearly causing considerable difficulty.

Latin

The continued decline in the number of candidates entered for examination in Latin in the 1970s and 1980s was a matter of considerable concern for examiners.[27] The number of candidates taking A level fell from 197 in 1970 to 64 in 1986, while the total entered for O level fell from 1,984 in 1970 to 236 in 1986.

Those who pursued the A level course sat three papers. Paper A1 tested their ability to translate and analyse a book of prose and another of verse which had been studied in class; a second paper focused on comprehension and composition; while a third paper measured proficiency in unseen translation. The quality of the answers varied. In 1972 examiners noted that translation from Latin was poor in comparison with previous years, although the quality of answers on syntax had improved and candidates increasingly produced answers of a high standard in response to questions on the passages which had been set for comment.

At O level, candidates sat two papers, each lasting two-and-a-half hours. The first paper included a comprehension exercise, a passage for translation from English or Welsh, and a passage of verse for translation from Latin. In the second paper candidates were expected to translate texts which they had studied and to demonstrate understanding of those works in answer to an essay question. On the whole the quality of the work was satisfactory. Translations of Latin texts were sometimes exemplary, although some lacked the close attention to detail expected by examiners, and it was felt some candidates could have achieved a better grade had they studied the set books in greater detail. In 1986 a new examination was introduced which sought to cater for the whole of the ability range through differentiated papers, and the syllabus was revised in order to devote greater attention to Roman life and civilization. But despite the best efforts of those who were committed to retaining Latin as part of the school curriculum, it was clear that it was unlikely to remain popular and widely studied. An educational climate had emerged which demanded that each subject had to be justified on the grounds of its usefulness, and there was little room for those such as Latin which were considered to be little more than an academic exercise.

Geography

As we have seen previously, the syllabus in geography owed much to the inspiration of the exciting work undertaken by those who taught and researched aspects of the subject at the universities. The role of the University of Wales in developing an interesting and topical syllabus was maintained, and more scientific approaches to the subject, evident in studies of landscape, environmental patterns, and interpretative techniques, were introduced into the classroom. The location of phenomena, spatial interaction, distribution patterns and global interdependence, which emphasized individual enquiry, field investigation, data collection and interpretation, became an accepted part of the geography syllabus.[28]

At A level, candidates studied a combination of general physical and human geography as well as the detail of different global regions, and a practical examination tested their proficiency in work based both on Ordnance Survey and land utilization maps. Periodic syllabus revisions sought to keep pace with changing approaches to the subject at A level.

During the early 1970s, however, several worrying features were identified. Work submitted from some centres was markedly inferior to that from others; the fact that candidates often did better in one paper than in another suggested that the whole of the syllabus was not being covered; and too many candidates confined their answers to the bare facts. For instance, a question requiring the comparison of two agricultural systems was often answered by means of a description of those systems. Many scripts lacked critical analysis of factual information and, while some answers included maps drawn in intricate detail, others contained only a solitary, hastily drawn cartographic effort designed to satisfy the demands of the rubric.

By the end of the decade examiners were more positive. It was noted that the analytical aspects of the subject had received more attention. Questions on population growth and economic geography were generally well answered, and there were some excellent answers on the United States, the British Isles and western Europe, but few candidates had mastered the complexities of physical geography and answers on geomorphology were particularly poor.

At O level, candidates were given three hours to answer a geography paper which contained five sections: a study of maps and a test of recall of Ordnance Survey symbols and skill in measurement, and interpretation of information about relief, drainage features, communications, settlement patterns and the distribution of population; the movements of the earth, including latitude and longitude, land forms and the impact of the weather and erosion; agriculture and industry in England, Wales and Scotland; knowledge and understanding of the United States, the Soviet Union and western Europe; and similar study of Africa, Latin America and the Indian sub-continent, with special reference to issues such as natural resources and demographic issues.

In general, examiners were satisfied, and they attributed the improvement in the physical geography section to the decision to reduce the amount of factual material required. It was noted that sketch maps were used more appropriately as the decade progressed and there was less evidence of rote learning of factual material. In the human geography section examiners found that questions on hill farming and the economic structure of south Wales were often answered well, but that sections on other regions, such as the West Midlands region, produced vague and disappointing answers. The extent to which the O level syllabus was covered was also questioned. Answers on the economic and social issues confronting the United States were often impressive, but knowledge and understanding of the continent of Africa tended to be pedestrian and out-of-date. This uneven level of attainment continued to characterize performance during the 1980s. In 1981 it was noted that a great deal was known about 'modern geography' and that some excellent answers had been written on questions on the economies of the Ruhr, farming in Denmark and manufacturing industry in the United States. However, spatial understanding was often weak, mathematical work was poor, and the command of geographical terms was inadequate.

The CSE examination centred on the practical ability to handle source material such as photographs, maps and statistics, and in particular the study of Ordnance Survey maps. The syllabus stipulated that Wales should be studied with particular reference to the immediate locality, and topics such as tourism, settlement, language, power and communication formed an integral part. The section on the British Isles considered specialization in agriculture and industry through detailed case studies of representative areas, while the section on world geography examined communication and the influence of the environment on man's activities in areas such as the monsoon lands and the desert.

Examiners expressed considerable satisfaction with the way candidates performed during the early 1970s. Map interpretation and photograph reading were reckoned to be excellent in many instances. The arguments in favour of and against the construction of new roads had been well understood and there were some excellent answers on regional economies such as that of the Ruhr. The main weaknesses arose through lack of fieldwork and direct practical experience. Yet, as was the case in other subjects, the promising signs evident during the early 1970s were not sustained. By the next decade examiners were increasingly disappointed with the quality of work submitted. They pointed to the proliferation of unacceptable phrases such as 'good soil' and 'suitable climate', and terms such as 'basic industries' caused confusion. In 1981 examiners noted that knowledge of geographical locations in Wales was scant and candidates were unable to visualize even the major features of the relief of the Ordnance Survey extract. It was against this background that the O level and CSE papers were replaced by a Common Syllabus examination in 1983. Pupils pursued a course which focused on skills and knowledge, tested on the basis of graded questions. The initial response to the new format proved positive, with the individual project portion of the examination being particularly well received.

Geology

The study of geology was largely confined to those who were deeply interested in the subject and therefore the standard of work was generally of a very high quality. Candidates were required to take two papers. Paper A1 dealt with palaeontology, stratigraphy, earth movements and structural geology, while paper A2 examined crystallography and mineralogy, applied geology and petrology and petrogenesis. As in other scientific disciplines, a high premium was placed on practical skill. The main criticism of examiners referred to the presentation of examination work rather than the content of the answers themselves. The quality of the work on aspects of the syllabus such as plate tectonics and on physical and chemical processes was highly praised. In the practical test the most pleasing work occurred where experiments were based on personal observation, and fieldwork used as an integral part of the teaching process. In 1979 a new examination format was introduced which confirmed the high standard achieved in previous years. There were some good answers to the structured questions and the majority of candidates proved adept at drawing sketch maps and cross-sections. Even so, lack of interpretative power meant some failed to appreciate anything but the most obvious points relating to unconformities and igneous rocks. Questions on economic geology were sometimes poorly answered, not least because of the tendency of some candidates to confine their answers to the south Wales coalfield.

History

Those involved in any aspect of the history syllabus regularly drew attention to the need for reform. Throughout the 1960s, historical scholarship sought to break new ground by abandoning the anglocentric view of the subject which led to undue concentration on the political history of England. Yet, despite a growing chorus of disapproval, numerous aspects of the history syllabus remained unchanged, an issue which will be considered in detail in Chapter 5. Throughout most of the 1970s and early 1980s, factual knowledge was emphasized far more than the acquisition of skills and there was little emphasis on field and project work among the 14–16 age group. O level examinations continued to be based on the formal five-question examination paper, with only one answer devoted to Welsh history. This stipulation that candidates had to answer a question on Wales was a matter of considerable debate. It was resented by some teachers but vigorously defended by those responsible for the recent unprecedented renaissance of scholarly study of Welsh history which had led to an outpouring of publications on the economic, social and political history of the nation. Many commentators, including some teachers, maintained that this vibrancy should be reflected in the school syllabus if history was to be seen as an interesting and lively subject.

A level students had to sit two separate papers, one on the history of England and Wales and the other on Europe. This meant that most of those pursuing the course spent one year examining European history in a particular period and the second year focusing on the experience of England and Wales during the same chronological span. Examiners expected the work to be based on sound factual knowledge coupled with an ability to analyse and consider issues in a mature and reasoned way. In addition, an awareness of contemporary debates in history, and the process of revising and reinterpreting historical evidence, were required. Those who examined the subject at A level found little evidence of this approach. Standards fluctuated widely in the 1970s, and reached a particularly low point in 1974 when the very high percentage of scripts which contained poor or indifferent answers prompted examiners to question whether some of the candidates should have been entered for the examination:

> The Advanced level is and always has been primarily an examination designed to provide the Universities with promising entrants and, therefore, cannot and should not be adapted to meet the requirements of many candidates who are not by aptitude suitable to tackle Advanced level work.[29]

The fact that only a small number of papers were deemed excellent continued to disappoint the examiners. A very large proportion of papers contained answers which were little more than satisfactory. It was clear that candidates had mastered a mass of information which they were determined to use without taking account of the demands of the questions. Few were able to use facts critically, and there was little evidence of independent reading. Poor expression, spelling and grammar blighted many answers.[30] Answers on both British and European history clearly demonstrated that the syllabus was not being studied as a whole in many schools. For instance, economic history was neglected, the life and works of John Calvin were known, but those of Huldrych Zwingli were often ignored. More was known of the Tudors than of the Stuarts, and most of the answers on the period 1603–60 were confused and old-fashioned, while the history of Wales was rarely studied in sufficient depth.

The problems identified during the 1970s prompted examiners to advocate a radical reassessment of the aims of teaching history. In 1980 it was maintained:

> Teachers must be encouraged to present history, not as a body of revealed fact, but as an exercise in 'problem solving' using historical situations and data. This must involve the student in both the studying of specific issues and in gaining a panoramic view of the development of human affairs over an extended period.[31]

A similar pattern of dissatisfaction with the work of candidates was reflected in the reports of those who examined the subject at O level. Seven different syllabuses were provided by the WJEC in history, five of which concentrated on the experience of England and Wales. Each year a small number of those entered responded extremely well to the challenge of the examination, but a great deal of indifferent work was produced. The problems fell into three main groups. First, few candidates could use the facts they had learned effectively. Many produced long, detailed and irrelevant biographical accounts whenever the name of an individual appeared in the question. Secondly, many answers did not relate to the demands of the question. Answers to questions on battles and social conditions were too descriptive and basic terms such as social reform, elementary education and domestic policy were confused and misused. The third problem identified was directly attributable to the way in which the subject was taught. Candidates from some centres tended to answer questions from the same group, suggesting that only a portion of the syllabus had been taught, and the misuse of words and phrases indicated many teachers used dictation as their main teaching method.

As well as expecting candidates to produce short essays, the CSE papers in history included several questions which could be answered by one word or in a short sentence. Candidates were invited to produce a folio which could be taken into account when awarding the final grades. Overall during the early 1970s, examiners found much to praise in the work they marked. Scripts and projects were well presented and revealed a sound grasp of factual material. The main faults highlighted were a failure to devote sufficient attention to the whole syllabus (and particularly those aspects of Welsh history which should have been covered), confusion about dates and events, and a tendency to be too descriptive. For instance, in 1975 it was noted that many candidates lacked a firm grasp of the chronology of the Depression. Answers on Adolf Hitler were too biographical and lacked analysis, and those on the events at Peterloo failed to relate the incident to the wider movement for electoral reform. The quality of the work identified in the 1970s was not maintained, however, and by the early 1980s examiners found disturbing evidence of haste and confusion in the answers. Concepts such as 'the poor', the 'distribution of population' and 'rural society' caused many problems, while Welsh history remained a neglected area of study.

Scripture

Those who studied scripture at A level sat two examinations. Paper A1 tested knowledge of the Old Testament, including the history, religious beliefs and literature of the Hebrew nation, while Paper A2 posed similar questions on the New Testament. Although the work produced in the examination was generally considered satisfactory, few students of a high calibre studied at this level. The main strengths were factual recall and historical knowledge. For instance, candidates were often well versed in the history of the Hebrew nation and the culture of the ancient Near East; but questions which required discussion of theological issues were rarely answered satisfactorily. Few candidates were able to make perceptive comments on the meaning of divinity and many had great difficulty in selecting material appropriately.

These problems were not ameliorated as the study of scripture gave way to religious studies during the 1980s. The syllabus was broadened and considerable attention was devoted to non-Christian faiths and the influence of philosophers such as Freud, Durkheim, Weber and Marx. Textual study remained part of the examination, but those questions were rarely answered directly and many candidates could only produce vague suggestions concerning the origins of the texts included in the examination. The overall standard of the work declined, and issues such as the humanity of Christ and the nature of salvation were treated superficially.

An identical division into two papers, one on the Old Testament and the other on the New Testament, was adopted in examining O level. The main emphasis was placed on the content of the Gospel and general information on its background. During the 1970s examiners found that the quality of work varied considerably. On the one hand some answers were inspired, reflecting a commitment to the subject and a thorough knowledge of the texts studied. On the other hand, examiners complained that many candidates had studied the subject as an easy option and lacked the necessary skills to answer contextual questions, or the knowledge which derived from the detailed study of set texts.

The CSE examination focused on two areas of study. Sixty per cent of marks were awarded for the section on 'The Life and Teaching of Jesus Christ' while the remainder of the marks were awarded for answers on one of three options: 'The Story of the Covenant', 'Prophets and Prophecy' and 'The Growth of the Early Church'. Candidates were expected to answer by means of one essay, two shorter compositions, and a question testing comprehension of a text studied in class. Examiners noted that some excellent work was submitted on Biblical extracts, and some projects were models of diligent research, thoughtful preparation and lively presentation. Yet it was also apparent that both the quality of the teaching and learning were often deficient. There was evidence that commentaries on the Bible had been studied at the expense of the text itself, religious terminology was confused and many answers were vague and general.

The place of scripture in the curriculum was itself a matter of discussion. The decline in religious observance and the increase in the proportion of the population adhering to non-Christian faiths meant that the WJEC, in common with other examining bodies, was under mounting pressure to broaden the syllabus by replacing the subject with religious studies, a subject which might include, for example, a consideration of the Moslem, Hindu and Jewish faiths alongside Christianity. These issues, which featured prominently in the discussion about the introduction of the National Curriculum, will be considered in detail in Chapter 5.

Mathematics

As has been noted above, changes made to the curriculum during the late 1960s and early 1970s generated heated debate and this was reflected clearly in the arguments about the role and objectives of studying mathematics in secondary schools. Demands for reform during the 1960s challenged traditional assumptions about the relationship between teaching mathematics and mental discipline. Critics referred to the use of obsolete methods, maintaining that the syllabus was out-dated, narrow in its focus, and irrelevant to the majority of those who studied it. The concept of 'the architecture of mathematics', advanced by a group of French mathematicians, influenced the notion of a modern approach which viewed the subject as a practical activity involving the understanding of basic numerical concepts and the study of statistics.

Such ideas were a stimulus for programmes such as the School Mathematics Project, the Nuffield Mathematics Project and the Schools Council's *Mathematics for the Majority* report, published in 1967. They contained a syllabus which centred on spatial relationships, geometric, algebraic and arithmetical reasoning, and practical work involving discovery and learning, observation, measurement and number relationships.[32] Many teachers welcomed the approach as an opportunity to move away from the unrewarding grind of traditional methods. Yet, for opponents of change, most notably the authors of the *Black Papers* on education, it highlighted a malaise at the heart of the education system. In 1978 the government appointed a Committee of Inquiry into the teaching of mathematics in schools. Its report, *Mathematics Counts* (the Cockcroft Report) published in 1982, acknowledged that many school-leavers and adults lacked confidence in the use of mathematics. It emphasized the importance both of knowledge and skills, the need for enquiry and experiment in practical work, the importance of problem solving and the ability to identify relationships. Crucially, however, the Cockcroft Report rejected the argument of those who believed weaknesses in mathematical ability were a result of new syllabuses.

Examiners of mathematics for the WJEC during the early 1970s expressed satisfaction with the quality of the work which had been produced at A level. It was admitted that the papers set were 'searching', given that candidates were expected to demonstrate both an understanding of the basis of different aspects of the subject and an ability to apply principles to novel situations. While acknowledging the quality of a large portion of the work, examiners drew attention to the need to give closer attention to topics such as the manipulation of algebraic expressions, simple harmonic motion and vectors. In addition, candidates were urged to give more consideration to the way in which they tackled certain questions in order to ensure that their methods were economical and their answers sensible and precise.

The compartmentalized way in which the subject was considered also elicited comment. In pure mathematics it was found that many candidates were reluctant to attempt questions which required them to apply familiar concepts to an unfamiliar setting. The response to theoretical questions was generally poor and it was noted that answers to questions on logarithms and the properties of integrals suggested that those topics had not been studied in depth. Similarly, in applied mathematics, examiners attributed the difficulties experienced by candidates to their failure to relate one part of the syllabus to another. For instance, few experienced any difficulty in handling differential equations, but students were unable to solve those problems when they appeared as part of broader questions. During the 1980s it was noted that candidates showed a better understanding of basic processes and there was evidence of excellent work in some aspects of the syllabus. Lack of accuracy remained one of the main problems: candidates tended to approximate results very early in questions involving numerical calculations. Questions relating to probability and statistics were rarely satisfactorily answered.

The O level syllabus covered an immense range of topics, including ordinary arithmetical processes, weights and measures, fractions, percentages and decimals. In geometry, the syllabus included the measurement of rectangles, triangles, pyramids, circles and cylinders, while algebra encompassed the use of formulae and indices, the remainder theorem, linear equations and matrices. While those who examined the subject at A level were generally satisfied with the performance of pupils, their colleagues who assessed O level were alarmed at much of the work produced. Algebra was a particularly weak area: candidates were unable to apply basic processes such as squaring binomial equations, removing brackets, and adding or subtracting unlike terms. Questions on geometry, especially on angle proportions and the ratios of areas of triangles, prompted mediocre answers; vectors were not understood and the responses to the remainder theorem were mostly poor. Pythagoras's theorem was known, but the principles governing its application were not understood. These problems were not eradicated during the period studied in this chapter, but the reports suggest that in general the work submitted had improved.

The decision to allow the use of calculators in some mathematics papers, where applications and understanding rather than computation skills were tested, resulted in more accurate work, and examiners commended improvements in presentation and organization. Yet it was clear that the level of basic knowledge and skills remained variable.[33] Subtraction and the use of the decimal point caused many difficulties, diagrams were often poor, and there was confusion about the general concept of algebra and the procedure of simplifying, factorizing and solving equations. The notion of 'percentage increase' was misunderstood by a large proportion of candidates and there were some careless errors in the use of matrices.

The aim of the CSE mathematics examination was to test understanding of basic concepts and the ability to apply those in different circumstances. Papers contained short answer questions as well as more searching tests. Among the topics studied were the binary scale, the metric system, percentage, ratio and simple proportion as well as basic algebra and geometry. Overall, examiners were disappointed with the quality of work. Algebra submissions were poor – beset by manipulative errors and a failure to grasp even the basic features of the topic. Common faults included the belief that obtaining a square root of a number meant dividing by two, and confusion between a requirement to factorize and to solve.

The quality of the work in the separate CSE arithmetic examination was likewise noticeably low. Work suffered from poor presentation and failure to understand basic mathematical terms. Much of the work was marred by carelessness. Many candidates had not even attempted to answer questions which required some thought and others failed to recall information even at the most basic level. Clearly, the decision to enter as many candidates as possible for the GCE O level examination meant that only the weakest sat the CSE examination. Yet, results at O level were also generally disappointing. Throughout the period after 1945 commentators had emphasized the central importance of mathematics and the need to improve performance in the subject. Initiatives had been launched to recruit teachers of a high calibre, and the Department of Education and the Welsh Office had emphasized the need to train serving teachers in more effective methods. However, neither these efforts nor the introduction of a revised syllabus succeeded in overcoming weaknesses which were endemic throughout the twentieth century.

Science subjects

Commentators both within the teaching profession and in other spheres of public life increasingly questioned the objectives informing the teaching of science during the 1950s and the 1960s. They criticized the way courses focused on factual information, and the neglect of experimental work and scientific method in schools. The importance of science in the modern world was evident, not least because the decline of traditional industries and processes demanded a workforce orientated towards the use of technology and scientific application. The work of the Nuffield Foundation and the Schools Council proved crucial during the 1960s, as their projects provoked thorough debates about the content of science courses, teaching methods and the way in which the subjects were examined.[34] The notion of promoting understanding and the acquisition of skills through participation and engagement in the school laboratory, advocated at the end of the nineteenth century, were revived, and a renewed emphasis was placed on ensuring that pupils understood concepts and processes through investigation, observation, experiment, predicting, estimating, classifying, generalizing and judging. Moreover, schools were encouraged to view science as an integrated subject rather than one to be pursued on the basis of separate areas such as physics, chemistry and biology. While new projects undoubtedly exerted a strong influence on the way in which science was taught within secondary schools, the notion of teaching it as an integrated whole was resisted by some. Most schools adopted the practice of studying physics, chemistry and biology as separate subjects in the upper forms, partly because qualifications in general and integrated science were not widely accepted by employers and institutions of higher education.[35]

Physics

Of the sciences, physics was undoubtedly the one which showed greatest promise, according to those examining for the WJEC during the 1970s. Pupils entered for A level were tested on their knowledge of mechanics and the properties of matter, vibration and vibratory motion, electricity and magnetism, atomic physics and optics. Questions were set which demanded a thorough understanding of physical principles and their application.

In general, candidates were commended for their understanding of the basics of the subject and examiners highlighted areas of the syllabus such as the definition of factors, including simple harmonic motion, for particular praise. The main weaknesses were in many ways similar to those identified in relation to mathematics: confusion reigned when familiar principles were presented in unusual situations, and numerical work was generally unsatisfactory.

At O level, examiners found evidence that the performance of candidates was praiseworthy. A new syllabus was introduced at the beginning of the 1970s, to be tested by means of three papers. The first considered the particular nature of matter and mechanics, and included the study of the structure of solids, liquids and gases, while in mechanics candidates were expected to show their understanding of velocity and acceleration, and the laws of motion and momentum. The second section considered heat and energy, waves and light, and also included a study of wavelengths, frequency, and velocity. The third section focused on electricity and magnetism. Factual recall was found to be impressive and the work in the practical test indicated that key principles had been understood. Some very good accounts of free fall experiments were produced, and answers to questions on the swinging pendulum, the electromagnetic clock, the optical system and molecular theory were sensible and accurate. The main weaknesses arose when candidates were required to apply mathematical concepts, especially algebra, thereby reinforcing concern about this aspect of education in Wales.

Candidates studying for a CSE in physics focused on knowledge, comprehension and application. They investigated topics such as matter and measurement, force and motion and energy, including wave motion and electromagnetism, magnetism, radioactivity, reflection, transfer of heat and practical skills such as the method of wiring electrical plugs. Examiners commended the quality of the routine aspects, but familiar problems arose whenever candidates were expected to apply the principles that they had learned. There was confusion between convex and concave mirrors, answers on the electromagnetic spectrum were poor and numerical work was weak. Diagrams rarely satisfied the examiners and work on velocity-time relationships was poor.

Chemistry

The examination in A level chemistry tested knowledge, understanding and the application of basic principles. Topics such as atomic structure, bonding, states of matter, equilibrium and chemical kinetics were studied alongside those of metals and alloys, inorganic ion exchanges and synthetic organic polymers. Throughout most of the 1970s examiners found that few candidates were proficient in the written paper and only those questions which dealt with routine matters elicited satisfactory answers. As with other sciences, very few of the candidates were able to cope with a question which tested familiar principles in an unfamiliar situation, and poor examination technique, notably the tendency to spend too much time answering a question on a popular and well-understood topic, meant that some promising candidates failed to achieve their full potential. Many of those who had an essentially sound knowledge of chemistry were often unable to provide even the most basic definitions and very few were adept at making deductions.

At O level, candidates were introduced to concepts such as the characteristics of the solid, liquid and gaseous states, changes in the composition of materials, and air and combustion. Atom structures and valency were studied, as well as issues such as the effect of electricity on matter, the properties and compounds of metals, oxidization and reduction, and water. Quantitative chemistry was taught as a means of proving the validity of concepts, especially in relation to atom structure and valency.

As was the case with A level, examiners were disappointed by the standard of the work submitted during the early 1970s. The main faults identified fell into three broad categories. First, experience of laboratory work was lacking, some of the diagrams produced suggesting that the actual apparatus had never been seen. Secondly, technical terms such as 'element', 'compound', 'ion' and 'atom' were often confused and this affected the accuracy of answers. Thirdly, the standard of mathematical work was alarmingly poor – marred by inaccuracy and a failure to understand basic concepts.

The overall quality of the work in CSE chemistry was found to be of a satisfactory standard during most of the period. In 1973 the examiners found that factual and theoretical issues had been mastered and that new areas of the syllabus had been understood thoroughly. The quality of the work deteriorated during the second half of the 1970s, largely because some candidates had been entered who were unable to meet the challenge of the examination, but there was a marked improvement noted during the early 1980s. It was found that most candidates could give accurate descriptions of experiments and that the majority had gained a sound understanding of the basic features of the subject.

Biology

The performance of pupils in biology was a cause for concern throughout the 1970s and 1980s. At A level, the syllabus contained topics such as the nature and activities of the protoplasm, heredity and evolution, plant and animal form and function, and the inter-relationship of plants and animals. A great deal of importance was attached to proficiency in practical work but the examiners' reports highlighted recurring weaknesses. A substantial number of candidates were unable to answer more than two or three questions reasonably well; few produced appropriate illustrations and the quality of diagrams was often poor. Words such as 'mineral' were misunderstood and problems in applying theoretical knowledge and in solving numerical problems abounded. Even basic factual knowledge was found wanting, and questions on standard topics such as evolution and natural selection elicited a catalogue of evidence which bore little relation to the nature of the question. Although some improvement was seen during the 1980s, most notably in the quality of the work on biochemistry and physiology, examiners remained disappointed with the quality of answers, especially those involving mathematics and unfamiliar processes.

Those studying the subject at O level examined issues such as the basic cell in plants and animals and their work included consideration of chromosomes and genes. Candidates were introduced to outline classifications of the plant and animal kingdoms, the concept of evolution and the general structure and biology of mammals and flowering plants. They were expected to understand nutrition, respiration, excretion, locomotion and support, as well as the inter-relationship of organisms and their environments, and the ecology of man and his environment. The main strengths of the work produced during this period lay in the ability to recall information, especially in parts of the syllabus such as excretion in mammals, organs and their functions, and pollination and fertilization. However, once again application of this material in unfamiliar circumstances proved beyond most candidates. The manner in which the subject was taught was highlighted as a major cause for concern. Pupils lacked experience of laboratory work and some centres clearly concentrated on certain aspects of the syllabus at the expense of others.

Three types of question were set in the CSE paper in biology. The first was to be answered by one word or a sentence, the second called for structured enquiry, while the third was based on traditional methods of testing knowledge and understanding. Candidates were expected to be familiar with matters such as the characteristics of living organisms, the similarities and differences between plants and animals, and to be aware of matters such as nutrition, energy release, movement and support, and reproduction. The standard of work submitted, however, was uneven. Examiners complained of a substantial number of very poor answers, often attributable to a failure to read questions carefully, and it was evident that few of those entered had undertaken any real practical work. Only a small number responded to the notion of biology as an inspiring topic concerned with living organisms, and it appeared to some examiners that it was chosen by school pupils as an easier alternative to either physics or chemistry.

Art and design

One of the most important changes which occurred in the life of secondary schools following the introduction of comprehensive education was the rejection of the notion that subjects such as woodwork, metalwork, cookery and dressmaking were merely handicrafts. It was recognized that the study of crafts was valuable as a means of acquiring skills and developing innate talent. Both the DES and the Inspectorate maintained that pupils should be given confidence in identifying, examining and solving problems in the use of materials. Design problems were selected which prompted involvement with mathematical, scientific, social, political and ethical issues, and the scientific methods of identification, examination and testing. Aesthetic principles were emphasized, together with the importance of pupils being able to communicate their ideas effectively. Central to the teaching of these subjects was the manipulative skill of exercising control by hand or tool in order to execute designs.

Similarly, the notion that art was a refuge of children without the aptitude for academic subjects was challenged forcefully. It was viewed as a means of promoting an appreciation of the work of the artist and the relationship of art to society. Pupils pursuing art courses were to be introduced to a variety of techniques, including painting, drawing, printmaking, ceramics, textiles and photography, and to be encouraged to show an awareness of shape, colour, and texture. Notions of art as the pursuit of the beautiful, or as a means of transmitting a cultural heritage, were ignored in favour of expression and demonstration of skill.

In art and design courses, candidates at A level sat three tests. The first required them to produce a pair of two-dimensional works. Paper A2 tested proficiency in one of nine crafts, including lettering and layout, calligraphy, pottery, modelling, puppetry and printmaking. The final paper, A3, was a written examination on the history and appreciation of art and architecture. It was stipulated that both art and kindred topics should be studied in relation to the needs of society, and a specialized knowledge of one part of the syllabus was required. Those who examined art and design courses during the 1970s found the work extremely wide-ranging in quality. It was clear from the variety of some submissions that candidates felt a 'deep awareness of the tragedy of human life', and had used the period of study allowed before the examination to good effect. A more disturbing aspect of the work, however, was found in the response to questions on the history and appreciation of art. Many candidates appeared to possess limited knowledge, with few being able to link the practical work to its underlying social and political theory:

> There appears to be a need for candidates to have the opportunity to discuss art more generally; to link painting with the other arts; to reach some conclusions about the value of artistic expression to man; to understand terms such as Romanticism, Classicism, and Realism more fully and to grasp some of the ideas behind an artist's work.[36]

Matters did not improve. In 1977 examiners were alarmed by the poor quality in almost all aspects of the examination. It was suggested that candidates had little idea of composition or colour. These comments appear to have prompted a determined effort to improve the quality of the work submitted in the succeeding years but, even so, answers on the history and appreciation of art remained weak, with many candidates reported to be too heavily reliant on memorized notes which they failed to relate to the requirements of the question.

Performance was just as disappointing in the 1980s. A few candidates continued to make use of the examination as a means of producing imaginative and interesting work, but overall quality was mediocre. There were very few examples of excellence in calligraphy and the work in pottery was well below standard. Examiners complained that candidates lacked the maturity of vision and thought which was an essential hallmark of A level work, and poor expression and examination technique remained a feature of the written paper.

Candidates at O level sat four different tests. The first involved producing a composition in colour. In the second they were required to produce a two-dimensional design. The third section tested proficiency in drawing or painting from observed forms, such as natural or mechanical objects. The final section was a written paper on the history and appreciation of European painting and architecture.

Examiners were generally satisfied with the quality of the practical work produced during the period. Few submissions were below standard, and many showed evidence of a lively and original approach to the subject material. Other forms of art work, however, notably collage and two-dimensional designs, were generally of a lower standard. As with A level, the quality of the work in the written paper caused greatest concern. Candidates were criticized for including too much irrelevant material and this aspect of the subject was clearly poorly taught. For instance, most Welsh schools concentrated on studies of the work of Italian painters, even though few such works could be seen in Wales.

Despite some examples of excellent work, the overall standard fell significantly during the 1980s. There was little to suggest that the local environment had been used as a source of inspiration and too much of the work produced was based on second-hand photographic material rather than on a personal reaction to an object which had been seen through a discerning eye.

In the CSE examination candidates were encouraged to develop an unrestricted and experimental approach to their work. Emphasis was placed on developing an awareness of the environment and a broad range of artistic techniques, including figure and still life composition, landscape painting and illustration. Again, examiners were generally disappointed and reiterated the complaint made in relation to O level that few candidates used their preparation time, or the inspiration of the local environment, to good effect.

Woodwork and metalwork

The A level examination in woodwork and metalwork included four components. The first comprised the history and technological aspect of the subject, including topics such as the development of furniture design, the evolution of machine tools since the mid-eighteenth century and bridge construction in the twentieth century; while the technology paper demanded detailed knowledge of materials, tools and construction processes. The second paper focused on design and drawing. The practical test gave candidates the opportunity to show their ability in the use and manipulation of material. The final paper required them to design and construct an item specified by the examiners. Reports on woodwork examinations reveal a general sense of disappointment. Practical work was the main area of strength, even though the designs selected were sometimes too ambitious and lacked attention to detail. The most depressing results were found in the section involving draughtsmanship and design. Little attention appeared to have been given to the details of plans, and most of the work was conventional and unoriginal. Similar observations were made by those who examined metalwork. Practical work was handled competently, but work on theory and design was poor, and rules such as British Standard 308 were not observed in drawing, while answers on the history and technology paper were superficial and mundane.

The O level woodwork examination tested skills in drawing, theory and practical application, with proficiency required in the construction of joints and the ability to use, turn and shape different types of wood. The overall quality of tool work was reckoned to be good, though it was hampered by a lack of general preparation and insufficient thought on issues such as the design of joints. As with A level, draughtsmanship was the weakest component of the examination. The work was handicapped by carelessness and failure to understand basic features such as elevation. Even after the examination schedules were changed in 1976 to reduce the emphasis on this element, answers to theory questions remained disappointing. Examiners maintained:

> Traditional and customary things in the workshop need to be questioned and investigated if the subject is to be used successfully for education in its true sense. The acceptance of more information disseminated by any means leads to complacency and lower levels of craftsmanship in the end.[37]

The quality of craftsmanship and practical work improved during the 1980s. A large number of ambitious and well-executed examples of carpentry were submitted which showed a mastery of construction methods as well as close attention to the finished product.

In metalwork, considerable emphasis was placed on the ability to set out and measure correctly, the removal of waste material, the skill of forging, joining materials and drilling, and lathe work and grinding. Practical work was carried out effectively, with most candidates evincing a sound knowledge of basic manipulative skills and a substantial minority of them produced outstanding work. The theory section, again, accounted for the poor performance of many candidates. Few were able to solve problems involving design considerations and solutions, especially when they were presented in a new context.

As with cognate subjects, greater emphasis was placed on practical skills in the CSE examination. A total of 35 per cent of marks was awarded for coursework, of which 25 per cent were for the quality of the finished product and 10 per cent for the design. A practical test under examination conditions represented a further 40 per cent of the overall marks. The focus of the work with metal was on simple forging, hammered metalwork, silversmithing, and simple machine operations and casting. The theory paper tested knowledge of safety in the workshop, an understanding of different types of metals and care of tools. Examiners found few satisfactory responses to the written paper. Descriptions of processes were often too brief and poor presentation marred the work of candidates who otherwise had a good grasp of general concepts. There was evidence that plans had been drawn up after the practical work had been completed and the answers on workshop safety reflected a dangerous level of ignorance. Nevertheless, the coursework consisted mainly of well-tried and proven small engineering jobs and some excellent examples of welding and foundry casting. Likewise, in woodwork, examiners were consistently impressed by the high standard of craftsmanship and the attention given to the finished product. Some complex technical aspects were handled competently and basic tool work was satisfactory. By the beginning of the 1980s, however, the number of candidates of moderate abilities had increased considerably, many of whom did not take the subject seriously.

Home economics

The home economics syllabus was divided into two parts. All candidates at A level studied a section examining the home and community, which included a consideration of the family in society. They, or their schools, then chose either to specialize in food and nutrition or clothing and textiles. During much of the 1970s the standard of the work in cookery disappointed the examiners. For instance, it was noted that little importance was attached to issues such as hygiene and economy in the use of materials. Similarly, few of those examined in dressmaking gave attention to the details of the work such as the reverse side of garments they had produced. Reports for the 1980s were more promising. The examiners reported that knowledge of issues such as nutrition had improved and answers on housing policy, inflation and the work of voluntary associations were of a very high standard.

Candidates at O level in cookery were expected to be familiar with the nature and value of different foodstuffs and with changes which occurred in food during the cooking process. Considerable emphasis was placed on the ability to plan meals for various types of people and occasions. The response to both sections of the examination varied considerably. In the practical tests examiners noted that few of those entered could prepare a meal to cost, and that vegetarian meals or salads were uninspiring. Orders of work were rarely completed satisfactorily and the use of materials was often extravagant.

The theoretical aspects of the subject were most disappointing. Not many candidates understood underlying scientific and nutritional principles, and many had been inadequately prepared for the written paper. Although more balanced meals were produced during the 1980s, poor examination technique and a tendency to be over-ambitious in choosing meals for preparation were factors which adversely affected performances in the subject. In dressmaking, candidates were commended for the great variety of garments produced and for the way their choice of materials had improved. The main variations were in the quality and standard of the theory paper, in which long and irrelevant answers failed to explain processes appropriately.

Practical work represented 60 per cent of the marks in the CSE paper. Candidates were expected to prepare a menu and order of work, and to be able to demonstrate an awareness of matters such as food value and cost. A separate theory paper tested knowledge of matters such as home management, the issues to be considered when purchasing a property, decoration, furnishing, safety and financial management. Again, this part of the examination was invariably the most disappointing aspect. The knowledge displayed was often rudimentary and many examinees experienced difficulty in writing a menu in the correct order. Moreover, little originality was shown in the practical work. For instance, there was a distinct lack of variety in the choice of dishes, garnish was not used appropriately and few gave a correct interpretation of the meaning of healthy eating.

Conclusion

The period from 1970 to 1988 was one of immense change in the educational system of England and Wales. By the 1980s some of the practical difficulties which arose out of the reorganization of secondary schools had been resolved and examiners were expressing greater satisfaction with the performance of candidates in external examinations. Their expectations did not change to any significant extent during this period. GCE A level remained primarily a test for those intending to pursue courses in higher education. Candidates were expected to show a detailed involvement with the subjects they had studied and to possess depth of knowledge and the ability to apply that knowledge through their studies in the classroom and independently. Throughout the period it was found that many candidates displayed a gift for memorizing factual material, but revealed weaknesses in understanding. Few had undertaken the background reading required by examiners and many relied almost exclusively on material provided by teachers as the basis for examination answers. Many focused on safe or relatively unchallenging topics. Poor grammar and expression, together with weaknesses in work involving numeracy skills, were matters that were commented upon throughout the 1970s and 1980s.

Teaching methods were also under scrutiny. Examiners' reports warned that the syllabus was not being regarded as a unified whole and that in some centres a broad range of topics had not been studied. The extent to which candidates had been given experience of practical work in science subjects varied. Performance in chemistry and biology was a matter of repeated comment, work on physical geography did not match that on the human aspect of the subject, and in English and Welsh candidates were often weak when commenting on issues such as style, language and grammar.

Moreover, there were few instances of knowledge or skills learnt in one subject being used to enrich work in others.

Some radical solutions to these problems were advocated. It was maintained that the A level examination should be considered as a qualification in its own right rather than as a test designed to assess those who wished to proceed to higher education, a view which met with strong resistance. Others maintained that its focus was too narrow and advocated the introduction of continental models which would enable candidates to pursue a much broader range of topics in less detail.[38] But the A level examination was preserved after the review of the curriculum and examinations at the end of the 1980s. It had undergone some modification in the 1980s with the first generation of 'common core' syllabuses, intended to address the perceived problem of undue diversity of content across the examination boards. Although the impact was variable across the subjects, it was the first acknowledgement that A level syllabuses carrying the same subject title should have some content in common.

The only substantial structural change occurred in those LEAs which decided to abandon the practice of teaching A level in secondary schools by developing tertiary colleges. This initiative was inspired by the belief that specialist teachers with an aptitude for A level work would be recruited to those institutions and that more effective teaching materials could be made available. Yet the changes were vigorously resisted by many within the teaching profession, not least by those who enjoyed the challenge and opportunity of providing advanced courses within schools.

GCE O level remained a central examination, taken by an increasing percentage of sixteen-year-olds, and was viewed as the goal for which to aim. The 1970s witnessed important innovations in the content of some subjects, but essentially candidates were expected to assimilate and regurgitate masses of information on a very broad range of topics. Reports suggest that some of those examined displayed a lively, imaginative and mature approach to their studies, but it was also clear that, for many of them, the experience was little more than a mechanical process of committing to memory notes provided by teachers, often in an uninspiring way.

Moreover, as with A level, candidates tended to focus on some parts of the syllabus at the expense of others, and there was a marked reluctance to answer questions on certain topics. The CSE examination struggled to gain recognition as a valuable qualification. A great deal of effort had been devoted to the concept of a second examination for school-leavers and the methods of teaching, assessment and the course contents and objectives were often pioneering. For instance, the CSE history examination focused on social and economic topics which received attention at the universities to a far greater extent than did the GCE examinations; pupils in English language and literature were expected to show evidence of personal involvement; work in modern languages recognized the value of oral proficiency. Yet throughout the period studied in this chapter, the CSE was believed to be an examination which catered for pupils who were not good enough for the O level course. Given the prevalence of this myopic view, its demise was inevitable. By the early 1980s a 'common core' syllabus examination, anticipating what would become, from 1986, the General Certificate of Secondary Education (GCSE), had been devised in mathematics, art and design, biology and geography, and the WJEC decided that separate O level and CSE examinations would not be held in those subjects after 1984. While the concept of a common examination was broadly accepted, the issue of differentiation remained a focus of considerable discussion.[39]

External examinations, and the standards which they were held to uphold, came under increasing scrutiny and criticism from professionals and media alike in this period. The GCE was the focus of concern for much of the 1970s, while the standard of the work at CSE was the main focus of comment in the 1980s. The most worrying feature was that 24.5 per cent of all sixteen-year-olds in Wales left school without any sort of certificate during most of the period studied in this chapter, a figure which was significantly higher than the average of 16.5 per cent in England during the same period. Schools were criticized for devoting too much attention to their most gifted pupils at the expense of a large number of the less able. As Illtyd Lloyd has suggested, the WJEC was criticized in some quarters for being too rigid and inflexible in its approach to the CSE, although he acknowledges that it was a local authority in Wales which pioneered the somewhat confusingly named but unique Certificate of Education examination geared solely to the less able pupil, and later taken up by the WJEC.[40]

Factors such as the growing impact of the mass media, economic problems, industrial unrest and an increase in social alienation and exclusion influenced the overall performance of pupils, and schools were expected to develop appropriate responses to the issues which confronted them. It was clear that the curriculum, syllabus and examination system needed to address these issues. Each year individuals were disappointed with their results. Some later re-entered the education system and flourished under different guidance and inspiration. Assisting those failing in, and failed by, the school system remained one of the objectives of the adult education service, and the number who fell into this category was alarmingly large. These issues were recognized by the WJEC during the 1970s and 1980s. As a body it constantly reiterated the importance of increasing the resources made available to enable Welsh schools to provide pupils with the support necessary to attain better results. Yet at no time was the integrity of the Board's qualifications compromised to enable pupils to achieve better grades. During the 1980s the WJEC, in common with other examining boards, faced the immense task of revising its schedules, syllabuses and assessment methods in readiness for the introduction of a new examination to replace the O level and CSE. The Board was convinced of the need for reform and had supported initiatives to develop a common syllabus in many subjects. Yet, like many others in the education service, the WJEC was to face an unprecedented challenge to notions about the purpose and objectives of education as central government began to assert its influence more determinedly than at any time since the Second World War.

References

1 Some of the authors of the Spens and Norwood Reports had expressed doubts about whether the creation of three different types of schools to serve children from the same community was a desirable option: Public Record Office, ED136/749.
2 For instance, pupils who did not gain entry into their local grammar school could be offered places at a neighbouring one if their marks were higher than those of candidates who had passed the test in the other school's catchment area. This meant, for instance, that some pupils who failed to gain entry into the Llanelli Grammar schools were allocated places at Gwendraeth Valley Grammar School which had room for a larger proportion of its cohort of pupils.
3 G. E. Jones, *The Education of a Nation* (Cardiff, 1997), pp. 143–4.
4 As a result, if comprehensive education was to be introduced, a major programme to build new schools was required. LEAs had to consider their plans against a background of limited resources and a criterion for the construction of new schools which gave priority to those areas where the population was expanding.
5 The conversion of single-sex schools to serve the needs of all pupils required the construction of new workshops, toilet blocks and changing rooms.
6 Illtyd Lloyd, 'A period of change – working for progress: Secondary education in Wales, 1965–1985', in G. E. Jones (ed.), *Education, Culture and Society: Some Perspectives on the Nineteenth and Twentieth Centuries* (Cardiff, 1991), pp. 84–106.
7 These problems were compounded by an increase in the incidence of arson of school buildings during the 1970s.
8 Welsh Office, *Comprehensive Schools in Wales: Year I, II and III. Education Issues 1* (Cardiff, HMSO, 1978), pp. 6–10.
9 David H. Hargreaves, *The Challenge for the Comprehensive School: Culture, Curriculum and Community* (London, 1982), pp. 1–30.
10 Hargreaves, pp. 20–5.
11 G. E. Jones, *The Education of a Nation* (Cardiff, 1997), p. 140.
12 Jones, *The Education of a Nation*, pp. 148–54; G. E. Jones, *Which Nation's Schools: Direction and Devolution in Welsh Education in the Twentieth Century* (Cardiff, 1990), pp. 195–7; Paul Francis, *Beyond Control? A Study of Discipline in the Comprehensive School* (London, 1975), pp. 1–58; Phillip Whitehead, *The Writing on the Wall, Britain in the Seventies* (London, 1985), pp. 202–20; Rhodes Boyson, *Speaking my Mind: the Autobiography of Rhodes Boyson* (London, 1995), pp. 83–106; Rhodes Boyson and Charles B. Cox, *Black Paper 1975: the Fight for Education* (London, 1975), pp. 1–5.
13 In 1966 the National Association for the Teaching of English published its report, *English Examined: a survey of O level Language Papers*, which challenged the notion of a division between language and literature and maintained that key elements of English examinations should be revised.

14 Frances Stevens, *English and Examinations: What Is and Is Not Formally Examinable, and What Is and Is Not in Fact Examined; With Special Reference to Examination at 11 and 18* (London, 1970); Geoffrey Thornton, *Language at Work (Schools Council Programme on Linguistics and English Teaching Vol. 2)* (Harlow, 1972); Ian Forsyth, *Language, Classroom and Examinations (Schools Council Programme on Linguistics and English Teaching Vol. 4)* (London, 1974).
15 *A Language for Life: Report of the Committee of Inquiry Appointed by the Secretary of State for Education and Science under the Chairmanship of Sir Alan Bullock* (London, 1975).
16 Her Majesty's Inspectorate, *Curriculum 11–16: Working Papers by HM Inspectorate: A Contribution to Current Debate* (London, HMSO, 1977), pp. 19–52.
17 During the 1970s the syllabus included the work of authors such as Browning, Chaucer, George Orwell, Jane Austen and E. M. Forster.
18 WJEC, *Annual Reports of the Examiners*, 1974, 1977, 1979, English.
19 WJEC, *Annual Reports of the Examiners*, 1976, English. In the essay question candidates were invited to consider issues such as the state of religion in Wales, alcoholism, the problem of vandalism, poor housing and corruption in public life.
20 The suggested reading list included a broad range of novels, including works by Charlotte Brontë, Gerald Durrell, C. S. Forester, Anne Frank, William Golding, D. H. Lawrence, Arthur Conan Doyle, Neville Shute and Charles Dickens.
21 WJEC, *Annual Reports of the Examiners*, 1983, CSE English.
22 WJEC, *Annual Reports of the Examiners*, 1974, 1979, 1980, 1987, Welsh. Few candidates were able to compose an effective essay which presented a factual argument or personal standpoint, not least because of the tendency to use the opportunity to vent their convictions without basing their argument on reasoned judgements.
23 WJEC, *Annual Reports of the Examiners*, 1976, Welsh Language.
24 WJEC, *Annual Reports of the Examiners*, 1987, Welsh Language.
25 WJEC, *Annual Reports of the Examiners*, 1972, French.
26 WJEC, *Annual Reports of the Examiners*, 1977, 1979, German. Significantly the quality fell markedly in 1977, a feature attributed by the examiners to the decision not to appoint language assistants during the previous academic year.
27 WJEC, *Annual Reports of the Examiners*, 1972, 1974, Latin.
28 F. R. Dobson, *A New School Geography* (London, 1967); E. L. Marchant, *The Teaching of Geography at School Level* (London, 1971); Department of Education and Science, *School Geography in the Changing Curriculum* (London, HMSO, 1974).
29 WJEC, *Annual Reports of the Examiners*, 1974, History.
30 WJEC, *Annual Reports of the Examiners*, 1977, History. Stock answers derived from notes which had been dictated were commonplace, a comment both on the effort of the pupils and the methods adopted by a significant number of those charged with teaching the subject.

31 WJEC, *Annual Reports of the Examiners*, 1980, History.
32 Schools Council, *Report of the Working Group on Mixed-ability Teaching in Mathematics: a survey of current practice* (London, 1977).
33 WJEC, *Annual Reports of the Examiners*, 1986, Mathematics. Some 2,000 candidates failed to gain more than 30 per cent of marks in this year.
34 Dorothy J. Alexander, *Nuffield Secondary Science: an evaluation* (London, 1974).
35 Her Majesty's Inspectorate, *Curriculum 11–16: Working Papers by HM Inspectorate: A Contribution to Current Debate* (London, HMSO, 1977) pp. 19–52.
36 WJEC, *Annual Reports of the Examiners*, 1972, Art.
37 WJEC, *Annual Reports of the Examiners*, 1976, Woodwork.
38 Schools Council, *Report of the Second Working Party on the Sixth Form Curriculum and Examinations* (London, 1973).
39 Schools Council, *A Common System of Examining at 16+* (London, 1971).
40 Illtyd R. Lloyd, 'A period of change – working for progress: Secondary education in Wales, 1965–1985', in G. E. Jones (ed.), *Education, Culture and Society: Some Perspectives on the Nineteenth and Twentieth Centuries* (Cardiff, 1991), pp. 85–106.

Chapter 5
Examining the New Wales 1988–2000

Introduction

The end of the 1980s witnessed major changes in the education system in England and Wales, reflected both in the curriculum of the schools and in the method of examination and testing. Schools became subject to the control of central government to a far greater extent than had been the case since the end of the Second World War, while the influence and autonomy of the local education authorities (LEAs) and the teaching profession over policy was eroded substantially. LEAs had devoted considerable resources to planning educational services on the basis of educational, social and economic need, a process aided by the fact that all schools served a fixed catchment area. Support services, such as free school meals and education welfare provision, had been developed, and research and evaluation work was undertaken to assist with the development of policy. The creation of this structure was viewed by many professional bodies and individual educationists as essential to the maintenance of an effective education system. During the late 1970s and early 1980s, however, there were vociferous demands from the right of the political spectrum for the introduction of measures to increase parental choice and to remove the power of the LEAs and professional bodies, criticized as wasteful by right-wing commentators. For instance, in a pamphlet published in 1988, Sheila Lawlor, a leading figure on the far right, denounced the LEAs as 'bureaucratic' and urged that their role should be diminished to that of agencies charged solely with administering the transfer of funds to schools.[1] She maintained that too much money was being spent on support services at the expense of schools, so producing a 'dull uniformity' in the education system and undermining the autonomy of schools:

> For as long as LEAs continue to have unquestioned responsibility for running the system, they will continue to undermine the autonomy of schools, prejudicing the prospects of excellence and diversity; and continue to direct resources from schools in the interests not of higher standards of teaching, but of high levels of support.[2]

Right-wing opinion also wanted the division of administrative and support services into competing, privatized, commercial groups, with school building programmes based on a competitive market rather than on a survey of need, and educational research limited to the compilation of information for parents on details of schools, their character, ethos and examination results. In addition, it was suggested that all responsibility for developing teaching resources should fall on the individual teacher in order to encourage initiative and diversity. Sports centres, swimming pools and 'games-pitches' should become sports clubs, established as independent charitable trusts.[3]

These arguments were forcefully opposed by representatives of the LEAs, the unions and most of those with professional expertise in the field of education.[4] Yet the Conservative government proceeded to introduce a succession of measures aimed at transforming the education system, beginning with the Education Act of 1986. First, it reduced the influence of the LEAs by increasing the representation and role of parents and local businesses on governing bodies, and by devolving greater responsibilities to those bodies through Local Management of Schools (LMS).[5] Second, although the notion of schools competing for capital finance was not introduced, LEAs had to adopt a new funding mechanism which included an element of competitiveness in attracting capital for development. Third, by the 1988 Education Act, schools were given the opportunity to become independent grant maintained institutions, free of LEA control. Bodies such as the Welsh LEAs and the WJEC objected strongly to many of these changes which, they maintained, were inimical to the ethos which underpinned the education service in Wales. Commenting on the proposals contained in the 1993 Education Bill the WJEC stated:

Major aspects of the Bill will prejudice the community ethos of education in Wales, and nullify the spirit of co-operation as between schools . . . it is only a system built on a true partnership of the various interests – parents, teachers, governors, and local education authorities, which will allow the essential community needs of schooling to flourish and grow. The intensified market ethos is not the appropriate vehicle; the competitive ethos should not predominate. Surely the twenty-first century requires young people who have attained high academic standards, but also young people who have been imbued with a co-operative ethos and with a cultural identity reflecting their role both as citizens of their local communities and of the wider national and international communities.[6]

The structure of the examinations system was itself under review. Schools were given freedom to enter pupils for examinations set by different boards in different subjects, so that the virtual monopoly enjoyed by bodies such as the WJEC was ended. The WJEC had always prided itself on being an examining board for Wales, working in partnership with schools and colleges.[7] In 1995 it declared:

There are facets of public service in general, and education in particular, where the competitive ethos is inappropriate. The prime objective of any system of public examination must be the maintenance of education standards. It is critical for students and the public to have confidence in the consistency of standards year on year. It has been, and continues to be, the view of the WJEC that an examination marketplace with different examination boards competing for candidate entries is in conflict with the maintenance of standards.[8]

Fears were continually expressed that the changes heralded the introduction of a free market in education and that policy would be geared solely towards assessment and examinations. Yet in Wales the impact of these changes were ameliorated somewhat by the country's distinctive characteristics. Demographic considerations meant that parental choice was severely limited in many parts of Wales, including most rural counties and some valley areas.[9] Opposition to grant maintained status was strong. Most LEAs successfully resisted attempts to induce schools to opt out of LEA control and they promoted a vision of the education system which emphasized the importance of a unified, community-based approach rather than the competitive ethos advocated by central government. Although the education system which evolved in Wales during this period could not be regarded as distinctive, the fact that only a few schools chose to become grant maintained meant that by the mid-1990s the school structure was substantially different from that in England.[10] And, ironically, the WJEC has become a net beneficiary of the market system in examinations, examining more pupils from England than the numbers of Welsh pupils examined by English boards.

The second major change witnessed during this period affected the curriculum and the way in which pupils were assessed. We noted at the end of the previous chapter that scrutiny of the examination system had become a national pastime among politicians, professionals and the media. During the 1980s it had become evident that the quality of the work submitted in the CSE examination had deteriorated, not least because schools took the decision to enter as many candidates as possible for the O level examination.[11] The notion that the top 20 per cent of pupils would be entered for O level and that the CSE examination would be taken by some 40 per cent of the cohort had largely been abandoned. It was also clear that greater provision should be made for pupils at the lower end of the ability range. These issues were particularly prevalent in Wales where the Schools Council Committee for Wales' report, *The Curriculum and Assessment in Wales*, published in 1981,[12] concluded that examination results at the lower end of the ability range in Wales were noticeably poor in comparison with those in England. The report highlighted the fact that the WJEC had given little encouragement to school-based Mode III CSE examinations and had promoted its own standardized examinations instead; it concluded that schools were too academic in their approach and that the rigid division of examinations hampered the provision of an adequate service for 'borderline' candidates. These views were echoed by many advocates of comprehensive schools who maintained that the principle of an integrated education was undermined by the separate examinations and that the separation of O level and CSE was an obstacle to the development of mixed-ability teaching methods. As a result, a powerful coalition, including the Schools Council, teachers' unions and some examining boards such as the WJEC, became convinced of the need for radical changes in the examination structure during the 1970s and 1980s, and began the work by developing common syllabuses in geography, biology, art and design and mathematics.[13]

The Conservative government was, however, initially reluctant to support the change to a common examination at 16 and it viewed the organizations responsible for educational research and curricular innovation with some suspicion. In 1981 it announced the abolition of the Schools Council, which had been criticized by the authors of the *Black Papers* on education as an unaccountable body of professional educationists, out of touch with the wishes of parents and the needs of industry.[14] It was replaced by the Secondary Examinations Council (SEC), appointed by the Secretary of State and responsible mainly for the development of examinations. This change indicated that in future the emphasis would be placed on examining, assessing and testing rather than upon broader notions of curriculum development.[15]

The abolition of the Schools Council coincided with the announcement of consultation over the future of examinations. Two principles were to be considered. The first was whether public examinations should be based on standard criteria; the second, whether a common examination should be introduced for those aged sixteen. In both cases the government decided that the evidence warranted action. Concern had been expressed that examinations set by some bodies were less demanding than those of others, and it was decided to adopt a uniform set of criteria against which expectations would be judged. These would be determined by the SEC. This meant abandoning the cohort reference system whereby candidates were awarded grades depending on comparisons with the overall quality of the work submitted in a particular year. In the event, technical difficulties in awarding grades on the basis of generalized criteria, rather than on total marks, proved insuperable, so the ambition of making the new GCSE examination 'criterion-referenced' was not realized.

Furthermore, the GCSE assessment method emphasized the importance of testing what pupils knew rather than identifying weaknesses in their learning. Differentiation would be secured either through graded questions or separate examination papers, with the result that, although all candidates might sit for the same examination qualification, they could be streamed into ability-based groups. The task of developing the new examinations proved immensely difficult, especially as it was intended that the best features of O level and CSE should be retained. A central place was to be given to coursework, syllabuses were to be made more practical and less theoretical, and an emphasis placed on oral as well as written skills. Significantly, although teachers and other education professionals were represented on subject committees, there was no attempt to engage the broader community in discussion either of the curriculum, or of the syllabuses for individual subjects, or for the methods of assessment.

The introduction of the GCSE was rapidly followed by the decision to develop a specified school curriculum which would be studied by all pupils from the age of five until they sat the examination at sixteen. Commentators on the right of the political spectrum, concerned that 'liberal' subjects had been introduced at the expense of English, mathematics and science and that basic skills had been neglected, advocated a core curriculum.[16] Yet the proposals outlined by Kenneth Baker, Secretary of State for Education and Science from 1986 until 1989, went much further than the notion of this common core. Under the terms of the 1988 Education Act, mathematics, English and science were to be core subjects, together with Welsh in Welsh-speaking schools, while history, geography, technology, music, art, and physical education were to be foundation subjects, together with one modern language for pupils aged 11–16.[17] It was intended that this National Curriculum would aim to satisfy two basic objectives. First, it should 'promote the spiritual, moral, cultural, mental and physical development of pupils at the school and of society'; and, second, 'prepare such pupils for the opportunities, responsibilities and experiences of adult life'.[18] School life was to be divided into key stages: Key Stage 1 (pupils aged 4–7), Key Stage 2 (pupils aged 8–11), Key Stage

3 (pupils aged 12–14) and Key Stage 4 (pupils aged 15–16). At each stage children were to be provided with:

a) the knowledge, skills and understanding which pupils of different abilities and maturities are expected to have by the end of each key stage;
b) the matters, skills and processes which are required to be taught to pupils of different abilities and maturities during each key stage;
c) an assessment at the end of each key stage to ascertain what they had achieved in relation to set attainment targets for that stage.[19]

The implementation of the proposals was to be directed in England by the National Curriculum Council (NCC), and, after some discussion, a separate Curriculum Council for Wales (CCW) was established.[20] The NCC was to review the curriculum and establish subject panels to consider what should be included in each syllabus.[21] Significantly the nation was defined as 'England and Wales'. Most of the early initiative came from the Department of Education and Science (as it was known until 1992) and, although the Welsh Office was involved in the early planning of the new concept, there was little consideration of the desirability of a completely separate and distinctive National Curriculum for Wales. Indeed, initially it was believed that the National Curriculum in Wales would differ only marginally from that in England, with the exception that Welsh would be a core subject.[22] Nevertheless, the CCW rapidly developed a more distinctive approach and insisted that the National Curriculum in Wales be amended to take account of issues specific to the nation's needs and experiences. Only in history, however, was Wales accorded a separate curriculum working committee, equivalent to England's history working group, a significant factor in view of the controversy surrounding the syllabus for the subject in England.[23]

As a result of the CCW's initiatives, the National Curriculum eventually included separate orders for Wales in four subjects – history, geography, art and music – which specified that Welsh dimensions should be considered in studying these subjects. The main differences lay in the programmes of study, issues that are discussed below. The CCW also recognized that the curriculum in Wales as a whole should be distinctive and appointed a committee which published a consultation paper, *Developing a Curriculum Cymreig*. In its introduction it was stated:

> The great variety in its topography, history, language, occupations, social customs, traditions and outlook have led to differences in shades of opinion and perspectives. Nevertheless, Wales undoubtedly has its own distinctive cultural dimension which manifests itself not only in those areas of Wales where Welsh is the main spoken language of the community, but also in those areas of Wales which have become more culturally diverse.[24]

The Curriculum Cymreig review studied subjects for which there were separate orders for Wales and also considered those subjects which had common orders with England. In some subjects such as mathematics, science and technology it was acknowledged that identifying a Welsh perspective would be difficult, although Welsh contributions to these areas of study could be recognized. It was emphasized that the ethos of every school in Wales should reflect the nation's cultural inheritance, in both Welsh and English, and that pupils should be introduced to a variety of experiences that promoted an understanding of their own national identity while developing an awareness of cultural diversity and broader perspectives.

Underpinning the assessment arrangements for the new National Curriculum was a system initiated by the government-appointed Task Group on Assessment and Testing (TGAT). Its report had proposed a system which assessed how pupils progressed at the end of each key stage. Ten levels of attainment in each subject were to be drawn up, setting targets against which pupils' work would be measured.[25] The GCSE was not replaced by a new Key Stage 4 assessment as it was accepted that it would be unwise to replace the GCSE after such a short existence. Sir Ron Dearing was asked by the government to undertake a review of the National Curriculum and assessment ahead of his appointment as Chairman of the newly established School Curriculum and Assessment

Authority. One of the recommendations of this review, carried out in Wales jointly with the Curriculum Council for Wales, was that the ten-level scale would not be appropriate for use in grading GCSE examinations.[26] It was authoritatively claimed that the GCSE had established itself as a rigorous and standard test for children aged sixteen and over. According to Her Majesty's Inspectors:

> The GCSE has proved to be a successful examination. It has resulted in marked improvements in the quality of learning and the boards are certain those standards have been maintained. The examination has increased pupils' motivation and raised teachers' expectations, both of which are crucial to effective learning. The individual subjects of the curriculum have been enriched and many of the disadvantages of the previous dual system of examination have been removed. The increased requirement for assessed coursework has helped to raise the level of achievement and has provided a fairer and more solid system of assessment.[27]

Although the GCSE was to remain the assessment for Key Stage 4 it was acknowledged that it would have to be amended to meet the requirements of the National Curriculum and that the A level schedules would also have to be revised.[28] It was recognized that, in some subjects, radical changes would be required to make the transition as smooth as possible.

The Dearing Report also considered the scope and manageability of the National Curriculum.[29] Critics on the political right used the opportunity to reiterate their view that the scope of the National Curriculum was too wide. For instance, Robert Skidelsky, a former chairman of the School Examinations and Assessment Council, maintained it should have been confined to the core subjects of English, mathematics and Science and that its focus should have been on reasserting traditional teaching methods and subject content.[30] Skidelsky also made pointed criticism of the recent emphasis on assessment methods, most particularly the emphasis on testing what pupils could do. The Dearing Report found that, despite the government's intention to the contrary, the National Curriculum was taking up almost all teaching time in most schools and that, if this was to be changed, then the degree to which the curriculum was prescribed would have to be changed and the number of statements of attainment reduced.[31] There was a widespread feeling that assessment, recording and reporting was placing too much strain on teachers. As a result, it was proposed that the number of mandatory subjects at Key Stage 4 should be reduced.[32] It also proposed that the ten-level scale, adopted to provide a structure for progression in learning, should be modified by replacing statements of attainment with 'broad descriptions of the standard of work required' and enabling teachers to exert a stronger degree of professional judgement. The argument in favour of abandoning the notion of positive testing was, however, rejected.[33]

The CCW undertook a parallel investigation in Wales and, in common with the Dearing Report, it found evidence of broad support for a statutory curriculum within a range of options at Key Stage 4. It also found that there was a great deal of support for the emphasis on developing skills alongside factual knowledge and that coursework was accepted as an integral part of the assessment methods. It was also clear that a majority of teachers and others involved in the delivery of the education service wanted a period of stability in order that changes to the curriculum and assessment techniques could be assimilated.[34]

The WJEC, in common with other examining bodies, addressed the need to amend its assessment techniques for GCSE, while ensuring that the grades awarded to candidates reflected their capabilities, both in factual knowledge and in an array of skills. As overall results in GCSE improved in both England and Wales during the 1990s, critics of the new system both within the education profession and elsewhere voiced concern that standards had been allowed to decline and that the assessment methods used both for the National Curriculum and for GCSE lacked rigour. The furore was far more evident in England than in Wales. Nevertheless, before devolution, Wales was drawn in. In England, the Office for Standards in Education (OFSTED), headed by the Chief Inspector of Schools, Chris Woodhead and cheerleader for government policy, launched a determined effort to overcome weaknesses in the schools service. He emphasized the need for regular testing, reiterated the importance of basic skills and looked favourably upon the notion of a standard teaching method which reduced the amount of discretion enjoyed by teachers over what methods to employ in the classroom. It was emphasized that the education received by each pupil should be tailored to meet his or her individual needs, which resulted in a greater weight being given to issues such as differentiation of work. This system sought to identify by means of league tables and 'special measures' those 'failing' schools in which pupils did not attain a satisfactory performance. The notion that financial problems and social or economic factors could explain poor performance was increasingly rejected.

The Labour government elected in May 1997 proved reluctant to challenge Woodhead's approach and supported many of OFSTED's initiatives as a means of improving educational standards. Significantly, little effort was made to restore the notion of comprehensive education; grant maintained schools were not returned to LEA control and the future of existing grammar schools was to be determined by limited ballots, not of all parents in a given area. Furthermore, prominent Labour politicians increasingly emphasized the desirability of diversity within the education system and some of them questioned the notion of one secondary school catering for the needs of all pupils from a certain area.

In Wales the establishment of the National Assembly for Wales in 1999 offered the prospect of a more distinctive approach to education policy. The structure of education was different, not least because Wales had few grant maintained and faith schools, and, as has been noted above, the notion of parents choosing where to educate their children was impractical in many areas. One significant step was the decision, taken in the summer of 2001, to abandon the practice of publishing league tables of secondary schools based on examination results. This was to be the first of numerous measures initiated by the Welsh Assembly which increasingly differentiated practice in Wales from that in England.

English

The examination schedules for A level English continued to emphasize the need for candidates to be introduced to a broad range of English literature, including prose, verse and drama, together with works from the medieval and early modern periods and contemporary works.[35] As in previous years, one paper included a requirement for some detailed study of texts by 'major authors' (Chaucer, Milton, Shakespeare) while the second paper offered a broader choice and approach to study. In 1979 a third paper testing critical appreciation through unseen poetry, prose and drama (two to be answered) was introduced. Another innovation in 1984 was assessment of coursework in place of the second paper – first offered by a consortium of schools and, in due course, incorporated as an option within the main syllabus.

Having stayed at around 3,000 during the 1980s the number of candidates entered for examination had increased to 3,801 in 1992. Overall performance improved slightly. Grade C or above was obtained by 45.5 per cent of candidates in 1989, rising to 49.8 per cent in 1994. The percentage securing a grade A also increased, from 8.0 per cent in 1989 to 11.1 per cent in 1994. Examiners found that textual knowledge was generally sound, although many candidates had difficulty in shaping information to meet the needs of the question. Poor expression, spelling and grammar remained a source of difficulty. In 1994 it was noted that where candidates had been invited to make connections between their own life experiences and the issues being discussed in the texts, interesting and relevant discussions had been produced, and the open text method of examination paper A2, where general response rather than textual knowledge was tested, was commended. It was also noted that an increasing proportion of candidates were familiar with issues such as style and literary technique neglected by previous generations, and that background knowledge of the history of the period in which texts had been written had improved.

The move to a single GCSE examination (graded A–G) in 1988, replacing GCE O level and CSE, was preceded by a pilot 'common syllabus', providing experience in meeting the challenge of setting papers accessible to the full range of ability. The first GCSE examinations offered a choice between 50 per cent or 20 per cent written coursework; briefly, between 1990 and 1993, an option assessed entirely through coursework was offered. With GCSE, the inclusion of speaking and listening (until then assessed for CSE but not O level) became a feature: this has remained since, with a variety of methods of reporting this either as a separate grade or contributing to the overall English grade.

In the first GCSE examinations no separate statutory orders for Wales were issued and it was intended that pupils would be introduced to the same broad range of literature as their counterparts in England.[36] There was, for instance, no specific instruction that a module on Anglo-Welsh literature should be pursued.[37] The examiners found that the overall performance in the examination was good. For instance, in 1992, of 35,385 candidates entered, nearly one half (47.1 per cent) gained grade C or above, while 7.3 per cent obtained the highest grade. Examiners found that many candidates had shown interest in the subject, and an imaginative response was engendered by some questions.[38] The poetry section showed a sound mastery of the texts, many of the essays being stylish and showing a good command of vocabulary.

The format of the examination was changed in 1994 to accommodate differentiated papers (equating to grades A*–E and F–G, though from 1998 onwards, in line with a large number of subjects, differentiated papers covered grades A*–D and C–G) and to limit written coursework to 20 per cent. Examiners praised the response to the tier 1 paper, which was acknowledged to be demanding, not least because it required sixteen-year-olds to write in a variety of forms under examination conditions. The reports on the tier 2 papers were also favourable. Many scripts impressed the examiners and indicated that candidates had enjoyed the course and had been genuinely interested in the subject. The examiners found that:

> In some cases, GCSE *English* seemed to leave the candidates drained of all emotion as they first worried about the fate of the child in the supermarket and then experienced guilt and outrage on behalf of the Amazonian Indians.[39]

Similarly in English literature examiners found that many candidates had responded sensitively to the texts and there were fewer instances of regurgitation of classroom notes. During the early 1990s more than half of the entry each year obtained a grade C or above, with more than 10 per cent obtaining grade A. Teachers were commended for having set appropriate coursework assignments which regularly showed a remarkable degree of maturity and sophistication. The main weaknesses were found in empathy tasks (writing from the point of view of a particular character) which limited candidates' ability to comment on matters such as form and style. The reform of the examination schedules in 1994 reduced the number of questions and allowed candidates access to some texts during the examination. The response confirmed the evidence that the study of English literature had been an enjoyable experience and the use of tiered papers was found to have enabled less able candidates to perform creditably.

Welsh

During the late 1980s the method of assessing A level Welsh was changed. The difficulty of writing creative prose under examination conditions was recognized and candidates were now expected to produce a folio which included a selection of different forms of creative writing produced during the two years of their A level course.[40] The formal examination concentrated on testing candidates in matters such as language and reading comprehension, and a selection of literature which included the work of medieval and early modern authors, as well as a varied selection of more recent writing. It was expected that candidates should be able to express their thoughts in a clear, accurate and lucid style and that their answers should be inspired by a familiarity with a broad range of Welsh literature, beyond that studied as part of the course.

In addition to studying certain texts in depth, candidates were expected to be able to respond at a more general level, to evaluate complete works and to comment on style, literary allusions and content. The reports suggest that, although some excellent responses were submitted, the overall quality varied considerably. There was a small number of excellent candidates each year, for instance the number who obtained a grade A stood at 11.5 per cent in 1989, 10.9 per cent in 1990, 10.4 per cent in 1992 and 12.5 per cent in 1994. On the other hand, the percentage securing a grade C or lower stood at 61.0 per cent in 1989 and 61.5 per cent in 1994. Many answers were marred by poor expression, limited vocabulary and grammatical inaccuracies.[41] Particular problems were identified with the use of negatives and apostrophes, and few candidates paid heed to the conventions of underlining the name of the book or using inverted commas when referring to a poem.[42] It was also noted that the folio work in too many centres concentrated on a very limited range of tasks.

At the GCSE stage the aims of the Welsh language course for those for whom Welsh was their first language were described as being:

> ... to foster positive attitudes towards the Welsh Language by stimulating interest in and enthusiasm for it, to show its study brings enjoyment and satisfaction to the mind, the imagination and the intellect and to encourage the candidates' attachment to it ... [and] to develop accurate, appropriate and clear expression in both the written and spoken language.[43]

Candidates were required to demonstrate their skill at written composition by producing a folio which included two pieces based on their imagination, two presenting information and two discussing an idea or a standpoint. The written examination tested comprehension, and an oral test assessed the ability to communicate effectively in order to convey information, discuss thoughts and standpoints, and describe experiences and feelings. Examiners were, in general, pleased with the response to the GCSE examination. The number of candidates awarded a grade A rose from 9.3 per cent in 1990 to 12.7 per cent in 1994, and there was an improvement in the percentage who obtained grade C or above, which increased from 47.2 per cent to 57.6 per cent during the same period. Examiners found that the quality of oral work improved steadily, with more candidates being familiar with Welsh idioms and modes of speech.[44] The creative work submitted as coursework was often impressive, and examiners expressed satisfaction that the new method of assessment assisted less able candidates to perform creditably.[45] Nevertheless, some irritating mistakes continued to cause concern to the examiners. Knowledge of sentence structure was sometimes weak and many candidates tended to compress words together, suggesting that little attention was devoted to the study of the structure of the language.[46] Some of the topics chosen for factual presentation were inappropriate because of their superficial nature, and folios tended to concentrate on certain genres of writing at the expense of others.[47]

The Welsh literature syllabus sought to generate interest in a wide range of genres and to encourage those who pursued the course to read widely and study examples of standard literature in depth in order to foster an awareness of both style and content. It was expected they would be able to respond intelligently both orally and in writing, and be familiar with the nation's literary heritage and the way in which it was conveyed through television, radio, tape and film. The examination was structured in such a way as to assess ability to read an extended piece of prose, together with knowledge and understanding of literary texts.[48] Examiners found that some of the coursework was particularly perceptive and the quality of the presentation often impressive.[49] The response to poetry suggested candidates had a deeper involvement than in the past, even though answers on style remained weak and some candidates continued to devote more attention to content than analysis. In addition, it was found that candidates were very good at relating their literary studies to the issues confronting the modern world, indicating that they had a thorough understanding of the aims of authors and sympathy with the thoughts and experiences they sought to convey.

Modern languages

The syllabus in modern languages required A level candidates to study a common core which included translation, composition in the target language, reading and listening comprehension, as well as conversation. They were then allowed to choose one of two optional papers, one involving the study of literary texts, the other examining the language in greater detail.[50] Although the quality of oral work in French was satisfactory, examiners were not impressed by the overall standard of the written work.[51] In the literature section it was noted that answers were too vague and contained irrelevant material. Many pupils had relied on notes provided by their teachers, which they had committed to memory, and an alarmingly large number could not apply what they knew to the requirements of the question. Knowledge of French grammar was sometimes distressingly poor, many candidates had difficulty with the use of negatives and the future tense, and few had a sound command of idioms.

The quality of the work in German was also variable. Some candidates were found to have produced excellent compositions but translation into German proved challenging and many candidates produced work which lacked understanding of German syntax and grammar. In the literature section a few had not studied their texts thoroughly. For instance, in 1996 it was noted that some passages of translation could not be understood and oral work was hampered by limited vocabulary.

The GCSE courses in modern languages sought to promote the skills of oral and written communication, to provide sufficient knowledge for further study, work and leisure, and also to offer a glimpse of the culture and way of life of the relevant country. It was intended that all candidates would develop a core of basic skills while some would progress to a more advanced command of the language. The core objectives were to ensure pupils could understand specific details orally and in writing, while the more advanced objectives required them to be able to ask and respond orally and write brief compositions in the target language. The main topics included information about family and friends, the time, weather and dates, travel, food and drink, shopping, leisure and school routine.[52]

The number of candidates entered for examination increased. For instance, the total number entered for French rose from 8,398 in 1990 to 11,720 in 1994. Overall performance remained satisfactory. More than half of the cohort gained a grade C and over a fifth a grade A each year. The French examiners commended the work at the basic level.[53] In the oral test many candidates had been able to sustain simple conversations and most had shown a good command of vocabulary. In spite of this, examiners were regularly disappointed at the quality of the work at the higher stage where few candidates could converse at the expected level. In the written paper candidates were hampered by deficiencies in their knowledge of verb forms and tenses, and adjectival agreements. Few could write intelligent and creative prose, and the quality of translation was generally below what was expected. Similarly in German, which was taken by far fewer candidates than French, examiners found the overall quality of basic listening and oral work to be satisfactory but there was a very wide range of work produced at the higher level. Some of the writing was very simplistic, and marred by careless spelling and lack of attention to detail. Grammatical faults, such as inaccuracies in the use of verbs, widespread ignorance of the gender of common nouns, and a failure to use capital letters for nouns were regularly highlighted.

Geography

The aims of A level geography were to introduce students to a broad selection of environments and regions in differing stages of development, and to develop the practical and intellectual skills which were required to understand key ideas, models and theories in the context of the environment, conservation and human welfare. Candidates were required to study core subjects such as land formation, the weather and climate, and ecosystems, as well as aspects of human geography like agricultural systems, manufacturing geography and studies of the urban world. The emphasis on practical skills, including statistical analysis, was confirmed and candidates were expected to have had experience of fieldwork and individual study. An enrichment module required them to study one aspect of the course in greater depth and there was also a section devoted to individual work.

As in previous decades the examiners found that the work of a small number of those examined revealed an impressive body of knowledge and the ability to apply factual information appropriately.[54] The variety of the work clearly appealed to candidates who performed well in both the physical and human sections of the paper. This interest was reflected in the examination results. More than a quarter of candidates in 1992 gained a grade A or B, and in 1994 the figure stood at 34.4 per cent. At the same time examiners regretted that a high proportion of candidates produced work of inferior quality.[55] Knowledge of issues such as coastal erosion were often not adequate and many candidates failed to select appropriate material or organize it effectively.

The GCSE syllabus built on the success of the new initiatives introduced in the geography syllabus during the 1970s and 1980s. Six assessment objectives were identified. These included the ability to develop a sense of place and relative location; understanding of the characteristics of various types of environment and the processes that contributed to their evolution; the development of a range of skills associated with the use of data and maps; and an understanding of the impact of geography on economic, political and social issues. The examination was intended to measure the extent of factual recall, understanding, the ability to describe and seek explanations, and the use of basic techniques for observing, recording, clarifying, interrelating and analysing data, including source materials, maps, photographs and simple statistical information. The syllabus was presented in three sections. The first examined the physical environment and involved the study of selected landforms associated with rivers, coasts and glaciation. Weather, climate and ecosystems were also studied. The second section considered economic activity through case studies of agriculture and industry. The third section looked at population, settlement and urbanization and involved the study of world distribution, by examining issues like the density of population, migration, settlement and the process of urbanization.[56] The curriculum stipulated that pupils should be given an opportunity to understand themselves in relation to 'their local area, Wales and the wider world'. Wales was to be studied as a geopolitical entity. Welsh examples were to be included and experiences related to those of other parts of Britain and the wider world.

Candidates were found to have maintained the standard achieved in previous years. The percentage of candidates who gained a grade C or above increased to 51.0 per cent by 1994 and nearly a quarter of the cohort (24.1 per cent in 1992 and 24.5 per cent in 1994) were awarded a grade A or B. Some impressive work had been submitted on aspects such as the identification of geographical phenomena, the description of data, map and atlas work and the use of resource material.[57] The general standard of the projects was also high, especially where topics of local interest, such as the course of a river or a local industry, had been chosen. Some good use was made of information technology and many maps showed a command of cartographic skills. Examiners commended the way in which many had approached the examination with a positive and determined attitude. Nevertheless, many candidates were found to be careless in the use of statistical information. Many failed to confine their answers to the data provided, their knowledge of geographical skills was sometimes lacking and answers lacked sufficient detail. Candidates were fearful of familiar concepts when they were applied in unfamiliar situations, and answers on climate and weather were usually the weakest part of each paper.

History

Those studying history at A level were introduced to a course which focused both on the skills of historical research and the requirement to demonstrate mastery of a detailed body of factual knowledge of the topic studied. It was intended that all candidates would be introduced to current debates about the periods which were being studied and that they should be aware of the problems encountered in interpreting evidence. The traditional format, whereby candidates studied the experience of England, Wales and Europe, continued and most candidates pursued a course examining a specific period.[58] More than 2,000 candidates sat the A level examination in 1990. Of these 9 per cent gained a grade A and a further 13.3 per cent were awarded a grade B. A further 22.4 per cent gained a grade C.

One feature which was commended by the examiners was the way in which candidates showed greater care in the presentation of their work. Many answers were elegantly written and grammatical inaccuracies were less evident than in previous years. Even so, the problem of irrelevance, especially among weaker candidates, remained and it was apparent that the complete syllabus was still not being covered in some centres. Some candidates attempted to fashion the demands of the question to preconceived answers.[59] It was clear, however, that the emphasis on testing a broad range of skills and the attention which had been given to determining precise assessment objectives had enabled most candidates to demonstrate their potential in the examination and that they had derived considerable benefit from pursuing an advanced course in history.[60] The quality of the coursework submitted drew considerable praise, both for its content and presentation, and it was recognized that the introduction of this element in the assessment was something from which candidates had benefited in that many of them had enjoyed the exercise.[61]

As noted above, history was the only subject, other than Welsh, in which a separate National Curriculum committee was established for Wales. In many ways the decision to grant Wales its own group was an acknowledgement of the need for the syllabus to recognize the distinctive experiences of the nation. It was intended to introduce pupils to the concept of 'Welshness' and foster an awareness of the nation's distinctive political, economic, social and cultural experiences. At the same time it was stressed that the syllabus should enable pupils to understand Wales in the context of a wider study of Britain, Europe and the wider world. However, as with other non-core foundation subjects, when the WJEC history syllabuses were revised it was to the GCSE subject criteria that these had to conform, although the WJEC's committees may well have chosen to take account of the thinking of the National Curriculum History Committee for Wales.

The GCSE course sought to stimulate interest and enthusiasm, to provide pupils with an understanding of human activity and train them to use knowledge appropriately. A central place was accorded to work with historical evidence. Those pursuing the course were expected to be able to locate and extract information from a variety of primary and secondary sources, as well as to evaluate the evidence to ascertain reliability and bias, and to recognize differing standpoints. Four modules were to be studied. The first was to be a line of development; the second, a study in depth; the third, a Welsh history study, and the fourth, a modern world study produced through coursework. All candidates were encouraged to show what they knew, understood and could do, with differentiation achieved by outcome.[62] The overall response to the challenge of the GCSE examination in history was promising, although a very wide range of work was submitted.[63] More than 10 per cent of candidates obtained a grade A in 1990, 1992 and 1994, while the number who secured a grade C or above increased from 46.5 per cent in 1990 to 49.3 per cent in 1992 and 54.5 per cent in 1994. Many candidates showed a sound knowledge of the subject-matter and a range of appropriate skills. In general, examiners were pleased with the quality of the written work; the source-based questions indicated that the skill of analysing evidence was being taught and that many candidates clearly understood the meaning of history and the way in which historians worked. Nonetheless, examiners noted that factual knowledge was less impressive. There were many candidates who could not describe historical change or analyse different features of historical information. Crucially, the Welsh history module remained a neglected part of the syllabus.

Religious studies

The religious studies syllabus consolidated changes made during the previous decade. It sought to foster an understanding of religion as a phenomenon, and its role and significance in human life. Those studying the subject at A level were examined on their knowledge and understanding of the Christian gospel, together with other religions in the modern world. The quality of the work submitted during the early 1990s had improved. In 1989 only 28.5 per cent of candidates gained a grade C or above but nearly half (47.4 per cent) achieved those grades in 1994.[64] The examiners found that a large number of very competent scripts were produced, which addressed the requirements of questions more directly than in the past.[65] Questions on Martin Luther and world religions were answered well, and it was clear that most candidates had understood the main issues concerned. Examiners commended the maturity expressed in many of the answers.

A major fault identified was lack of care in explaining portions of the Old Testament. It was also emphasized that the study of church history required attention to the explanation and meaning of events as well as chronology, and that knowledge of narrative had to be supported by the ability to explain and interpret.

There was a similar improvement in the quality of work produced by those studying the subject at GCSE. The percentage of the entry gaining a grade C or above was 44.1 per cent in 1990; by 1994 the figure had risen to 56.2 per cent. A more striking increase was found among those who gained grade A, which increased from 8.7 per cent in 1990 to 18.1 per cent in 1994.

During their studies, candidates were introduced to a broad range of faiths, given an insight into the way in which religious belief changed and how different religious groups addressed questions about the meaning of life and morality. They also considered the contribution of religion to the formation of patterns of belief and behaviour and its role in war and conflict.[66] Candidates were expected to be able to show detailed knowledge of important individuals and the principal beliefs of the faiths studied.[67] Some topics, notably those concerning Jesus and the foundation of Christianity, were well-answered, and it was clear that candidates had been interested in the issues under consideration. Many showed a firm grasp of the texts and could handle context questions adroitly. Even so, few candidates were able to evaluate religious experiences and an increasingly large number of answers displayed a lack of any familiarity with religious concepts, suggesting answers had been written from a purely secular standpoint. Many were content with making sweeping statements without being able to support their point of view with rational argument or effective use of evidence.

Mathematics

Mathematics students at A level pursued a modular course based on a selection of two of four options, which included pure mathematics, mechanics, and probability and statistics.[68] Examiners found the overall standard of the work to be satisfactory. Some exceptional work was produced in response to questions requiring candidates to test hypotheses, but the quality of the work in other parts of the syllabus, notably mechanics, rarely reached the standard required.[69] Many candidates engaged in motiveless and lengthy calculations because they had failed to give sufficient thought to what was required, and poor manipulative skills and elementary mistakes due to premature approximation were a cause of frequent difficulties. In pure mathematics and applied mathematics the overall standard was commended, and it was reported that many outstanding candidates submitted work each year. As in previous years, however, algebra and integration continued to cause the greatest difficulties, and considerable concern was expressed at the decline in the total number of candidates taking applied mathematics.

The scope of the GCSE mathematics course was a matter of frequent comment, given that candidates were expected to master an immense range of topics, knowledge and skills intended to develop mathematical knowledge and a feel for numbers, the understanding of mathematical principles, the ability to read mathematics and to apply principles in a logical way. Candidates were expected to demonstrate factual recall and use their knowledge in a variety of situations to calculate, measure, estimate and approximate results.[70]

The subject was examined through differentiated papers and teachers were required to enter candidates at three levels.[71] During the early years of the GCSE, examiners noted that the quality of the work was promising. For instance, in 1992 it was found that 85.0 per cent of candidates had gained more than half of the marks, and there was a laudable improvement in work on areas of the syllabus such as trigonometry.[72] A grade C or above was obtained by 45.3 per cent of candidates in 1994, and 8.9 per cent were awarded a grade A, of whom 1.1 per cent gained a starred grade. Nevertheless, traditional weaknesses continued to affect performance in the examination. Candidates used compasses and protractors inappropriately in answering questions on geometry. Algebra was the source of many difficulties, with candidates often lacking a basic knowledge of the topic. Premature approximation and failure to show the process of arriving at a calculation meant candidates lost marks. Moreover, little confidence was shown when transferring principles from arithmetical problems to those involving algebra.[73] Examiners were also concerned that only parts of the syllabus had been studied and it was evident that many of those entered at the bottom of the ability range had worked in a haphazard and careless way.

Science subjects

The teaching of science was of central significance in the debates concerning the introduction of the GCSE and National Curriculum. Government ministers regularly highlighted the need for the subjects to be given greater attention, in the belief that the economy would only prosper if the workforce was trained in scientific methods and principles. At A level the arguments in favour of integrating science were rejected, and candidates pursued separate courses in biology, physics and chemistry. The schedules were based on the principle that study at A level would be appropriate for those who intended to study the subjects at a higher level but would also provide other candidates with a thorough body of knowledge, understanding and skills.[74]

Physics

The A level course in physics was presented in three sections: fields, forces and energy, molecules and matter; waves and vibrations and atomic physics; and electricity and magnetism and electronic systems. The course was examined by a combination of a written paper and practical tests of manual skill, the use of apparatus and the ability to handle numerical data. The impressive quality of much of the work produced remained a matter of satisfaction for examiners. A large number of able candidates impressed examiners with their content knowledge and also with the dexterity they showed in applying principles.[75] Yet, as was the case in previous years, a weakness in mathematics, in particular the manipulation of algebraic equations, meant some candidates failed to fulfil their potential, and the tendency of some to provide vague and loose descriptions suggested that they had failed to master the basic principles of what they had studied. This was particularly so for some candidates at the bottom of the ability range.

Chemistry

The syllabus in chemistry focused on topics such as atomic structures, energetics, bonding and structure, the states of matter, equilibria, chemical kinetics, the periodic table, industrial processes and the chemistry of carbon compounds.[76] During the 1970s and 1980s examiners expressed concern at some of the work submitted, but they found that the standard improved during the early 1990s. Answers in the written paper indicated that knowledge and understanding of physical and organic chemistry, in particular, had improved.[77] Nevertheless, weaknesses in handling numerical information continued and many of those who sat the examination were unable to write chemical equations correctly. According to the examiners, the difficulties in quantitative chemistry could be related to changes in the syllabus as a result of the introduction of GCSE:

> It is of course impossible to be certain why candidates are experiencing such difficulties with these more quantitative areas, but it may be that they are now tending to have a later and therefore shorter exposure to such ideas in their GCSE work, leaving insufficient time for these concepts to mature.[78]

Biology

The quality of the work in A level biology remained a matter of considerable concern for examiners, and their reports in the 1990s indicate that overall performance did not improve. Candidates pursued a syllabus which included consideration of the structure and functions of cells, their chemistry and metabolism, respiration and photosynthesis. The complexity, variety and classification of organisms were studied as well as subjects such as the ecosystem, genetics and ecology. One of the main weaknesses identified in the reports was the failure of many candidates to grasp basic factual knowledge. Too many of them left questions unanswered and some approached the practical test with preconceived ideas which undermined the spontaneity of experimental work. Even basic principles appeared to have been misunderstood and few candidates were found to have shown genuine interest and commitment to the subject.

The central aim of the biology course was to generate a life-long interest in living organisms, to arouse curiosity through scientific enquiry, to provide candidates with basic knowledge, to develop manipulative skills, to convey an understanding of the relationships between living organisms and to nurture a respect for all forms of life. Candidates studied the diversity of organisms, the organization and maintenance of the individual, including plant and animal nutrition, respiration, excretion and sensitivity, the development of organisms and the relationship between organisms and the environment, including population size and control, cycles of matter, human interactions and the environment, and parasites and pathogens.[79]

As was the case in other single science subjects, the number of candidates gradually declined, but unlike other subjects this did not result in an immediate improvement in the quality of the work. The number obtaining a grade A fell from 7.8 per cent in 1990 to 6.1 per cent in 1992, although the performance in the succeeding years improved considerably. It was found that a large number of candidates were unable to provide adequate descriptions of basic processes such as photosynthesis and the processes of life.[80] The general standard of the diagrams was poor, many being inaccurate and poorly labelled. The coursework submitted was also below the standard expected by examiners. The quality of the work improved during the 1990s as the number of candidates entered for the examination fell. Examiners found evidence of more accuracy and better knowledge of experimental processes. The quality of the coursework was higher but it was found that in too many instances the tasks set had been inappropriate and often trivial, with the result that little benefit had been gained from them.

Integrated science

Although the advocates of an integrated approach to science failed to have an impact at A level, their ideas exerted greater influence over GCSE courses. It was clear that those pupils who had a talent for scientific enquiry would benefit from the study of each subject separately. Even so, because science was deemed to be an essential part of a holistic education which should be part of the experience of all school pupils there were clear advantages in developing an approach which introduced all candidates to the three branches of the subject. Furthermore, the National Curriculum ensured that science became compulsory for all pupils at Key Stage 4. This meant that, for the first time, schools had to make provision for the whole of this cohort and were thus faced with the question of what form this provision should take – integrated science or separate sciences. A dual system emerged whereby candidates could be entered either for a subject-based examination or for a modular test which could be taken either as a single or a double award. As a result, the number of candidates entered for biology fell from 13,458 in 1990 to 2,642 in 1994, those in chemistry from 9,106 in 1990 to 2,155 in 1994 and those in physics from 10,540 to 2,323. On the other hand, 21,746 candidates were entered for the double award examination in science in 1994 and 2,363 for the single award. One common theme in all schedules was the emphasis that science was a practical subject which required candidates to gain skills and to be able to conceptualize issues, as well as to master a body of factual information.

Thus the physics course was intended to promote an awareness of the impact of the subject on society, the economy and the environment and to portray it as a changing structure of knowledge based on proven theories.[81] As the number of candidates entered for 'single physics' declined there was a marked improvement in the general quality of the work produced.[82] Whereas 9.1 per cent of candidates obtained a grade A in 1990, no fewer than 21.8 per cent secured the highest grade in 1994. The examiners' reports commended the way in which candidates had responded to questions on molecular theory and it was noted that the quality of the work involving mathematics had improved substantially.

The chemistry syllabus was divided into four assessment objectives: experimental and practical work; recall and knowledge; understanding, application and analysis; and synthesis and evaluation. The syllabus stipulated that, in experimental and practical work, candidates should learn about safety, manipulation, measurement, observation, recording, interpreting and designing. In the written test they were expected to demonstrate knowledge and understanding of patterns and classifications, organic structure and bonding, energies, reversible reactions, speed of reactions, oxidization and reduction, electrochemistry, quantitative chemical reactions, metals, gases of the air, aminia and food, acids, petroleum, natural gas and coal, ethanol, sodium chloride and calcium carbonate, water and radioactive chemicals.[83] The average performance during the early 1990s was found to be satisfactory. A total of 69.8 per cent of those entered in 1994 obtained a grade C or higher; more than a quarter (27.1 per cent) were awarded a grade A. Aspects of the syllabus, such as the corrosion of iron, elicited some excellent responses and candidates showed a greater proficiency at interpreting information in novel situations.[84] Nevertheless, it was noted that knowledge of certain topics such as the hardness of water and the contact process was generally superficial, and work with equations and with formulae continued to cause problems.

The modular course in science was organized into the three traditional groups of biology, chemistry and physics. Candidates had to study eighteen modules. For the double award it was compulsory to study the first six modules of each section; for a single award candidates were required to study nine modules, being the first three from each subject group. They were expected to demonstrate proficiency in observation and investigation, to be able to search for patterns, and to interpret, apply and communicate knowledge and understanding.[85]

Examiners found the response to be varied, with the standard of work in double award papers usually substantially below that found in the single award entries. For instance, only 6.3 per cent of those entered in 1994 gained a grade A and fewer than half (44.8 per cent) secured grade C or above. Weaker candidates experienced immense difficulty with the questions requiring factual recall, and candidates regularly performed better in those parts of the examination which asked them to demonstrate a grasp of processes and skills rather than those demanding knowledge and understanding.[86] Many candidates experienced difficulties with terminology and scientific vocabulary, and lacked the ability to solve problems when they were presented in new situations. In addition, examiners continued to highlight the very poor response to questions involving the application of mathematical principles, especially in the physics modules.

Art and design

The A level examination in art and design focused on three tests: drawing and painting; design and practice; and the history and understanding of art and architecture.[87] Nearly half (48.3 per cent) of candidates achieved grade C or above at A level in 1992, with 10.4 per cent achieving a grade A. In 1994, 52.1 per cent were awarded grade C or above and 12.7 per cent obtained an A grade. Examiners expressed satisfaction that the number of candidates increased and that the standard of work was generally being maintained.[88] Nevertheless, some concern was expressed with the quality of the personal records and observational and recording skills, and it was clear that some candidates relied on photographic material as their source. Work in graphics was hampered by lack of analysis and the quality of the three-dimensional work was generally not high.

The GCSE course sought to develop practical skills as well as theoretical knowledge. Candidates were expected to undertake personal work based on original research and to be able to demonstrate talent in using colour, tone, shape, drawing, designing and painting.[89] The CCW recognized that the environment in which the curriculum was taught in Wales was unique and that the arts played an increasingly important role in many aspects of national life. They noted that Wales had distinctive traditions and that those studying the subject should be given the opportunity to study examples of Welsh arts and crafts, which influenced the syllabus pursued in Wales.[90] In 1990, 9,570 candidates sat the examination: 47.2 per cent secured a grade C or above and 9.9 per cent were given a grade A. By 1994 the number of candidates had decreased to 8,429, of which 51.3 per cent were awarded grade C or above, 10.0 per cent obtained a grade A, with 2.2 per cent receiving a starred grade A. Examiners found much to commend. It was clear that many had enjoyed their study of the subject and some of the responses were honest and original.[91] On the other hand it was noted that the quality of the coursework was lower than expected. Many of the submissions lacked a sense of direction and suffered from a narrow conceptual framework, while some candidates continued to rely on photographs instead of original material.[92]

Candidates in craft and design were expected to display a combination of practical skills, together with proficiency at evaluation and the ability to design and analyse.[93] During the early 1990s the number of candidates entered rose from 362 in 1990 to 543 in 1994, and the number of candidates who obtained the higher grades increased: 7.3 per cent were awarded a grade A in 1990, a figure which rose to 9.1 per cent in 1992 and 13.1 per cent in 1994. Significantly, more than half those entered that year gained a grade C or higher. Overall it was found that analysis and evaluation work had improved.[94] Design methodology was handled more competently than in the past and there were similar improvements in the evaluative stage.[95] The problem-solving section remained the weakest part of the examination, candidates falling short of expectations through poor examination technique and lack of understanding.[96]

Three tests were set in the GCSE: a theory paper, a product design and a coursework folio.[97] Emphasis was placed on the ability to manipulate materials, and to use manual and machine tools and adhesives.[98] In 1994 a total of 8,460 candidates sat the GCSE examination. Of these, 11.6 per cent obtained a grade A and 41.7 per cent were awarded a grade C or above. Some projects were of excellent quality and indicated that candidates had spent considerable time planning and designing the tasks.[99] In the design and realization paper only the best candidates produced work of the quality expected and many were found not to have allocated their time properly in the examination.[100] Spelling and punctuation continued to cause problems. Analysis was often too hurried and suffered from poor presentation.[101]

Home economics

The A level syllabus in home economics introduced candidates to a core module covering the broad historical and sociological background to their work, and sought to promote understanding of issues such as home management and relevant social issues. Candidates specialized either in food and nutrition, or clothing and textiles.[102] Examiners were pleased with the quality of much of the work submitted.[103] They found a growing awareness of the inter-relationship between different parts of the syllabus, and that many candidates had used factual information appropriately.[104] The overall standard of the coursework was very high, and examiners took pleasure from the fact that so many creative and imaginative pieces had been submitted.[105] However, poor examination technique hampered some promising candidates in the written paper and investigative work suggested some had chosen topics which were too wide, with the result that their answers were too general.

At GCSE candidates were expected to be aware of the inter-relationships within the subject, and to develop a sensitive aesthetic appreciation and the skills of managing family resources. The theory paper accounted for 40 per cent of the marks, practical work for 40 per cent and an assignment for 20 per cent. Candidates studied topics such as human development, health, safety and efficient methods of working. In the food section the relationship between food and health, methods of cooking, transference of energy into food, and consumer protection were considered. In the textiles section they studied methods and trends in fashion and the way they impacted on health, taste and practicalities.[106] Examiners detected fewer rubric infringements in the theory paper, and the quality of the answers produced by weaker candidates had generally improved. The evaluation part remained the weakest section. In the 'food' section, candidates were generally well-prepared in the practical test and displayed greater confidence in the use of labour-saving devices. Orders of work were generally well done, with candidates demonstrating a logical approach to their work. A wide variety of equipment was used competently and good understanding was shown of the principles of safety and hygiene, but evaluation still tended to concentrate too much on the finished product rather than the planning and production stages. In investigation work, some very interesting and topical subjects were chosen for study but some attempted to cover an over-ambitious field and it was suggested that candidates were not receiving sufficient guidance in the initial planning. In 'textiles', examiners found the folios to be of a high standard and the work presented extremely well. The evaluation work was also generally acceptable and a very wide range of interesting and unusual artefacts were submitted.

Conclusion

During this period almost every year across the range of subjects a greater number of pupils achieved higher grades, and there was a noticeable improvement in the number who secured grade C or above at GCSE, a target which was a benchmark of achievement for central government. It is impossible to draw firm conclusions about how far improvements in pass rates, and the distribution of grades within these pass rates, resulted from grade inflation and how far there were genuine improvements in standards. The examiners' reports for this period indicate that those entered for examination by the WJEC produced work of an increasingly good quality. In some subjects, such as physics and chemistry, the improvement was significantly helped by the fact that only those with a particular gift for science were being entered due to a growing proportion of the cohort being entered for the double or single award in the modular science examination. Changes in the nature of what was examined, especially the increased emphasis on skills rather than factual recall, meant that some pupils were enabled to achieve a more creditable result, while the introduction of more coursework meant those who did not perform exceptionally well under examination conditions were able to demonstrate their abilities.

Inevitably, the general improvement in performance generated accusations that the GCSE examination lacked rigour, and similar criticisms were levied against the A level examination, albeit to a lesser extent. Undoubtedly, greater success owed much to the endeavour of the teaching profession and the efforts of individual candidates. Moreover, examinations were subject to rigorous analysis by independent adjudicators whose remit was to ensure the examinations were challenging tests of ability. The introduction of the National Curriculum meant school pupils studied a common syllabus from the age of five, while the emphasis on regular testing and assessment meant schools placed a continuous emphasis on addressing deficiencies in learning and teaching strategies, not least because of the importance of test results in the environment generated by school league tables.

Accusations of lack of rigour had been levied against other new examinations, including the GCE O level during the first years of its existence and, as was seen in Chapter 4, the CSE examination suffered from the emergence of a culture of derision. Moreover, those who maintained that the GCSE was not sufficiently challenging ignored the depressing fact that nearly 20 per cent of sixteen-year-olds in Wales left school in 1996 with no qualifications, and issues such as the status of more vocational and less academic subjects remained to be addressed. Other issues which continued to challenge all responsible for secondary education in Wales in the new millennium were the growing evidence that the performance of girls was better than that of boys, and that there remained a disparity of examination performance between schools, even in comparable socio-economic catchment areas.

Substantial change in the examination system is mooted, especially significant being the development of the Welsh baccalaureate. If ideas to remodel the structure of examinations for the 14–19 age group, heralded in the Welsh Assembly's *Learning Pathways* document, come to fruition, they will constitute the most radical change in external assessment and examinations since the system began in the late nineteenth century.[107]

References

[1] Sheila Lawlor, *Away with LEAs: ILEA Abolition as a Pilot* (London, Centre for Policy Studies, 1988).

[2] Lawlor, *Away with LEAs*, p 5.

[3] Lawlor, *Away with LEAs*, p 5.

[4] Association of County Councils, *The Way Ahead – Education: Report of a Sub-group Appointed by the ACC Officers Advisory Group* (London, 1986); ACC, *Education – What Price the Bill? The Association of County Councils' Response to the Consultation Paper Published by the Department of Education and Science* (London, 1987); ACC, *The Future Role of Local Education Authorities* (London, 1992).

[5] W. S. Fowler, *Towards the National Curriculum: Discussion and Control in the English Educational System 1965–1988* (London, 1988), pp. 88–92.

[6] WJEC, *Annual Reports*, 1980–8.

7   WJEC, *Annual Reports*, 1991–2.
8   WJEC, *Annual Reports*, 1994–5.
9   Morag Brown, *Mid Glamorgan School Catchment Area Profiles* (Cardiff, 1995); Catherine M. Farrell and Jennifer Law, 'Changing forms of accountability in education? A case study of LEAs in Wales', *Public Administration*, 77, No.2 (1999), pp. 293–310.
10 *Western Mail*, 14 August 1995; *South Wales Echo*, 8 September 1995, 23 September 1995, 5 October 1995, 9 October 1995.
11 WJEC, *Annual Reports of the Examiners*, 1983, CSE Mathematics.
12 F. A. Loosmore, *The Curriculum and Assessment in Wales: An Exploratory Study* (Cardiff, 1981).
13 WJEC, *Annual Reports*, 1980, 1981. In 1980 a decision was taken to move towards further integration through the establishment of one examinations committee to replace the separate GCE and CSE committees and to appoint single panels for all subjects. In addition, the WJEC cooperated with other examining bodies in forming a set of criteria and standardizing the syllabus of the new examination.
14 W. S. Fowler, *Towards the National Curriculum: Discussion and Control in the English Educational System 1965–1988* (London, 1988), p. 73.
15 Such an approach could hardly have been further removed from that of those who had influenced and formulated education policy during the immediate post-war years: G. E. Jones, *The Education of a Nation* (Cardiff, 1997), p. 151; E. C. Wragg, 'The slippery slope to statethink' in P. F. W. Preece (ed.), *Perspectives on the National Curriculum* (Exeter, 1987), pp. 23–8.
16 Sheila Lawlor, *Correct Core: Simple Curricula for English, Maths and Science* (London, 1988); Mervyn Hiskett, *Choice in Rotten Apples: Bias in GCSE and Examining Groups* (London, 1988); Cyril Taylor, *Raising Educational Standards: A Personal Perspective* (London, 1990).
17 Department of Education and Science and the Welsh Office, *The National Curriculum 5–16: A Consultative Document* (London, 1987).
18 Denis Lawton and Clyde Chitty, 'Two concepts of a National Curriculum' in Preece (ed.), *Perspectives on the National Curriculum*, (Exeter, 1987), pp. 10–14.
19 Education Reform Act 1988.
20 Department of Education and Science, *National Curriculum: From Policy to Practice* (London, 1989).
21 Welsh Office, *The National Curriculum in Wales* (Cardiff, 1987).
22 G. E. Jones, *The Education of a Nation* (Cardiff, 1997), pp. 155–6.
23 Association of History Teachers in Wales, *History in the National Curriculum: A Report on the Views of History Teachers in Wales on 'Proposals for a Core Curriculum in History'* (AHTW, 1982); Stuart Broomfield, 'History and the Curriculum Cymreig', *Welsh Historian*, 31 (2001), pp 17–19. Department of Education and Science, *National Curriculum History Working Group Final Report* (London, 1990);

Alan Beattie, *History in Peril: May We Preserve It* (London, 1987); Stewart Deuchar, *History on the Brink* (York, 1992).
24 Curriculum Council for Wales, *Developing a Curriculum Cymreig (CCW Advisory Paper No.18)* (Cardiff, 1993), p. 2; Brinley Jones, 'A Curriculum Cymreig', *Welsh Journal of Education*, 4, 2 (1995), pp. 22–35.
25 Department of Education and Science and the Welsh Office, *Report of the National Curriculum Task Group on Assessment and Testing* (London, 1988).
26 School Curriculum and Assessment Authority, *The National Curriculum and its Assessment* (London, 1993), p. 70.
27 WJEC, *Annual Reports*, 1988–9, p. 6.
28 WJEC, *Annual Reports*, 1989–90; the WJEC appointed syllabus committees which were to prepare draft submissions to the School Curriculum and Assessment Authority by 1991, so that courses could begin in September 1992 for examination in 1994.
29 School Curriculum and Assessment Authority, *The National Curriculum and its Assessment*, pp. 21, 28–39, 40–52.
30 Sheila Lawlor (ed.) *The Dearing Debate: Assessment and the National Curriculum* (London, 1993).
31 School Curriculum and Assessment Authority, *The National Curriculum and its Assessment*, pp. 28–9, 40–52.
32 School Curriculum and Assessment Authority, *The National Curriculum and its Assessment*, pp. 40–52.
33 WJEC, *Annual Reports*, 1991–2.
34 School Curriculum and Assessment Authority, *The National Curriculum and its Assessment*, pp. 22–3.
35 WJEC, *Regulations and Syllabuses*, 1986.
36 WJEC, *Regulations and Syllabuses*, 1986.
37 Curriculum Council for Wales, *Curriculum Cymreig* (Cardiff, 1993), pp. 21–31.
38 WJEC, *Annual Reports of the Examiners*, 1992, English.
39 WJEC, *Annual Reports of the Examiners*, 1996, English.
40 WJEC, *Regulations and Syllabuses*, 1986.
41 WJEC, *Annual Reports of the Examiners*, 1992, 1994, 1996, Welsh.
42 WJEC, *Annual Reports of the Examiners*, 1992.
43 WJEC, *Regulations and Syllabuses*, 1986.
44 WJEC, *Annual Reports of the Examiners*, 1992, 1994, Welsh.
45 WJEC, *Annual Reports of the Examiners*, 1992.
46 WJEC, *Annual Reports of the Examiners*, 1994, 1996.
47 WJEC, *Annual Reports of the Examiners*, 1996.
48 WJEC, *Regulations and Syllabuses*, 1986.
49 WJEC, *Annual Reports of the Examiners*, 1992, Welsh Literature.
50 WJEC, *Regulations and Syllabuses*, 1986.
51 WJEC, *Annual Reports of the Examiners*, 1992, 1994, French.
52 WJEC, *Regulations and Syllabuses*, 1986.
53 WJEC, *Annual Reports of the Examiners*, 1992, French.
54 WJEC, *Regulations and Syllabuses*, 1986.

55 WJEC, *Annual Reports of the Examiners*, 1992, Geography.
56 WJEC, *Regulations and Syllabuses*, 1986.
57 WJEC, *Annual Reports of the Examiners*, 1992, Geography.
58 WJEC, *Regulations and Syllabuses*, 1986.
59 WJEC, *Annual Reports of the Examiners*, 1992, History.
60 WJEC, *Annual Reports of the Examiners*, 1994, History.
61 WJEC, *Annual Reports of the Examiners*, 1992, 1994.
62 WJEC, *Regulations and Syllabuses*, 1986.
63 WJEC, *Annual Reports of the Examiners*, 1992, History.
64 WJEC, *Regulations and Syllabuses*, 1986.
65 WJEC, *Annual Reports of the Examiners*, 1993, 1994, Religious Education.
66 WJEC, *Regulations and Syllabuses*, 1986.
67 WJEC, *Annual Reports of the Examiners*, 1992, Religious Education.
68 WJEC, *Regulations and Syllabuses*, 1986.
69 WJEC, *Annual Reports of the Examiners*, 1996, Mathematics.
70 WJEC, *Regulations and Syllabuses*, 1986.
71 The examination schedules included a clear definition of the competencies which were required to gain specific grades. For instance, it was stated that those awarded grade F would be able to demonstrate a thorough knowledge of the content of the syllabus and to apply principles in familiar situations, while those awarded a grade C were expected to show a similar mastery of the syllabus but be able to apply principles and processes in situations which they had not previously encountered, including some situations where they had to use more than one process to arrive at a solution. Those entered at level 1 sat papers 1 and 2. Those entered at level 2 sat papers 2 and 3 while those entered at level 3 sat papers 3 and 4: WJEC, *Regulations and Syllabuses*, 1986.
72 WJEC, *Annual Reports of the Examiners*, 1992, Mathematics.
73 WJEC, *Annual Reports of the Examiners*, 1992. Differentiation, which had been an integral part of the mathematics examination, was consolidated in 1994 with the introduction of tiered papers.
74 WJEC, *Regulations and Syllabuses*, 1986.
75 WJEC, *Annual Reports of the Examiners*, 1992, 1994, 1996, Physics.
76 WJEC, *Regulations and Syllabuses*, 1986.
77 WJEC, *Annual Reports of the Examiners*, 1992, Chemistry.
78 WJEC, *Annual Reports of the Examiners*, 1992.
79 WJEC, *Regulations and Syllabuses*, 1986.
80 WJEC, *Annual Reports of the Examiners*, 1992, Biology.
81 WJEC, *Regulations and Syllabuses*, 1986.
82 WJEC, *Annual Reports of the Examiners*, 1992, Physics.
83 WJEC, *Regulations and Syllabuses*, 1986.
84 WJEC, *Annual Reports of the Examiners*, 1994, Chemistry.
85 WJEC, *Regulations and Syllabuses*, 1986.
86 WJEC, *Annual Reports of the Examiners*, 1992, Combined Science.
87 WJEC, *Regulations and Syllabuses*, 1986.
88 WJEC, *Annual Reports of the Examiners*, 1992, Art.

89 WJEC, *Regulations and Syllabuses*, 1986.
90 Curriculum Council for Wales, *Curriculum Cymreig* (Cardiff, 1993), pp. 10, 28–9.
91 WJEC, *Annual Reports of the Examiners*, 1994, Art.
92 WJEC, *Annual Reports of the Examiners*, 1992, 1994, 1996, Art.
93 WJEC, *Regulations and Syllabuses*, 1986.
94 WJEC, *Annual Reports of the Examiners*, 1992, Craft Design Technology.
95 WJEC, *Annual Reports of the Examiners*, 1994.
96 WJEC, *Annual Reports of the Examiners*, 1996.
97 WJEC, *Regulations and Syllabuses*, 1986.
98 WJEC, *Annual Reports of the Examiners*, 1992, Craft Design Technology.
99 WJEC, *Annual Reports of the Examiners*, 1992.
100 WJEC, *Annual Reports of the Examiners*, 1992.
101 WJEC, *Annual Reports of the Examiners*, 1992, 1994, 1996.
102 WJEC, *Regulations and Syllabuses*, 1986.
103 WJEC, *Annual Reports of the Examiners*, 1992, Home Economics.
104 WJEC, *Annual Reports of the Examiners*, 1992.
105 WJEC, *Annual Reports of the Examiners*, 1992.
106 WJEC, *Regulations and Syllabuses*, 1986.
107 Welsh Assembly Government, *Learning Country: Learning Pathways, 14–19* (Cardiff, 2002).

Index

A level examination
  qualification in own right, as 190
  see also General Certificate of Education
Aberdare Committee Report 2–3
  curricular blueprint 5
  recommendations 3
algebra, 49 *see also* mathematics
art 118
art and design
  1970–1988 182–5
    A level tests 183
    CSE examination 185
    falling standards in 184–5
    introduction of 182
    O level tests 184
    quality of work 183–4
    techniques 183
  1988–2000 226–8
    A level art examination 226–7
    craft and design 227–8
    GCSE course 227
    GCSE examinations 228
    pass rates 228
    quality of work 227
    Welsh traditions, and 227
art of précis
  English, and 17

Beloe Committee 121
bilingualism
  effects 77
biology
  1918–1949 105–7
    two subjects, as 106–7
  1949–1970 142–5
    credibility gap 144
    criticisms 144–5
    deficiencies in 143
    examinations, structure 144
    examiners 142
    number of candidates 143–4
    quality of candidates 143
    standard of work 143
    University of Wales, role 142
  1970–1988 180–2
    A level 180–1
    application of 181
    CSE paper 181–2
    O level 181
    poor performance in 180
    practical work 181
  1988–2000 223–4
    aim of course 223
    number of candidates 224
    pass rates 224
    quality of work 223, 224
    syllabus 223
Blue Books 2
botany 55–6
  1896–1918
    accuracy, need for 55
    examination criteria 55
    gender, and 56
    quality of teaching 55
  1918–1949 105–7
    examination methods 105
    perennial deficiencies 105–6
    replacement with biology 107
    standard of work 105

INDEX

1949–1970 140–2
  A level examinations 140–1
  criticisms 141
  practical work 141–2
  standard of work 140
  verbose answers 141
  see also biology; zoology

Central Advisory Council for Education (Wales) 117
  arts and culture 118
  manual skills and practical work 118–19
  role 117–18
  curriculum, and 117–18
Central Welsh Board 6
  creation 6
  criticisms 74
  exams administered by 8
  inspection responsibilities 7
  main purpose 6
chemistry
  1896–1918 53–5
    defects in achievements 54
    First World War, and 55
    philosophical side 54
    practical work 54
    quality of teaching 53
    standards of attainment 53–4
    syllabus 53
    theoretical knowledge 53
  1918–1949 103–5
    equipment shortages 104
    perennial deficiencies 104
    practical work 103
    standard of work 103–4
  1949–1970 139–40
    practical experience 139–40
    standards in 139
  1970–1988 179–80
    A level 179
    CSE examination 180
    examination technique 179–80

    O level 180
    standard of work 180
  1988–2000 222–3
    standard of work 222–3
    syllabus 222
classical bias
  Latin, and 29
commercial arithmetic 47
comprehensive schools
  approval of 151
  arrangement of existing schools, and 151–2
  building programme for 152
    temporary arrangements 152
  concept of 150–1
  curriculum, and 152–3
  proposals for 151
Cowper Temple clause 40
Crosland, Anthony 149
CSE examination
  recognition of 191
culture 118
curriculum
  assessment of pupils, and 200–1
  changes to, 1990s 197
  comprehensive schools 152–3
  regulation of 6–7
  specified school curriculum 202
    core subjects 202
  status of schools, and 5
  university demands, and 8–9

Dearing Report 205
devolution 2
  Welsh Department of Board of Education, and 2
Direct Method alternative syllabus 24

economy
  disasters of 1920s and 30s 107

Education Act 1944 115
  effect 115

INDEX

English
  1896–1918 12–18
    art of precis 17
    attributes of successful essays 15
    'composition' 13
    examination criteria 13
    First World War, prior to 13
    grammar 14
    inspectors' reports 17
    literary appreciation, and 17–18
    literature 14
    literature examination criteria 15
    quality of teaching of 15–16, 18
    second language, as 16
    spelling and punctuation 14, 16
    syllabus for examination 12
  1918–1949 75–9
    ability to write precis 77
    effects of bilingualism 77
    errors of idiom 77
    examiners' reports 76–7
    formal grammar 77
    liberal approach 76
    Newbolt Report 76
    teaching methods 75
    traditional approach 76
  1949–1970 121–4
    A level syllabus 122
    essays 123–4
    literature 122
    nature of subject 121–2
    School Certificate examinations 123
    traditional syllabus 123
    vocabulary 122
  1970–1988 153–8
    committee investigation 154
    coursework 158
    CSE 156–7
    examination criteria 155
    formal grammar 154
    O level 155–6
    pass rates 156
    reforms 154
    set texts 157–8
    testing methods 154
    WJEC schedules 155
  1988–2000 208–10
    coursework assignments 210
    empathy tasks 210
    examination schedules 208
    format of examination 209
    GCSE examination 208–9
    literature 209, 210
    number of candidates 208
Evans, Frederic 72
examinations
  influence of 72
  interplay of curriculum, and 6–7
  postwar reform 121
  rationalization of system 11
    negotiation on 11–12
  school certificates system 11
  scrutiny of system 191–2
  standard criteria for 201
  structure of system 10, 199
    exam boards 199
    review 199

fees 66
  exemptions 66
First World War
  education system during 63
Fisher, H. A. L. 64
  investigation of education system 64
Fleure, H. J.
  recognition of geography, and 32–3

INDEX

French
  1896–1918 22–9
    academic status of 22–3
    benefits of 23
    conversation lessons 28
    Direct Method alternative syllabus 24
    English idiom, and 25
    First World War, and 28
    grammar 27
    literature 27
    meaning of passages 25–6
    oral work 24, 27
    quality of work 26
    reading and dictation 27
    syllabus for, emphasis 24
    teaching methods 23–4
    translation 25
  1918–1949 81–4
    conversation 83
    Direct Method 83
    literature 82
    new techniques 83
    oral French 82, 84
    paraphrasing 82
    pronunciation 83
    standard of work 83–4
    translation skills 81–2
    visits to France 83
    vocabulary 84
  1949–1970 126–8
    deficiencies in standard 126–7
    literature 127
    number of candidates 127
    quality of translations 127–8
    unseen translations 127
  1970–1988 162–3
    A level examination 162
    O level 162–3
    oral work 163
    quality of work 162–3
  1988–2000 213
    quality of work 213

GCSE examination
  assessment method 202
  creation of 202
  National Curriculum, and 205
  pass rates 230
gender
  science subjects, and 51
General Certificate of Education (GCE) 119
  autumn supplementary examinations 120
  introduction 120
  levels of 119
geography
  1896–1918 31–6
    academic study of 31–2
    general geography paper 33
    H. J. Fleure, and 32–3
    lack of attention of 32
    local geography 35
    new approach to 32
    'New Geography' 32
    physical geography 33
    resources 35–6
    scientific subject, as 34
    specialist teachers 35
    study of relationships 34–5
    syllabus studied 33
    Wales, study of 34
  1918–1949 87–90
    examination criteria 88
    local geography 89–90
    new approach to 88
    performance of girls 90
    political climate, and 87–8
    poor performance in 89
    practical work 88–9
  1949–1970 129
    quality of work 129
    'reality' of study 129
    revised syllabus 129

INDEX

1970–1988 165–8
  A level 165
  analytical aspects 166
  candidates' performance 167–8
  CSE examination 167
  economic and social issues 167
  factual material 166
  human geography 166–7
  O level 166–7
  quality of work 165–6
  University of Wales, role 165
1988–2000 214–16
  aims of A level course 214
  GCSE assessment objectives 215
  GCSE syllabus 215
  pass rates 216
  practical skills 215
  standard of projects 216
  standard of work 215
sense of nationhood, and 73
geology
  1970–1988 168–9
    economic geology 168–9
    practical test 168
    quality of work 168
geometry 49 *see also* mathematics
George, David Lloyd
  education system, on 63
German
  1970–1988 163–4
    A level 163
    O level 164
    oral work 163–4
    translation 163
  1988–2000 213
    quality of work 213
Gruffydd, W. J. 79
  Welsh language, and 79

Hadow Report 94, 96
Haldane Commission 65

Higher Certificate examination 8
history
  1896–1918 36–9
    'amateur teachers' 38–9
    examiners, role of 36
    factual knowledge 36
    inspectors' reports 37
    lesson planning 37
    specialist teachers for 38
    status of 37–8
    understanding 36–7
  1918–1949 90–3
    emphases in interpretation 91–2
    irrelevant material 91
    literary subject, as 92
    maps and wall charts 92
    medieval period 91
    style and language of candidates 92
    syllabus 90
    terminology and quotations 93
  1949–1970 129–31
    criticisms of work 129–30
    history of Wales 130
    medieval Wales, work on 130–1
    range of textbooks 130
    stylistic weaknesses 130
  1970–1988 169–72
    A level 169–70
    aims of teaching 170
    anglocentric view 169
    CSE papers 171
    factual knowledge 169
    O level examinations 170–1
    quality of work 170, 171
    standards 170
    syllabus reform 169
  1988–2000 216–18
    A level 216–17
    GCSE course 218

INDEX

GCSE pass rates 218
presentation of work 217
traditional format 217
'Welshness', concept of 217–18
rural life, and 73
home economics
1970–1988 187–9
CSE paper 188–9
O level cookery 188
standard of work 187–8
syllabus 187
theoretical aspects 188
1988–2000 228–9
A level syllabus 228
evaluation part 229
food section 229
GCSE course 229
inter-relationships within subject 229
quality of work 228–9
textiles 229
honours examination 8
Hughes, Ernest
history teaching, on 38

independent grant maintained institutions 198–9
integrated science 224–6
1988–2000 224–6
advantages of approach 224
aims of physics course 225
chemistry syllabus 225
compulsory subject, as 224
dual system 224–5
modular course 226
number of candidates 225
pass rates 226
intermediate secondary schools 6
creation 6

joint education committees 3
creation 3
junior examination 8

debate surrounding 66–7
Labour Party
access to schools, and 75
Education Act 1944, and 108
Latin
1896–1918 29–31
case construction 30
'classical bias' 29
examination papers 29–30
idioms 30
loose phrasing 30
position in curriculum 29
prepared passages, translation 31
quality of teaching 30
quality of translations 30–1
systematic study 29
translation 29
1918–1949 84–7
accuracy 86
central feature of curriculum, as 84
examination criteria 86
grammar 85, 87
learning translations 87
Norwood Report 85
prepared translation 86
Spens Report 84
unprepared translation 86
varying quality of work 85
1949–1970 128–9
number of candidates 128
quality of work 128–9
quotations 129
translation, importance 128
vocabulary 128
1970–1988 164–5
A level course 164
decline of 164
O level 164–5
revised syllabus 165
standard of work 164, 165
translations 165

INDEX

Welsh language, and 21
Lawlor, Sheila
  LEAs, on 197–8
league tables 207
leaving age 69–70
  statistics 69–70
    England and Wales compared 69–70
Lewis, Saunders 117
local education authorities (LEAs) 116
  capacity of 116
  Education Act 1944, and 116
  erosion of influence of 197
  privatization, and 198
Local Management of Schools (LMS) 198

mass media
  impact of 192
mathematics
  1896–1918 45–50
    algebra 49
    application of basic principles 47
    commercial arithmetic 47
    deterioration in performance 49–50
    emphasis on centrality of 46
    examiners' reports 48
    geometry 49
    place in curriculum 45–6
    practical illustrations 47
    reason 47
    reform of syllabus 46
    rote learning 48
  1918–1949 96–100
    algebra 97–8
    arithmetic 97
    examiners' reports 100
    geometry 98
    Hadow Report 96
    Norwood Report 97
    number of candidates examined 99
    reform of curriculum 96
    Second World War, during 99–100
    standard of work 97
    trigonometry 99
  1949–1970 132–4
    algebra 133
    applied mathematics 132
    arithmetic 133
    geometry 133–4
    O level work 132–3
    trigonometry 134
  1970–1988 173–7
    A level 174–5
    calculators, use of 176
    changes to curriculum 173–4
    compartmentalized approach 175
    CSE examination 176
    lack of accuracy 175
    new methods of teaching 174
    O level results 177
    O level syllabus 175–6
    obsolete methods 174
    programmes for 174
    quality of work 174–5, 176–7
    recruitment of teachers 177
  1988–2000 220–1
    A level modular course 220
    GCSE examinations 221
    GCSE pass rates 221
    scope of GCSE course 220–1
    standard of work 220, 221
    traditional weaknesses 221
  postwar reform 118
metalwork *see* woodwork and metalwork
mining
  population growth, and 1
modern languages

INDEX

1970–1988 161–4
  realization of importance 161
  syllabus reform 162
1988–2000 213–14
  A level syllabus 213
  GCSE courses 213–14
  number of candidates 214
Modern Languages Association 22
  campaign by 22
Morant, Robert
  segregation of middle-class education, and 7
municipal secondary schools 6

National Assembly for Wales 207
  education policy, and 207
National Curriculum 202–3
  aims 202
  Dearing Report 205
  implementation 203
  key stages 203
  scope and manageability of 205–6
  strain on teachers 206
  Wales, in 203–4
  assessment techniques 206
  Curriculum Cymreig review 204
  separate orders for 203–4
  support for 206
Newbolt Report 76
Nonconformists 2
Norwood Report 85, 97
Nuffield Foundation 136
  science subjects 177

parental choice
  limitations on 199–200
parsing 19
  grammatical training, and 19
part-time instruction 65
  introduction of 65
Perry, John
  reform of maths syllabus 46

physics
  1896–1918 51–3
  areas of 51
  facilities 52
  inaccuracy in answers 52
  laboratory practice 52
  1918–1949 102–3
  broad view of subject 103
  practical work 102
  standard of work 102
  understanding of fundamental principles 102
  1949–1970 135–9
  A level pass rates 136
  critical feedback 138
  criticisms of candidates 137
  CSE examination 136
  equipment and resources 138–9
  growth in entries 136
  marking policies 135–6
  number of candidates 135
  number of good candidates 138
  O level pass rates 135
  1970–1988 178–9
  A level 178
  CSE examination 179
  O level 178–9
  quality of work 178, 179
  1988–2000 222
  A level course 222
  quality of work 222
population growth 1
prosperity, and 1
privatization
  administrative and support services 198

radio programmes
  schools, for 117
religious studies 219–20
  A level criteria 219

INDEX

explanations of New
  Testament 219
GCSE course 219
GCSE criteria 219–20
quality of work 219
syllabus changes 219
introduction of 172
see also scripture 1988–2000

School Certificate 12, 67
  groups of subjects 12, 67
  pass criteria 68
  postwar reform 119
schools museums service 117
science subjects
  1896–1918 50–6
    facilities and equipment 50–1
    gender, and 51
    teaching methods 51
    Welsh economy, and 50
  1918–1949 101–7
    practical application 101
    Report of Thomson
      Committee 101
    restrictive nature of 101
    syllabus content, criticisms
      101–2
  1949–1970 134–45
    examination structures 135
    number of candidates 134
    reform of curriculum 134
    teaching practices 134
  1970–1988 177–82
    laboratory work 177–8
    Nuffield Foundation 177
    objectives of teaching of 177
    study of separate subjects
      178
  1988–2000 221–4
    A level schedules 221–2
    debates over teaching of 221
  postwar reform 118
scripture 39–45
  controversy in 39

Cowper Temple clause 40
curriculum 41
denominational rivalry 39–40
examiners' reports 42–3
factual knowledge and
  analysis 42
geography of Bible 44
level of sophistication 43
numbers studying 40–1
role of examiners 44
scholarly biblical criticism
  43
set biblical texts 42
spiritual significance of work
  44
Welsh language, in 44–5
'Welsh revolt' 40
1918–1949 93–6
  controversy regarding 93
  geography, and 95
  Hadow Report 94
  knowledge of biblical texts
    94
  knowledge of facts and texts
    95–6
  lack of interest in 94
  modernist approach 95
  recent scholarly study 95
  standard of work 94–5
1949–1970 131–2
  doctrinal teaching 131
  improving standards in 131
  number of candidates 132
  validity of subject 131
1970–1988 172–3
  A level examinations 172
  CSE examination 173
  easy option, as 173
  O level examinations 172–3
  place in curriculum 173
  religious studies 172
  see also religious studies
    1896–1918

INDEX

Second World War
  effects 107
secondary education system
  accessibility 9
  aims of 72
  anglicized ethos 73
  creation 1, 3
    intermediate schools 3
    legislation 3
    religious affiliation, and 39
    subjects studied, and 3
  external examinations 8
  fees 66
  grade status of schools 4
  grammar schools, number of 146
  grants for 4
  municipal secondary schools 6
  population growth, and 107–8
  purpose of schools 75
  reform 64
  Second World War, effect 108
  standards in 10
    'quality of mind' 10
  tripartite system 149–50
    failings with 150
  Welsh society, and 4
Secondary Examinations Council (SEC) 201
Secondary Schools Examination Council 12
  function 12
senior examination 8
special schools
  expansion 116–17
Spens Committee 75
Spens Report 84
  recommendations 115

Task Group on Assessment and Testing (TGAT) 204–5
Taunton Report 4
teaching
  methods 9
  comprehensive schools 153
  history 37
  introduction of standard 207
  modern languages, reform of 23–4
  scrutiny of 189–90
  quality of 18
trigonometry 99 *see also* mathematics

Wales
  gwlad y menyg gwynion, as 2
  industrialization 1–2
  secondary education system, creation 1
Welsh (language) 18–22
  1896–1918 18–22
    examination criteria 18–19
    Latin, and 21
    parsing 19, 20
    precarious status of 22
    quality of work in 19–20
    scientific training, as 19
    specialist teacher training for 22
    study of literature 19
    translation into English 19, 20
    translation into Welsh 21
  1918–1949 79–81
    competence in translation 80
    composition 80
    English idioms 80
    grammar 79–80
    recognition of status of 79
    standard of understanding 79
    use of English 79
    Welsh literature 81
  1949–1970 124–6
    colloquial Welsh, use of 126
    failings in 124–5
    formal grammar 124
    literary criticism 125

INDEX

literature papers 126
traditional values 125
1970–1988 158–61
  CSE examination 161
  grammatical errors 160
  literature 161
  O level 159–60
  quality of essays 159
  revised schedule 158–9
  second language, as 160–1
  Welsh language C1 160
1988–2000 210–12
  A level pass rates 211
  aims of GCSE course 211
  assessment at A level 210
  coursework 212
  evaluation of complete works 210–11
  GCSE pass rates 211
  literature syllabus 212
decline of spoken language, and 74
O levels 120

Welsh Department of Board of Education 6
  conflict with CWB 7
  inspection of schools 6
Welsh Joint Education Committee 109, 116
  1993 Education Bill, on 199
  creation 109, 116
  resources, and 192
  responsibilities 116
Wheeler, Olive 117
woodwork and metalwork
  1970–1988 185–7
    A level examination 185
    answers to theory questions 186
    coursework 187
    CSE examination 186–7
    O level 186
    quality of practical work 186
    standard of work 185–6

zoology
  1918–1949 105–7